C++

FAQs

FREQUENTLY ASKED QUESTIONS

Marshall P. Cline

Greg A. Lomow

Paradigm Shift, Inc.

Addison-Wesley Publishing Company

Reading, Massachusetts ▪ Menlo Park, California ▪
New York ▪ Don Mills, Ontario ▪ Wokingham, England ▪
Amsterdam ▪ Bonn ▪ Sydney ▪ Singapore ▪ Tokyo ▪
Madrid ▪ San Juan ▪ Paris ▪ Milan

Deborah R. Lafferty: Sponsoring Editor
Jim Rigney: Production Supervisor
Bob Donegan: Marketing Manager
Roy E. Logan: Senior Manufacturing Manager
Vicki Hochstedler: Copy Editor
Diana Coe: Cover Design
Benchmark Productions: Interior Design and Production

The Library of Congress Cataloging-in-Publication Data

Cline, Marshall P.
   C++ FAQs : frequently asked questions / Marshall P. Cline, Greg A.
Lomow.
     p.   cm.
   Includes bibliographical references and index.
   ISBN 0-201-58958-3
   1. C++ (Computer program language)   I. Lomow, Greg A.   II. Title.
QA76.73.C153C55   1995
005.13'3--dc20   94-10798
                                              CIP

The programs and applications presented in this book have been included for their instructional value. They have been tested with care, but are not guaranteed for any particular purpose. The publisher and authors do not offer any warranties or representations, nor do they accept any liabilities with respect to the programs or applications.

1 2 3 4 5 6 7 8 9 10—MA—98979695

Printed on recycled paper stock

For MaryElaine, David, Elizabeth, Gabrielle, Peter, and Katherine.
You too, Pepper (woof).

—Marshall

For Bennie, Mac, Lonnie, and Barb.

—Greg

Chapter Nine—Specifying Observable Behavior

Chapter Ten—Proper Inheritance

For MaryElaine, David, Elizabeth, Gabrielle, Peter, and Katherine.
You too, Pepper (woof).

—Marshall

For Bennie, Mac, Lonnie, and Barb.

—Greg

Table of Contents

v

Chapter Three—Fundamentals of Extensibility

Chapter Four—Fundamentals of C++

Chapter Five—Designing Classes and Objects

CHAPTER NINE—Specifying Observable Behavior

CHAPTER TEN—Proper Inheritance

Chapter Thirteen—Static and Dynamic Typing

Chapter Fourteen—Constructors and Destructors

Chapter Fifteen—Initialization Lists

CHAPTER SIXTEEN—The Big Three

CHAPTER SEVENTEEN—User-Defined Assignment Operators

CHAPTER EIGHTEEN—Designing for Testability

CHAPTER NINETEEN—Friend Classes and Friend Functions

CHAPTER TWENTY—Strategic Advice for Exception Handling

CHAPTER TWENTY-ONE—Tactical Advice for Exception Handling

CHAPTER TWENTY-TWO—Templates

CHAPTER TWENTY-THREE—References

CHAPTER TWENTY-FOUR—New and Delete

Chapter Twenty-Eight—Operator Overloading

Chapter Twenty-Nine—Exploiting Inline Functions

Chapter Thirty—Reference and Value Semantics

Chapter Thirty-One—Performance Tuning

CHAPTER THIRTY-SIX—Coding Standards

CHAPTER THIRTY-SEVEN—Leaf Classes

CHAPTER THIRTY-EIGHT—C++ and Smalltalk

CHAPTER THIRTY-NINE—Private and Protected Inheritance

CHAPTER FORTY—Pointers to Member Functions

CHAPTER FORTY-ONE—Source Code

CHAPTER FORTY-TWO—Miscellaneous

CHAPTER FORTY-THREE—Getting More Information on C++

ACKNOWLEDGMENTS

An unusually large number of people were involved in making this book a reality.

First, we would like to thank the tens of thousands who read the electronic FAQ and the thousands who have graduated from Paradigm Shift, Inc. training and consulting sessions. Thank you for giving us the opportunity to be part of your personal paradigm shift; you helped steer our thoughts toward questions that are relevant to the "real world" of object-oriented software development.

Special thanks to Bjarne Stroustrup and Andrew Koenig, who have been supportive of this work from the earliest days of the electronic FAQ right through to providing helpful guidance as early reviewers of the FAQ book. Thanks also to William Bulley, Stephen Clammage, James Coplien, Delano Stevens, and Stephen Vinoski for your support and insightful suggestions.

Deborah Lafferty, thank you for going far above and beyond the call of duty to persuade us to create this book, and for displaying more than normal amounts of patience during the months of preparation.

We would also like to acknowledge the many people who have helped with the copyediting and organization necessary to produce this book. Much appreciation to our students who suffered through early drafts; to Melony L. Katz, copyeditor, for reviving the book after it was shelved for a time; to Wm. Dennis Horn for his input on the project; to David Itkin and Larry Mellon for introducing us to the term "voodoo debugging"; to Pete Schommer for inventing the term "remote ownership"; to Andrea G. Mulligan; to Mike Girou; and to the office staff at Paradigm Shift, Inc.: John D. Meyers, Madeleine E. Moore, and John M. Wicke.

Our appreciation also goes to Clarkson University for providing cycles on your machines for posting and for FTP-ing the electronic FAQ.

Special thanks from Marshall: to David W. Bray for showing me the realities of self-directed thinking; to Doug Lea for daily email at 5:30 a.m. (you get an A++); and to Jamshid Afshar, Jr. for a million and one suggestions via email; and to my colleagues at Clarkson University. Most of all, thank you to MaryElaine and to David, Elizabeth, Gabrielle, Peter, and Katherine; you make it worth the trouble.

Special thanks from Greg: to Brian Unger and Graham Birtwistle for introducing me to Simula 67 and object-oriented programming in 1981, long before it became fashionable. Thank you to Brian Unger and Marshall Cline for giving me the opportunity to pursue interesting projects in stimulating work environments. Also, thanks to my colleagues from the University of Calgary, Jade Simulations, and Paradigm Shift, Inc. for their assistance and support over the years. Thank you, Barb, for all of your support and for putting up with my unusual work arrangements and bizarre schedules.

Marshall
Greg

PREFACE

What is the purpose of this book?

F A Q

0.1

The purpose of the book is to change the way you think.

Changing the way you think is much more challenging than learning the syntax of a programming language. For example, learning *when* and *why* you should use a particular construct is much harder than learning the syntax for that construct. Learning when *not* to use a particular construct is even harder.

This book gives specific advice and directions to help you properly use C++ for object-oriented programming. If you are new to object-oriented programming, our aim is to convert you to the object-oriented way of thinking. If you are a seasoned veteran, our aim is to have you question some of your ingrained practices and possibly adopt new approaches to using C++— approaches that will scale better.

F A Q

0.2

What is unique about the style and format of this book?

To achieve the book's goals, we used a novel style and format. Here are the key elements of that style and format.

- *A question and answer format:* This book contains answers to Frequently Asked Questions (or FAQs) about using C++ for object-oriented programming. These FAQs are the product of several years of teaching others to use C++ effectively, as well as an embarassingly large number of hours corresponding with the international C++ user community via the Internet news group, comp.lang.c++.

- *A focus on principles and concepts rather than syntax:* Rather than focusing on the syntax and semantics of various C++ language features, this book shows how to combine features properly and why to combine them.

- *A consistent programming and design philosophy:* As with any programming language, there are numerous ways to use and combine the various features of C++. Some of these uses and combinations lead to comprehendable, maintainable, extensible, and reusable software; other uses and combinations only work in small examples and are, in reality, abuses of the language. These FAQs identify which uses and combinations are preferred and promote a consistent programming and design philosophy that has good scaling properties.

- *Lots of programming examples:* This book contains almost 200 programming examples, most of which are complete, runnable programs rather than program fragments. Readers are encouraged to dissect and execute the examples because this will enhance the learning experience.

- *Extensive cross referencing:* The FAQs in this book are extensively cross referenced to other FAQs, as well as to other C++ books. Since the topic of using C++ for object-oriented programming is too large to be completely covered by one book, we provide you with pointers into other books where complementary material can be found. Three books we selected for cross referencing: Stroustrup's *The C++ Programming Language, Second Edition,* an excellent description of the language; Ellis and Stroustrup's *The Annotated C++ Reference Manual,* an authoritative and comprehensive definition of the language; and Lippman's *C++ Primer, Second Edition,* an excellent introductory book.

- *A lighthearted style:* We want to change the way you think, so we have to debunk many common assumptions. This leads to the questioning of common practices and—to take the edge off—humor. Another reason for the lighthearted style is that this book has roots in comp.lang.c++, where the communication style is direct and unforgiving, and where humor is used to calm people's passions and cajole people into seeing your point of view :-)

FAQ 0.3

Where did these FAQs come from?

We made them up.

Surprisingly, most of the FAQs contained in this book are not questions that anyone ever asked us directly. Instead they come from our experience training developers in object-oriented technology and from corresponding with readers on comp.lang.c++. Topics that come up again and again, whether during training sessions or on `comp.lang.c++`, were coalesced into a series of questions.

Is every topic treated with equal emphasis?

No.

Some topics are covered in greater depth than other topics. We focus more energy on topics that historically have been most difficult for people to get right, and we almost completely ignore placement of semicolons and other issues that the compiler will tell you about. The more subtle the problem, the more we focus on it—especially practices that are accepted by the compiler and appear to function correctly, but which increase the overall cost of the software.

How should you use this book in combination with other books?

It depends on what you're trying to achieve.

This book is not intended to be a tutorial introduction to C++. Each example is meant to illustrate a single idea relevant to that FAQ. Many introductory aspects of the language, such as the syntax of a *for* loop, are assumed. If you want to cover the fundamentals of C++, we recommend using this book in conjunction with either *The C++ Programming Language, Second Edition* or *C++ Primer, Second Edition.* Our FAQs provide extensive cross references into both of these texts.

This book is not intended to be a reference manual for C++. It does not pretend to cover all aspects of the language in encyclopedic detail. If you want such a reference manual, we recommend using this book in conjunction with *The Annotated C++ Reference Manual.* Our FAQs provide extensive cross references into this text.

How is the book organized?

The FAQs are organized into more than 40 chapters, each of which is organized into ascending complexity.

The FAQs in each chapter all deal with a specific topic. Usually the questions near the beginning of a chapter deal with basic questions and fundamental concepts; later questions deal with advanced issues and complex topics.

The first third of the book deals with object-oriented aspects of C++ such as inheritance, dynamic binding, and polymorphism. The middle portion of the book deals with a variety of C++ facilities ranging from templates to exception handling to the proper management of pointers. The last portion of the book contains chapters that deal with environmental topics such as training, coding standards, and Smalltalk.

FAQ 0.7

Why did we create the electronic FAQ?

To bring order to chaos.

First, the electronic FAQ presents the facts (pun intended) about C++ in a more concise and focused manner than the somewhat chaotic discussions on comp.lang.c++. Second, the number of developers switching to C++ is amazing, and the electronic FAQ answers many basic questions for these new users. Third, without a FAQ list, seasoned veterans would become irritated by answering the same questions over and over; the electronic FAQ encourages the veterans to act more like ambassadors. In the end, the electronic FAQ makes comp.lang.c++ a kinder, gentler news group, where people are less likely to be "flamed" (a technical term for posting a particularly scathing, blistering, and sarcastic response to something that is posted to an electronic bulletin board).

FAQ 0.8

Why did we write this book?

To further spread the good news.

We decided to write this book for several reasons. First, Addison-Wesley expressed interest in such a project. Second, it would make the FAQs available to a wider audience since not everyone has access to Internet and comp.lang.c++. Third, a book permits the material to be presented in a more professional manner than can be easily done with the electronic FAQ. Fourth, this project spurred us to expand the material vastly beyond what is provided by the electronic FAQ. In the end, after adding all the new

FAQs, examples, and internal and external cross references, the book contains five times more material than the electronic FAQ.

Are Marshall's and Greg's motivations based on language bigotry?

No.

For the record, we are not now—nor have we ever been—C++ language bigots. We love Smalltalk, Eiffel, C, Lisp, CLOS, Prolog, Simula, Ada, Modula, Pascal, perl, awk, sed, csh, ksh, REXX, COBOL, FORTRAN, RPG, etc. At the same time, we adopted the philosophy that since we're writing a book about C++, we might as well throw ourselves into the project even if it means that we look like C++ fanatics. It certainly has made for more exciting and provocative writing and, we hope, reading.

Our main goal is to get you to think about what you are doing and how you might improve on it. If we accomplish this, then we will be satisfied.

How can you communicate with us?

Email and FTP.

We'd love to hear from you. Our email address is clinefaq@aw.com. Send us your questions. Send us your comments.

You can acquire a free, machine-readable copy of the code sections in this book via FTP (ask your favorite network guru for help on how to access FTP with your software). The code sections will be available via FTP aw.com in the directory aw.computer.science/clinefaq. Use anonymous as your user ID, and use your email address as your password.

Enjoy!

What are FAQs?

Frequently Asked Questions you *should* ask about object-oriented programming and C++.

Each FAQ provides specific guidance in the form of in-depth answers. Many FAQs also provide a complete, runnable program which illustrates the principles.

How is "FAQs" pronounced?

Like "facts."

This book is full of C++ FAQs.

What do you mean when you say, "FAQs are questions I *should* ask"?

FAQs are questions and answers that guide you in proper usage of C++. Developers need a guidebook to help them use C++ effectively and to take them beyond simply knowing the syntax and features of the language.

F A Q

4

Why do I need a C++ guidebook?

Learning to properly use C++ is a long journey with many pitfalls.

Because of the sophistication and complexity of C++, developers need a road map that shows how to properly use the language. For example, inheritance is a powerful facility that can improve the clarity and extensibility of software, but it can also be abused in ways that result in expensive design errors.

The field of object-oriented technology is large, evolving, and heterogeneous. Under these circumstances, a guidebook to using C++ is essential.

These FAQs introduce you to the latest innovations so that you don't have to stumble around for years learning the same lessons others have already learned. The FAQs also expose incorrect and questionable practices so that you will not fall victim to them.

■

Cross references—
FAQ: 412, 413

F A Q

5

What kind of guidance is given in the answers to these FAQs?

Explanations of language features, directions for using these features properly, and guidelines indicating programming practices to avoid.

The FAQs can be divided into roughly three categories. First, FAQs that explain what a particular language feature is and how to use it in compliance with C++ semantics. Second, FAQs that explain how to use C++ properly. Some of these answers deal only with a single language feature, while others explain how to use several different language features in concert. Combining language features allows sophisticated designs that can simultaneously satisfy multiple technical and business goals. Third, FAQs that expose poor programming practices. These show design and programming practices that are legal in C++, but should be avoided because they can lead to incorrect programs, or programs that are hard to comprehend, maintain, extend, and reuse.

F A Q

6

Where did these FAQs come from?

Very few of these C++ FAQs were questions that anyone ever asked us explicitly. Inspiration for most of them comes from our experience teaching and consulting in the areas of C++ and object-oriented design. We noticed that many software developers were able to learn the rules of the language, but that they needed help learning how to use and combine its features properly.

F A Q

7

What is the electronic FAQ?

A set of C++ questions and answers, originally prepared and distributed on the Internet by Marshall Cline. The Internet version is currently updated and distributed by Marshall Cline and Greg Lomow, and is available through the news group comp.lang.c++.

This book and the electronic FAQ were inspired by a seemingly unquenchable thirst among C++ developers for more and better information about C++.

F A Q

8

How is this book related to the electronic FAQ?

A number of years ago, Marshall Cline, the proud parent of both FAQs, decided to collect some of his teaching examples, and make them freely available to the readers of comp.lang.c++. Many hours and nights later, the electronic FAQ was born.

Several years and tens of thousands of comp.lang.c++ readers later, Marshall, Greg, and Addison-Wesley decided to rewrite and expand the material and make it available in book form.

FAQ 9

Why should I buy this book if I can get the electronic FAQ for free?

This book has 5 times as much material as the electronic FAQ.

Relative to the electronic FAQ, this book covers a broader range of topics and goes into greater depth.

This book highlights the key points with extensive new examples, and it is thoroughly cross-referenced to other topics within this book and to other books on C++.

Most of the programming examples are working, stand-alone programs, complete with their own main( ), all necessary #include files, and so on. All examples have been compiled directly from the source text of the book; those that have a main( ) have also been run.

FAQ 10

What conventions are used in this book?

This book uses a number of conventions. They are as follows:

We use the undecorated word "inheritance" to mean "public inheritance." Whenever we speak of private or protected inheritance, we say so explicitly.

Similarly, we use the phrase "derived class" to mean "publicly-derived class." Derived classes produced via private or protected inheritance are explicitly designated "private derived class" or "protected derived class," respectively.

We use the class names Base and Derived as hypothetical class names to illustrate the general relationship between a base class and one of its (publicly) derived classes.

We use the term "out-lined" function to indicate a function that is called via a normal CALL instruction. In contrast, when an "inlined" function is invoked, the compiler inserts the object code for that function at the point-of-call.

We use the term "remote ownership" when an object contains a pointer to an allocation that is owned by the object. The default destruction and copy semantics for objects that contain remote ownership are incorrect, so explicit controls are needed.

We use "OO" as an abbreviation for "object-oriented."

We use "K&R" as an abbreviation for "Kernighan and Ritchie."

We allow the compiler to supply an implicit int return type for main(); all other functions have an explicit return type.

We use the (new) intrinsic data type bool, which has literal values true and false. If your compiler doesn't have a built in bool type, insert the following at the beginning of each example:

```
typedef char bool; const bool false = 0; const bool true = 1;
```

We assume that new will throw an exception if it runs out of memory (in particular, we assume new never returns NULL); this is new C++ behavior.

We recommend that library developers don't use protected data, since it allows derived classes to do things that they shouldn't be allowed to do. However for most C++ developers, protected data is ok, and for this reason we often use protected data in the examples. Library designers should use private data with protected access functions.

Class names start with a capital letter; preprocessor symbol and global enumerations are all capitals; all other indentifiers start with a lower case letter. Data member names and class scoped enumerations end with a single underscore.

The following priorities were used in designing the examples: 1) unity of purpose, 2) compactness, and 3) self-contained functionality. In other words, each example demonstrates one basic point or technique, is as short as possible, and, if possible, is a complete, runnable program. The examples are not intended for plug-in reuse in industrial strength settings since balancing the resultant (subtle) tradeoffs would conflict with these priorities.

Specifically, to avoid complicating the discussions with finding the optimal balance between virtualness and inlinability of member functions, virtual is used more often than strictly necessary (see FAQ-90). To achieve compactness, some member functions are defined in the class body even if they wouldn't normally be inline, or even if moving them down to the bottom of a header file would improve specificability (see FAQ-108). Uncalled functions are often left undefined. Some functions that are called are also undefined, since compactness is a higher priority than self-contained functionality. Also for compactness, examples are not wrapped in preprocessor logic that prevents multiple expansions (see FAQ-356).

■

Cross references—

FAQ: 202, 349

What are the fundamental concepts of object-oriented technology?

Objects, classes, and inheritance.

By definition, object-oriented programming must provide those tools. However, in our experience, polymorphism and dynamic binding are also required. Together, these tools fulfill the real goals of OO: abstraction, encapsulation, comprehensibility, and reusability.

Now for a few definitions. An object is a region of storage with associated semantics. An object is like a house. It has state (whether the lights are on, ambient temperature, and so on), and it provides services (a button that opens the garage door, a thermostat that controls the temperature, an alarm system that detects intruders, and so on).

To carry the house metaphor a bit further, a class is like a blueprint that describes how to construct and use an object. An object is an instance of a class. A blueprint describes what a house will look like; but you can't live in a blueprint. Similarly, you need to create an object before you can use its services.

A class has a name, and it describes the state (member data) and services (member functions) provided by its objects. The class too can have state and services (static member data and functions, respectively).

Simple data types such as int and float can be thought of as classes; variables of these types can be thought of as objects of the associated class.

Classes can be related by inheritance. In C++, inheritance facilitates polymorphism and dynamic binding. Polymorphism allows objects of one class to be used as if they were objects of another, related class. Dynamic binding ensures that the code that gets executed is always consistent with the type of the object. Rather than selecting the proper code fragment by some *ad hoc* technique such as complex decision logic, the proper code fragment is automatically selected in a manner that is always correct, and is extensible. Together, these allow old user code to call new server code; new classes can be added to a working system without affecting existing code.

■

Cross references—

FAQ: 15, 16, 19, 20, 56, 57
See Stroustrup: 1.4, 1.5, 5.2, 6.2, 12.2
See Ellis & Stroustrup: 9.1, 10.1c, 10.2

F A Q
12

What is prompting people to adopt OO technology?

Money.

The former paradigm (structured analysis, design, and programming) enabled the design and construction of huge software systems. However, the resultant systems lack the flexibility required to meet the demands placed on software in today's rapidly changing business environment. Thus, the old paradigm died from its own success. It created a market hunger that it couldn't satisfy.

As consumers demand more and more from software, pragmatism required a better paradigm. Enter object-oriented analysis, design, and programming.

■

Cross references—

FAQ: 11
See Stroustrup: 1.5, 11, 12.1
See Ellis & Stroustrup: 10.2

What are some specific reasons to use C++ for OO programming?

Large user community, multi-paradigm language, performance, legacy code, and professional development.

C++ is the most widely used object-oriented programming language. This large and thriving user community has led to high-quality compilers and other development tools for a wide range of systems. It has also led to the availability of learning aids, such as books, conferences, bulletin boards, and organizations that specialize in training and consulting. With that much support, investing in C++ is a relatively safe undertaking.

C++ is a multi-paradigm language. This allows developers to choose the programming style that is right for the task at hand. For example, a traditional procedural style may be appropriate for performing a simple task such as writing the code within a small member function.

C++ software can be performance and memory efficient, provided it is designed properly. For example, well-designed, object-oriented software is normally comprehensible and therefore amenable to performance tuning. In addition, C++ has low-level—and often dangerous—facilities that allow a skilled C++ developer to obtain appropriate levels of performance.

C++ is (mostly) backward compatible with C. This is useful in very large legacy systems, where the transformation to OO normally occurs a few subsystems at a time rather than all at once. In particular, C++'s backward compatibility makes it relatively inexpensive to compile legacy C code with a C++ compiler, allowing the old, non-OO subsystems to coexist with the new, OO subsystems. Furthermore, simply compiling the legacy C code with a C++ compiler subjects the non-OO subsystems to the relatively stronger type safety checks of a C++ compiler. In today's quality-sensitive culture, this makes good business sense.

C++ experience looks great on a résumé. This is especially valuable now as organizations continue to downsize. Job security has been replaced by skill security, and skill in OO/C++ is at a premium. But don't limit yourself to using C++ as only "a better C" or you'll miss most of its benefits.

■

Cross references—
FAQ: 388, 395
See Stroustrup: 1.3, 4.4

F A Q
14

What is the purpose of composition?

Composition allows software to be developed by assembling existing components rather than crafting new ones.

Composition (sometimes called aggregation) is the process of putting an object (a part) inside another object (the composite). For example, a FordTaurus can be composed from, among other things, an Engine, Transmission, InstrumentPanel, and so on. In other words, an Engine is *part-of* a FordTaurus (equivalently, a FordTaurus has an Engine):

```cpp
#include <iostream.h>

class Engine {
public:
  virtual void start()
    { cout << "starting Engine\n"; }
};

class FordTaurus {
public:
  virtual void start()
    { cout << "starting FordTaurus\n"; engine_.start(); }
protected:
  Engine engine_;     //an Engine is part of a FordTaurus
};                    //convention: "_" suffix on member data

main()
{
  FordTaurus taurus;
  taurus.start();
}
```

Building software objects by composition is a lot like building an airplane model from a kit. Some of the pieces already exist; your job is to add the glue. With composition, software ends up being assembled rather than crafted.

Sometimes developers incorrectly use inheritance (kind-of) when they should use composition. For example, they might make FordTaurus inherit from Engine, which confuses "kind-of" with "part-of."

■

Cross references—

FAQ: 15, 76
See Stroustrup: 5.2, r.9
See Ellis & Stroustrup: 9.2

What is the purpose of inheritance?

In C++, inheritance is for subtyping; it lets developers model the "kind-of" relationship.

Inheritance allows developers to make one class a kind-of another class. In an inheritance relationship, the derived class is the new class, and the base class is the original class from which the new class is being derived. All of the data structures and services belonging to the base class automatically become part of the derived class.

For example, suppose you have a class Stack with services push() and pop(), and you want to create a class PrintableStack. PrintableStack is exactly like Stack except PrintableStack also provides the service print(). Class PrintableStack can be built by inheriting from Stack—Stack would be the base class and PrintableStack would be the derived class. The services push(), pop(), and any others that belong to Stack, automatically become part of PrintableStack, so the only requirement for building PrintableStack is adding the print() service to it.

To do something similar in C, you would need to modify the existing Stack module (which is trouble if Stack is being used by others) or copy Stack into another file and then tweak that file. However, code copying is the least desirable form of reuse. It doubles the maintenance costs and duplicates any bugs in the original module. In C++ Stack remains unmodified, yet PrintableStack doesn't need to duplicate the code for the inherited services.

■

Cross references—
FAQ: 14, 76, 77
See Stroustrup: 1.5, 6.2, 6.3
See Ellis & Stroustrup: 10, 10.1c

What are the advantages of polymorphism and dynamic binding?

They allow old code to call new code in a substitutable fashion.

The real power of object-oriented programming isn't just inheritance; it's the ability to treat objects of derived classes as if they were objects of the base class. Polymorphism and dynamic binding are the mechanisms that support this.

Polymorphism allows a derived class object to be passed to a function that accepts a reference or a pointer to a base class. A function that receives such objects is a polymorphic function.

When a polymorphic function invokes a service using a base class reference or pointer, dynamic binding executes the code from the derived class even though the polymorphic function may be unaware that the derived class exists. The code that gets executed depends on the type of the object rather than on the type of the reference or pointer. In this way, objects of a derived class can be substituted for objects of a base class without requiring any changes in the polymorphic functions that use those objects.

■

Cross references—

FAQ: 89, 94
See Stroustrup: 1.5, 4.6, 6.2
See Ellis & Stroustrup: 10.1c, 10.2, 10.7c

How does OO help developers produce flexible and extensible software?

OO minimizes the ripple effect of enhancements.

Even in well-designed, structured systems, enhancements often require modifications to significant portions of existing design and code. In OO, we achieve flexibility by (1) allowing the past to make use of the future, and (2) designing for comprehensibility.

The past can make use of the future when old user code (the past) can reliably and predictably call new server code (the future) without any modifications to the old user code. We use inheritance, polymorphism, and dynamic binding to achieve this lofty goal.

Comprehensibility allows software to be understood not only by the original development team, but also by the team making the enhancements. We use abstraction and specification to achieve this lofty goal.

This contrasts with software developed using the traditional, structured approach, where enhancements or modifications often lead to a seemingly endless cycle of random modifications (a.k.a. hacks) until the system appears to work.

■

Cross references—
FAQ: 18, 70, 94, 105

How can old code call new code?

Magic.

In the traditional software paradigm, it is easy for new code to call old code using subroutine libraries. However, it is difficult for old code to call new code (unless you modify the old code so that it knows about the new code, in which case the old code is no longer old).

With object-orientation, old polymorphic functions can dynamically bind to new server code. A new derived class can be used by an existing polymorphic function without modifying the polymorphic function.

When compiling a polymorphic function, it is as if the compiler looks forward in time and generates code that will bind to all the classes that will ever be added.

For example, a graphical drawing package might deal with various shapes such as squares, circles, and polygons. Most of the drawing package's services deal with generic shapes rather than a particular kind of shape like square (for example, "if a shape is selected by the mouse, that shape is dragged across the screen and placed in a new location"). Polymorphism and dynamic binding allow the drag-and-drop code to work correctly regardless of the kind of shape being manipulated. To implement this, class Shape would declare virtual functions for drawing and moving. The derived classes would represent the various kinds of shapes: Square, Circle, and so forth.

```
#include <iostream.h>

class Shape {
public:
  Shape(int x, int y)                   : x_(x), y_(y) { }
  virtual ~Shape()                      { }
  virtual void draw()                   = 0;
  virtual void move(int x, int y)       = 0;
protected:
  int x_, y_;                           //convention: "_" suffix
  void operator= (const Shape& s)       { x_ = s.x_; y_ = s.y_; }
  Shape(const Shape& s)                 : x_(s.x_), y_(s.y_) { }
};

void
dragAndDrop(Shape& s)    //a polymorphic function
{
  s.move(42,24);    //dynamic binding calls the "right" code
  s.draw();         //as if the compiler predicted the future
}

class Square : public Shape {
public:
  Square(int x, int y, int width)
    : Shape(x,y), width_(width) { }
  virtual void draw()
    { cout << "Square::draw\n"; }
  virtual void move(int x, int y)
    { x_ = x; y_ = y; cout << "Square::move\n"; }
protected:
  int width_;
};

class Circle : public Shape {
public:
  Circle(int x, int y, int radius)
    : Shape(x,y), radius_(radius) { }
  virtual void draw()
    { cout << "Circle::draw\n"; }
  virtual void move(int x, int y)
    { x_ = x; y_ = y; cout << "Circle::move\n"; }
protected:
  int radius_;
};
```

```
main()
{
  Square s = Square(5, 20, 3);
  Circle c = Circle(10, 15, 7);
  dragAndDrop(s);
  dragAndDrop(c);
}
```

The `dragAndDrop(Shape&)` function above properly invokes the right services from class `Square` and `Circle`, even though the compiler didn't know about `Square` or `Circle` when it was compiling `dragAndDrop(Shape&)`. The output of this program is:

```
Square::move
Square::draw
Circle::move
Circle::draw
```

Suppose the function `dragAndDrop(Shape&)` was compiled on Tuesday, and a new kind of shape—say a `Hexagon`—was created on Wednesday, `dragAndDrop(Shape&)` will work with a `Hexagon`, even though the `Hexagon` class didn't exist when `dragAndDrop(Shape&)` was compiled.

What is the verb "abstract"?

F A Q
19

As a verb, to abstract is to identify the inherent qualities of some entity. Using the process of abstraction, developers identify the "abstract" properties of an object or a subsystem.

When building large, reusable software systems, abstracting allows you to separate the essential qualities of an object or a subsystem from incidental implementation details. These essential qualities are far more valuable and reusable than the code used to implement them.

The product of abstracting is one or more abstractions.

■

Cross references—
FAQ: 20, 23, 70
See Stroustrup: 1.2, 5.1, 12.2
See Ellis & Stroustrup: 9.1

F A Q
20

What is the noun "abstraction"?

An abstraction is a simplified view of an object in the user's own vocabulary.

In OO and C++, an abstraction is the simplest interface to an object that provides all of the features and services that the intended users expect.

An abstraction tells users everything they need or want to know about an object, but nothing else. It is the well-defined, unambiguously specified interface. For example, on a vending machine, the buttons and their meanings form an abstraction; users don't have to know about levers, internal counters, or other parts that are needed for the machine to operate. Furthermore the vending machine's price list implies a legally binding promise to users: if users put in the right amount of money, the machine promises to dispense the desired item.

■

Cross references—
FAQ: 19, 23, 70
See Stroustrup: 1.2, 5.1, 12.2
See Ellis & Stroustrup: 9.1

F A Q
21

What is the key to designing good abstractions?

Deep knowledge of the problem domain.

Good abstractions capture important elements of the user's problem domain. The key to finding which elements are important is a deep understanding of the problem domain. If you do not possess deep knowledge of the problem domain, consult with domain experts to prevent gross mismatches or shallow abstractions.

Should abstractions be user-centric or developer-centric?

User-centric.

New object-oriented programmers commonly make the mistake of thinking that inheritance, objects, and so on, exist to make it easier to build a class. Unfortunately, this self-centered view of OO software merely provides a short burst of improved productivity; it fails to produce a software-development culture that has "sustainable effectiveness." In other words, a flash in the pan, then nothing.

The only way to achieve long-term success with OO is for developers to focus on their users, instead of on themselves. Ironically, most developers eventually become users of their own abstractions, so they end up helping themselves through their efforts to help others.

What are the benefits of a good abstraction?

Simplified, stable user code.

A good abstraction allows users to use an object in a relatively safe and predictable manner. It reduces the learning curve by providing a simple interface described in terms of the user's own vocabulary.

A good abstraction separates specification from implementation. It doesn't expose too much nor does it hide features that users deem important. If an abstraction is good, users aren't tempted to peek at the object's implementation.

■

Cross references—
FAQ: 19, 20
See Stroustrup: 1.2, 5.1, 12.2
See Ellis & Stroustrup: 9.1

FAQ 24

What's the difference between encapsulation and abstraction?

Encapsulation protects abstractions. Encapsulation is the bodyguard; abstraction is the VIP.

Encapsulation provides the explicit boundary between an object's abstract interface (its abstraction) and its internal implementation details. Encapsulation puts the implementation details "in a capsule." Encapsulation tells users which services are stable, permanent features of the object, and which features are implementation details that are subject to change without notice.

For developers of an abstraction, encapsulation provides the freedom to implement the abstraction in any way consistent with the interface. (Encapsulation tells developers exactly what users can, and cannot, access.) For users, encapsulation provides protection by preventing dependence on volatile implementation details.

Abstraction provides business value; encapsulation "protects" these abstractions.

■

Cross references—

FAQ: 19, 20, 23, 27
See Stroustrup: 1.2, 5.1, 5.2, 12.2, 12.4
See Ellis & Stroustrup: 9.1, 11, 11.1c

FAQ 25

What are the consequences of encapsulating a good abstraction?

Peace and safety.

If a developer provides a good abstraction, users won't be tempted to peek at the object's internal mechanisms. Encapsulation is simply a safety feature that reminds users not to stray over the line inadvertently.

What are the consequences of encapsulating a *bad* abstraction?

Wasted money. *Lots* of wasted money.

There's nothing more frustrating than a lousy abstraction that is encapsulated. When a developer encapsulates a bad abstraction, users will continually attempt to violate the abstraction's encapsulation barrier. When that happens, don't waste your time trying to make it even harder for users to access the object's internals; fix the abstraction instead.

Don't think of encapsulation as a club with which the good guys (a class's authors) prevent the bad guys (a class's users) from looking inside an object. Remember, object-oriented design and programming is not a contest between developers and users.

What's the value of separating interface from implementation?

It's a key to reusable software.

Interfaces are a company's most valuable asset. Maintaining interface consistency across implementation changes is a priority for many companies. Keeping the interface separate from the implementation allows that consistency. It also produces software that is cheaper to design, write, debug, test, and maintain than other software.

Separating the interface from the implementation makes a system easier to understand by reducing its overall complexity. Each object only needs to know about the interfaces—not the implementations—of the objects with which it collaborates. This is in stark contrast to most systems, where it seems like every module knows about the implementation of every other module. In one extreme case, 157 different modules had direct access to a data structure in some other module (we're not making this up). Imagine how expensive it would be to change that data structure in response to a new customer requirement.

Separating the interface from the implementation also makes a system more flexible by reducing coupling between components. A high incidence of coupling between components is a major factor in systems becoming brittle. This makes it difficult to accommodate new customer requirements in a cost-effective manner. When coupling is strong, a change to one module affects other modules, so that they require changes as well. This produces a cascading effect that eventually ripples through a large part of the system. Since separating the interface from the implementation reduces coupling, it also reduces these ripples. The overall result is a more flexible software product, and an organization that is better equipped to keep up with market changes.

In addition, separating the interface from the implementation simplifies debugging and testing. The software that provides the interface is the only software that touches the implementation directly, and therefore is the only software that can cause nonsensical, incoherent, or inconsistent behavior by the implementation. For example, if a linked list caches its length, and the length counter doesn't match the number of links in the list, finding the code that caused this error is vastly simpler if direct access to the length counter is limited.

Finally, separating the interface from the implementation encourages software reuse by reducing education costs for those who want to reuse an object. The reusers of an object need only learn about the interface, rather than the (normally vastly more complicated) implementation.

■

Cross references—

FAQ: 19, 23, 24
See Stroustrup: 1.2, 5.1, 5.2, 12.2, 12.4
See Ellis & Stroustrup: 9.1, 11, 11.1c

F A Q
28

How can separating interface from implementation improve performance as well as flexibility?

Late life-cycle performance tuning.

Fact #1: The only objects worth tuning are the ones that create performance bottlenecks, and the only way to know which objects are the bottlenecks is to measure the behavior of a running system (profiling). Developers sometimes think they can predict where the bottlenecks will be, but many studies have shown that the actual bottlenecks were not accurately predicted by developers. Therefore don't waste your time tuning the performance of a piece of code until actual measurements have shown that it is an actual bottleneck.

Fact #2: The most potent means of improving performance is changing algorithms and data structures. Hand tuning the wrong algorithm or data structure has very little benefit compared to finding an algorithm or data structure that is a better match for the problem being solved. This is especially true for large problems, where algorithms and data structures must be scalable.

These two facts lead to an undeniable conclusion: the most effective performance tuning occurs when you change the product's fundamental data structures and algorithms late in the product's life cycle. This can only be accomplished if there is adequate separation of interface from implementation.

For example, it would be expensive to change a sorted array to a binary search tree in a typical software product today, since all the places that use integer indices to access entries would need to be modified to use node pointers. In other words, in typical software today, the interface *is* the implementation. The key to solving this problem is to focus on the similarity in the abstractions rather than the differences in the data structures: sorted arrays and binary trees are both containers that keep their entries in sorted order. In this light, they are merely alternate implementations of the same abstraction and they should have the same interface.

The key to late life-cycle performance tunability is to hide performance differences behind a uniform interface. This allows users to code to an abstraction rather than to a data structure. As a result, the data structure and algorithm can be replaced at any time.

Note that the real issues are much deeper than C++ versus C. It boils down to asking the right questions at the right time, which is the goal of a good software development process (SDP). Unfortunately, many SDPs cause developers to ask the wrong questions at the wrong time, often resulting in a premature commitment to an implementation technique. Even if an SDP uses OO terminology (for example, by using the term *object diagram* rather than *data structure*), your software will be inflexible if the bulk of your code is aware of relationships that may need to change.

The first programming technique that exploited these ideas was based on abstract data types. The OO paradigm is built on top of the abstract data type technique, in that OO adds the ability of the user code to work with all of an abstraction's implementations simultaneously. OO allows the data structures to be interchanged dynamically on a case-by-case basis, rather than forcing a statically chosen, one-size-fits-all approach.

■

Cross reference—

FAQ: 280

FAQ
29

What is an object-oriented programming language?

A language that supports objects, classes, and inheritance.

Languages that support only objects and classes (for example, the first release of the Ada language) are called object-based languages, to distinguish them from full object-oriented languages.

Note that supporting a technique is different from merely allowing that technique.

■

Cross references—

FAQ: 11, 13
See Stroustrup: 1.2, 1.3, 1.4, 1.5, 6.1
See Ellis & Stroustrup: 10.2

Which is more stable, the problem being solved, or the problem domain?

The problem domain.

The specification of the problem being solved is unstable, since it depends on the whims of the customer, but the problem domain is an artifact of the world in which the customer lives. The needs of customers change more rapidly than their world does.

For example, systems that control traffic lights must deal with vehicles, pedestrians, switches, magnetic vehicle detectors, and traffic lights. These entities represent the problem domain and are stable across all traffic light control systems. However, each particular traffic light system has different parameters. For example, delay a seconds after a pedestrian pushes button b; otherwise delay c seconds if a vehicle is detected in lane d, and so on.

Do customers ever change their requirements?

Ha, ha, ha! The only customers who don't change their requirements are dead customers.

In all of recorded history, no customer has ever changed his mind less than twice (and the poor guy who changed his mind only twice was hit by a truck on his way to send in his third set of changes).

We must write modern software so that changing the problem doesn't break the architecture. We do this by basing the architecture on the most stable thing we have: the problem domain.

Note that software can survive problem changes only within the confines of its problem domain. It's unreasonable to expect a system that was originally designed for the problem domain of compilers to work for cellular telephones, since this would be changing the problem *domain,* rather than just the problem.

F A Q

32

Would stable requirements make our jobs easier?

No—stable requirements would eliminate our jobs.

The software industry thrives on changing requirements. It's called a "line of business."

Most sales of legacy systems are to customers of previous versions, therefore enormous effort goes into differentiating version N from version $N-1$. Differentiation is another way of saying change.

The only way to have stable requirements is for the product to be so bad that no one wants to buy the next version. Stable requirements reflect a dead product. Stable requirements are an enemy, not a friend.

F A Q

33

How much effort should you expend to support change—that is, how much is extensibility worth?

You should support as much extensibility as you can afford, provided you still ship within the market window.

Having an extensible product isn't worth much if you have no market share. On the other hand, having market share without an extensible product means that enhancing your software will be an expensive proposition. An inflexible software product in today's rapidly changing business climate can be deadly.

The following is a real-life example that illustrates this issue. Two organizations had similar products. One used OO technology to achieve extensibility (a new release every six months); the other shipped a new release every two years. Not only did the rapid-fire organization create four times as many sales opportunities per customer than its slower counterpart, it also used its enhanced features to become the market leader.

The only products that never change are the failures. Successful products need to be changed. The strategic decision is to design for change.

Every product plan should have this line item: "Produce an extensible, domain-specific library of reusable software components."

What is an extensible, domain-specific library of reusable classes?

A competitive advantage.

A domain-specific, reusable class library models the key abstractions of the problem domain. These classes, along with the classes from a general-purpose class library, are the building blocks for solving the problems from that problem domain.

A domain-specific, reusable class library should have as much *domain*-specific knowledge as possible, while remaining as independent as possible from any single problem being solved. If the classes lack domain-specific knowledge, future developers must largely rediscover the problem domain. If the classes have too much *problem*-specific knowledge, future developers will always be fighting the problem-specific assumptions.

What characteristics make a class reusable yet domain-specific?

Mechanism-rich, policy-free.

The ideal domain-specific reusable class is rich in the mechanism of the problem domain, but free from policy within that problem domain. If it isn't mechanism rich, future developers won't get as much "oomph" (a technical term) as they might otherwise. If it isn't policy free, future developers will have to work around the obsolete policy.

■

Cross reference—

FAQ: 34

FAQ 36

Why isn't current technology producing software that is reusable and extensible?

Current technology produces software that is mechanism rich (good), but also, policy rich (bad).

Most software built using structured technology is policy rich. Current technology encourages developers to design their software based on data-flow diagrams (DFDs). DFDs are typically policy rich; they focus on the problem rather than the problem domain.

Although solving the particular problem is essential, programmers should define an architecture that is based on the problem domain, not on the problem.

■

Cross references—
FAQ: 31, 40, 45

FAQ 37

Why are some OO systems *non*-reusable and *non*-extensible?

Some OO software is policy free (good), but also mechanism free (bad).

One sure way to remain policy free is to provide nothing but get and set services. Although this prevents the class from imposing unnecessary policy, it also prevents the class from providing any mechanism.

Mechanism richness reduces the overall bulk of the system, because it moves mechanical complexity from users into the server (that is, from the many to the few). Classes that have a get and a set service for every datum do the opposite. They move mechanical complexity from the few servers to the many users. This results in "reuse by copy and tweak."

■

Cross reference—
FAQ: 38

What is reuse by copy and tweak?

The worst form of reuse.

Reuse by copy and tweak involves making a copy of a source file and then tweaking the source file until it matches the new set of policies for the new problem.

Although any reuse is better than none, reuse by copy and tweak is vastly inferior to the other techniques—such as composition—that don't require code copying. Reuse by copy and tweak copies bugs and increases maintenance costs.

■

Cross reference—
FAQ: 14

Is it insane to base software design on the policy of the problem itself?

Totally insane.

The policy of the problem is unstable. Software systems based on the least stable element (the problem) rather than the most stable element (the problem domain), are doomed to fail.

■

Cross reference—
FAQ: 40

What do data-flow diagrams have to do with the problem domain?

Nothing whatsoever.

Data-flow diagrams tell us what the product should do, not what the problem domain is like. They form the worst possible foundation for software development, because the policy of the problem (what the product should do) is destined to change.

■

Cross references—
FAQ: 33, 39

Should public inheritance reflect the problem being solved or the problem domain?

The problem domain.

The beauty of OO technology is that the architecture can be made to reflect the problem domain rather than the particular problem at hand. In other words, the public inheritance relationships should model the problem domain rather than depending on the fickle requirements of the even more fickle customer.

In C++, public inheritance relationships should reflect fundamental, immutable properties of the problem domain. Technically this is called subtyping.

OO technology provides flexibility when the domain analysis is solid and the software faithfully reflects that domain analysis. Under these circumstances, changing the details of the problem creates incidental disturbances, rather than fundamental disruptions.

F A Q
42

What happens if the domain analysis is incorrect?

It costs money.

Once a developer makes a domain analysis mistake, randomly patching the code makes matters worse. Instead, one should fix the domain analysis. Unfortunately, that fix often breaks existing code. That's why we say domain-analysis errors are 10 times more costly to fix than programming errors.

Domain-analysis mistakes shake the foundation of our public inheritance relationships.

∎

Cross references—
FAQ: 128, 130

F A Q
43

What happens if programmers abuse public inheritance?

It costs money.

If the public inheritance relationships don't faithfully model the domain analysis, the software will be just as brittle as if the domain analysis was faulty.

This is one of the most common problems for developers new to OO; they get so excited about using public inheritance that they use it when it isn't warranted, or they fail to use it when it is warranted. Either way, it costs money, since the resulting inheritance relationships don't accurately model the otherwise stable problem domain.

In C++, class D should inherit from class B if and only if there is a subtyping relationship between type D and type B.

∎

Cross reference—
FAQ: 42

FAQ 44

Is breaking existing code the ultimate evil?

No—failure to ship the product on time and within budget is the ultimate evil.

Fixing domain analysis errors often breaks existing code. Even though changing existing code is expensive, it is often far more expensive to continue building the software based on a faulty domain analysis, because domain analysis errors usually make software brittle.

If you must make changes, sooner is often much cheaper than later.

■

Cross reference—
FAQ: 42

FAQ 45

Is public inheritance primarily for code reuse?

No.

In C++, the primary reason for using public inheritance is to model the problem domain accurately. Usually this means interface reuse, because the interface reflects what something is, while the implementation tells how it is built.

Public inheritance should be used to model observable relationships, not merely for implementation reasons.

If the only goal is reuse of implementation code, composition is probably superior to public inheritance.

■

Cross reference—
FAQ: 131

What is C++?

FAQ

46

C++ is an object-oriented programming language.

C++ can be used as a better C, as an object-based programming language, or as an object-oriented programming language. Object-oriented programming is the preferred development technology for large, complex software systems.

■

Cross references—

FAQ: 11, 13, 29, 459
See Stroustrup: 1.2, 1.3, 1.4, 1.5, 6.1
See Ellis & Stroustrup: 10.2
See Lippman: 0.2

FAQ

47

Who uses C++?

Many corporations, government organizations, and universities use C++ for commercial products and research projects. The number of users is growing exponentially.

■

Cross reference—

FAQ: 48

F A Q
48

How often does a non-C++ programmer switch to C++?

Every 15 seconds.

The number of C++ users is difficult to measure, but Bjarne Stroustrup gave a "conservative" estimate of 400,000 in October 1991. At that time, the C++ community was doubling every 7.5 months. To be ultra-conservative, let's assume that the rate has slowed to doubling every 12 months.

Based on these assumptions, on May 17, 2005 every man, woman, and child on planet Earth will be a C++ programmer (and the following year, we'll have to discover life on Mars, no doubt).

■

Cross reference—

FAQ: 47

F A Q
49

Are there any efforts under way to standardize C++?

Yes.

ANSI (American National Standards Institute) and ISO (International Standards Organization) groups are working together to form one world-wide C++ standard. The ANSI-C++ committee is called "X3J16," ISO's C++ group is called "WG21."

The ANSI/ISO C++ standards process includes just about all the industry's major players: AT&T, IBM, Digital Equipment, Hewlett-Packard, Sun, Microsoft, Borland, Zortech, Apple, Open Software Foundation (OSF), and many others. About 70 people from all over the world attend each ANSI/ISO C++ meeting.

Optimistically, the standard might be finished by 1996, which is about as fast as the ANSI-C standardization process went.

As discussed in the remainder of this chapter, C++ has standardized ways to help beat the speed/safety trade-off, to exploit a user's intuition about the meaning of an operation, to simplify maintenance and increase code reuse, to handle errors, and to separate interface from implementation.

■

Cross reference—

FAQ: 470

How can inline functions help beat the performance/encapsulation trade-off?

In most programming languages, encapsulation must be sacrificed for performance. For example, an encapsulated C structure requires a function call to access even trivial fields. Function call overhead is small, but it can become unacceptable in performance-sensitive systems or applications. C++ provides a solution by allowing functions to be expanded inline. This allows:

1. the safety of encapsulation,

2. the convenience of multiple instances, and

3. the speed of direct access.

On the surface, inline functions are similar to #define macros; the compiler inserts the object code for the inline function at the call point without generating a CALL instruction.

Inline functions are an improvement over #define macros for two reasons. First, the compiler checks the parameter types of inline functions. Second, all arguments to an inline function are guaranteed to be evaluated exactly once. This second advantage eliminates an infamous category of defects typified by min(f(),g()), where min(i,j) is a macro that elaborates its arguments more than once, and where f() and/or g() have side effects.

```
#include <iostream.h>

#define     minMacro(i, j)          ( (i) < (j) ? (i) : (j) )
inline int minFunct(int i, int j) { return i < j ? i : j; }

int f() { cout << "f() called\n"; return 42; }
int g() { cout << "g() called\n"; return 24; }

main()
{
  cout << "using minMacro:\n";  minMacro(f(), g());
  cout << "using minFunct:\n";  minFunct(f(), g());
}
```

In the above code, the expansion of minMacro(f(),g()) will call f() once but g() twice. This can be an error when g() has side effects. However, the expansion of minFunct(f(),g()) will call both f() and g() exactly once.

■

Cross references—

FAQ: 350
See Stroustrup: 4.6, 5.3
See Ellis & Stroustrup: 7.1, 16.1c
See Lippman: 3.0

F A Q

51

How can operator overloading exploit a user's intuition about the meaning of an operation?

C++ allows user-defined types (for example, `Complex`) to look like predefined types (for example, `int`, `float`, and so on) by providing a way to overload the familiar operators. The compiler can be told what to do if it finds a + between two complex numbers, for example. Because the resultant syntax is familiar, it may reduce education costs and reduce defects.

The law of Conservation of Complexity says that software can be only so simple. Ultimately, complexity isn't actually reduced; it is moved. The advantage of operator overloading is that it moves the complexity from the many users to the few servers. For example, the arithmetic operators in class `Complex`, shown below, make the class more intelligent, but also make it more complicated than a simple `struct` that contains two floating point numbers. This example illustrates that reducing the software's overall complexity may actually increase the complexity of some portions of the code.

```
class Complex {
public:
  Complex(float real=0, float imag=0)
    : real_(real), imag_(imag) { }
  friend Complex operator+ (Complex a, Complex b)
    { return Complex(a.real_+b.real_, a.imag_+b.imag_); }
  friend Complex operator- (Complex a, Complex b)
    { return Complex(a.real_-b.real_, a.imag_-b.imag_); }
  friend Complex operator* (Complex a, Complex b)
    { return Complex(a.real_*b.real_ - a.imag_*b.imag_,
                     a.real_*b.imag_ + a.imag_*b.real_); }
  friend Complex operator/ (Complex a, Complex b)
    { float magB2 = b.real_ * b.real_ + b.imag_*b.imag_;
      return a * Complex(b.real_/magB2, -b.imag_/magB2); }
protected:
  float real_, imag_;  //convention: "_" suffix
};
```

The added complexity of the Complex class, however, is more than offset by the vastly simpler user code, below.

```
Complex
sampleUserCode(Complex a, Complex b, Complex c, Complex d)
{
  return (a*b + c*d) / (a*b - c*d);
}

main()
{
  sampleUserCode(Complex(2,3), Complex(4,5),
                 Complex(6,7), Complex(8,9));
}
```

Focusing complexity in a class reduces overall costs whenever the class is used in many places.

■

Cross references—

FAQ: 342, 343
See Stroustrup: 3.2, 4.6, 7
See Ellis & Stroustrup: 5, 8.3, 13.1, 13.2, 13.4
See Lippman: 6.3

FAQ
52

How can templates simplify maintenance and increase code reuse?

Templates permit definition of generic classes and algorithms independent of the actual types of data that they will manipulate.

Templates are frequently used to define container classes (linked lists, hash tables, binary trees, and so on). Because the underlying operations for maintaining a linked list, for example, are independent of the objects stored on the list, the algorithms can be defined once, and then instantiated for each type of linked list that is needed.

Templates are also used for generic functions such as sort(), swap(), min(), and so on, where the algorithm is independent of the type of object it manipulates. For example, the quicksort algorithm is the same whether sorting integers, complex numbers, or strings. It is easier and safer to write the algorithm only once.

Be aware, though, that every time you instantiate a template on a different data type, the compiler may generate a new set of functions to support that combination of template and data type. This can increase the size of the executable code.

■

Cross references—
FAQ: 275, 276, 278
See Stroustrup: 8
See Ellis & Stroustrup: 14
See Lippman: 7

FAQ
53

How can try, catch, and throw simplify error handling?

Code that may cause a fault is placed in a try block (as if to say, "let's try executing this code"). When a fault occurs, an exception is thrown (as if to say, "I can't handle this error so I'll throw it to someone else"). Code that is able and willing to handle the exception may elect to catch the exception (as if to say, "I'll catch the exception that was thrown").

This mechanism is generally more robust than returning error codes.

■

Cross references—

FAQ: 244, 245, 246
See Stroustrup: 15
See Ellis & Stroustrup: 9
See Lippman: Appendix B

How can access specifiers, abstract base classes, and private classes separate interface from implementation?

The simplest way to separate interface from implementation is via the access specifiers, `private:`, `protected:`, and `public:`. These allow the class designer to designate levels of access for individual class services. The compiler performs authorization checks whenever users access one of these services.

Although access specifiers are sufficient in many cases, the separation of interface from implementation they provide is generally not strong enough or flexible enough. For instance, malicious users can utilize pointer casts and unions to violate the encapsulation barrier produced by access specifiers.

When the implementation uses two or more distinct classes to support the same interface, abstract base classes (ABCs) and private classes can provide stronger and more flexible encapsulation barriers.

■

Cross references—

FAQ: 24, 27, 78, 243
See Stroustrup: 1.2, 5.1, 5.2, 12.2, 12.4
See Ellis & Stroustrup: 9.1, 11, 11.1c
See Lippman: 8.2, 8.6

Is C++ backward-compatible with ANSI-C?

Almost.

C++ is as close as possible to being compatible with ANSI-C, but no closer. In practice, the major differences are that in C++ function prototypes are required and that `f()` declares a function that takes no parameters. In ANSI-C, `f()` declares a function that takes any number of parameters of any type; that is, in ANSI-C, the declaration `f();` is equivalent to `f(...);`, but in C++, `f();` is equivalent to `f(void);`.

There are some very subtle differences as well. In C++, the size of a char literal (for example, `sizeof('x')`) is equal to `sizeof(char)`. In ANSI-C, `sizeof('x')` is the same as `sizeof(int)`. In C++, structure tags are in the same name space as other names. (C++ has a wart to handle backward compatibility here.)

```
void f();
//in C++, this declares "f" as taking no parameters
/*in C, "f" could accept any number of parameters of any type*/

struct Node {
  int elem;
  Node* next;    // Ok in C++
};               /* in C, would need "struct Node* next" */

main()
{
  int n = sizeof('x');  // in C++, n == sizeof(char) == 1
                        /* in C,   n == sizeof(int) */
}
```

■

Cross references—

FAQ: 388, 396, 422
See Stroustrup: 1.3, r.18
See Ellis & Stroustrup: 7.1, 18.1, 18.2
See Lippman: Appendix C.2

What is a class?

A class defines a data type.

The closest analogy in C is a built in type like int. In a mathematical sense, a data type consists of both a set of states and a set of operations that cause transition between those states. For example, int is a type because its objects have a set of states and a set of operations (such as +=, ++, printing, and so on). Similarly, a class provides a set of (usually public) operations and a set of (usually non-public) data bits that represent the abstract states in which instances of the class can be. From a C language perspective, a struct is a class whose data members are all public and which does not have any member functions.

```
class TV {
public:
  TV()                                : channel_(2),
                                        turnedOn_(false) { }
  void changeChannel(int channel) { if (turnedOn_)
                                        channel_ = channel; }
  void turnOn()                       { turnedOn_ = true;  }
  void turnOff()                      { turnedOn_ = false; }
protected:
  int channel_;  //convention: data members have "_" suffix
  bool turnedOn_;
};
```

```
main()
{
  TV recRoomTV;
```
L→ the constructor is called here
```
  recRoomTV.changeChannel(5);
```
L→ does nothing (forgot to turn it on first)
```
  recRoomTV.turnOn();
  recRoomTV.changeChannel(5);
}
```
L→ OK

The member function TV() is a constructor for class TV. It is called to initialize recRoomTV in main().

■

Cross references—

FAQ: 11, 63, 69, 82
See Stroustrup: 1.2, 1.4, 1.5, 5
See Ellis & Stroustrup: 9, 10
See Lippman: 5.1, 5.8

F A Q
57

What is an object?

That depends on who you are.

To a programmer, an object is a region of storage with associated semantics. To a designer, an object is any identifiable component in the problem domain. In the previous example, recRoomTV was an object of class TV.

After a declaration such as int i;, i is said to be an object of type int. In OO/C++, an object is usually an instance of a class.

■

Cross references—

FAQ: 11, 56, 58
See Stroustrup: 2.1, r.3
See Ellis & Stroustrup: 3.1, 3.3
Lippman: 5.2

What are the qualities of an object?

Objects are service providers that are alive, responsible, and intelligent.

Each object is an independent entity with its own lifetime, internal state, and set of services. Objects should be alive, responsible, and intelligent agents.

Objects are *not* simply a convenient way to package data structures and functions together. The fundamental purpose of an object is to provide services.

■

Cross references—

FAQ: 56, 57, 59, 60, 61
See Stroustrup: 2.1, 11.3, r.3
See Ellis & Stroustrup: 3.1, 3.3
See Lippman: 10.1, 10.2

Why should objects be alive?

So they can take care of themselves.

Objects are born (constructed), live a full and productive life, and die (destroyed). Objects are expected to do something useful and maintain themselves in a coherent state.

The opposite of "alive objects" is "dead data." Most data structures in procedural programs are dead in the sense that they just lie there in memory and wait for the functions to manipulate them.

■

Cross references—

FAQ: 57, 58, 60, 61

Why should objects be responsible?

So you can delegate to them.

Since objects are alive, they have rights and responsibilities. They have the right to look after their own affairs—programmers do not reach into their innards and manipulate them.

At the same time, they are responsible for providing one or more services. This means other objects ("users") can delegate work to them instead of having to do everything for themselves. You can then produce more modular and reusable software that consists of many objects, each of which does one thing.

Whenever you define a new class, the first thing you should do is write down its responsibilities. This helps you clarify why the class exists, whether or not it is needed, and what services it should provide. Defining the responsibilities of all objects prevents confusion and simplifies the design process.

■

Cross references—
FAQ: 57, 58, 59, 61
See Stroustrup: 11.4

Why should objects be intelligent?

Intelligent objects simplify user code.

An intelligent object provides services to its users. Thus, the knowledge of how to do some task (whether it is simple or complex) resides in only one place, inside the object. Users simply request the service; they concentrate on what needs to be done rather than how it's done.

An intelligent object moves complexity from the many to the few. For example, travelers need a safe, efficient means of getting from point A to point B. In theory, airlines could do what car rental companies do. They could get rid of all those expensive pilots and let the customers fly the airplanes for a rental fee. However, this would require that every traveler be trained as a pilot (among other things), making air travel both more complicated and more accident prone. Instead, airlines move the intelligence regarding cockpit controls from the many to the few—from every user of the airlines to the pilots. The result is simpler and safer for travelers (users), and cheaper for the airlines (servers).

■

Cross references—
FAQ: 57, 58, 59, 60
See Stroustrup: 11.4

Why isn't procedural software extensible?

Knowledge about changeable things is distributed to the users of those things.

In procedural software, users manipulate data. User code is more difficult to write and more error prone than it should be. It is more difficult to write, because users need to remember both what they are doing and how they are doing it. It is more error prone, because the authority to manipulate the "cockpit controls" of a data structure carries directly with it the responsibility and accountability of ensuring that the data structure remains self-consistent.

In today's technology, changing the layout of a data structure usually involves changing the code of the users of that data structure.

■

Cross reference—
FAQ: 61

How is a class a better structure than a struct?

Classes can be thought of as structs that are also alive and intelligent.

If you take away all the member functions from a class, make everything public, eliminate inheritance and remove all the static member data and functions, you have a traditional struct.

In C, `struct`s support multiple instances, but it is difficult to encapsulate their implementations properly. Classes support both multiple instances and encapsulation.

When a `struct` dreams of growing up, it wants to be a class.

■

Cross references—
FAQ: 27, 56, 57

How is a `class` a better module than a module?

Classes can be thought of as modules that also provide natural support for multiple instances and `inline` functions.

If you take away from a class all the non-static member data and the non-static member functions, and force all remaining static member functions to be non-`inline`, you have a traditional module.

Modules support encapsulation, but creating multiple instances of a module is cumbersome. Classes support both encapsulation and multiple instances.

When a module dreams of growing up, it wants to be a class.

■

Cross reference—
FAQ: 57

How is a `class` a better function than a function?

Classes can be thought of as functions that also maintain state between invocations of the function, and which provide multiple services.

If you make exactly one instance of a class, and take away all its services except for exactly one `public` member function, you'd have a traditional function. The object's member data would correspond to `static` data that is local to the function.

Functions support computation, but maintaining state between calls is cumbersome (using `static` local data is error prone in a multi-threaded setting). Classes support computation and they maintain state.

When a function dreams of growing up, it wants to be a class.

■

Cross references—

FAQ: 66, 67
See Stroustrup: 2.1, 4.2
See Ellis & Stroustrup: 3.5

What do you do with a global function that needs static variables?

F A Q
66

Make it into a functionoid.

■

Cross references—

FAQ: 65, 67
See Stroustrup: 2.1, 4.2
See Ellis & Stroustrup: 3.5

What is a functionoid?

F A Q
67

A function that grew up and became an object.

Functions that must maintain state between calls are really just objects in disguise.

In C, it was common to create a function that maintained state between calls by means of local, static data inside the function body. In C++, such a function should be implemented as an object, with the state stored in the object. This way you don't need to have *every* caller share the same state. Every calling function that wants its own copy of the function's state can simply create its own distinct object. Such an object is called a functionoid.

If you think of a function with local static data as a global functionoid object, it should become clear why the static data is expensive to model (global variables aren't fun!). For example, consider the rand() function, which remembers some state between calls:

```
int
rand()
{
    static unsigned long current = 1001;
    current = current * 22695477UL + 1;
    return int(current >> 12) & 0x7fff;
}
```

The single state variable current introduces subtle dependencies between users of the function. Any change in the calling pattern can alter the behavior of this routine. Such routines are notorious in shared memory, multi-threaded environments.

A better way to do this is with a class. Every user function that wants a pseudo-random stream of numbers can create its own object of this class.

```
#include <iostream.h>

class RandomSequence {
public:

    RandomSequence(int initialSeed=1001)
        : current_(initialSeed) { }

    int next()
        {
            current_ = current_ * 22695477UL + 1;
            return int(current_ >> 12) & 0x7fff;
        }

protected:
    unsigned long current_;
};
```

The user gets a sequence of random numbers by using the member function next().

```
void
printRandomSequence()
{
  RandomSequence rand;
  for (int i = 0; i < 10; ++i)
    cout << rand.next() << ' ';
}

main()
{
  printRandomSequence();
}
```

we used to use "rand( )"

Before, there was a global rand() function with a single state variable. Now there is a local rand object and as many state variables as there are user functions that want an independent pseudo-random sequence. The dependencies among callers (and especially among the various threads) are eliminated at the source. There is no more shared static data.

Another reason to create a functionoid object is when a function performs several distinct operations. In C, such a function would often accept a what-to-do parameter that selected the operation to be performed. In C++, such a "multi-operation function" should be implemented as an object. Each distinct operation performed by the original function should become a distinct service (member function) on the object. Such an object is also called a functionoid.

■

Cross references—
FAQ: 65, 66, 68
See Stroustrup: 2.1, 4.2
See Ellis & Stroustrup: 3.5

How can the function call operator help with functionoids?

F A Q

68

The function call operator lets users pretend that the functionoid is a function.

In the previous example, class RandomSequence is a functionoid. Unlike a standard function, RandomSequence can maintain state between calls without sharing that state between all of its callers.

Functionoids often use the function call operator (`operator()()`) rather than a named service such as `next()`. In the code below, `next()` has been replaced by `operator()()` in class `RandomSequence`.

```cpp
#include <iostream.h>

class RandomSequence {
public:

  RandomSequence(int initialSeed=1001)
    : current_(initialSeed) { }

  // "operator()" is the name of the member function
  int operator() ()
    {                              second "( )" are the parameters (none)
      current_ = current_ * 22695477UL + 1;
      return int(current_ >> 12) & 0x7fff;
    }

protected:
  unsigned long current_;
};
```

Given an object of class `RandomSequence` called `rand`, users can now use `rand()` instead of `rand.next()`:

```cpp
main()
{
  RandomSequence rand;
  for (int i = 0; i < 10; ++i)
    cout << rand() << ' ';
                              was "rand.next()"
}
```

■

Cross references—

FAQ: 65, 66, 67
See Stroustrup: 2.1, 4.2
See Ellis & Stroustrup: 3.5

What's the difference between the keywords struct and class?

Mostly perception.

The major difference between the keywords struct and class is the default access level assigned to members and base classes. The default access level assigned to members and base classes of a struct is public, while the default access level for members and base classes of a class is private. Regardless, we recommend that you should put an explicit public, private, or protected in your base class specifications, and that your class should start with an explicit public:. If you do that, these defaults are of little consequence in practice.

The perception, however, is very different. A struct is perceived as an open bucket of bits. Most structs have very few services (often they have only a constructor), and they are often entirely public:. A class, on the other hand, is a service provider that is alive, responsible, and intelligent.

■

Cross references—

FAQ: 55
See Stroustrup: r.9
See Ellis & Stroustrup: 9

How do you create a good interface to an abstraction?

Write user code.

When you build the implementation before you design the interface, the interface inevitably smells like the implementation. If you find yourself explaining the interface to your users in terms of the implementation, you're in trouble. If you can't justify your interface-design decisions based solely on the users' external perspective, you're in even bigger trouble.

■

Cross references—
FAQ: 11, 19, 20, 23, 123
See Stroustrup: 12.1, 12.2, 12.3, 12.4, 12.5
See Lippman: 10.2

How are get/set member functions related to poorly designed interfaces?

Get/set member functions are often used as bandages to patch broken interfaces.

Get/set member functions provide users with access to an object's internal data structures. Although get/set member functions hide the *name* of a member datum, they expose the member datum's existence, as well as the relationships between the member datum and all the other member data.

In other words, they expose the implementation technique. Ultimately, the resultant interface makes the user code dependent on the implementation technique. Changing the implementation technique will break user code.

If a `Container` class exports information about the binary tree that implements it (it exports services such as `getLeftChild()`, `getRightChild()`, for example), it will force users to think in terms of binary trees, rather than containers. The result is a cluttered interface in the implementor's vocabulary, instead of a simple interface defined in the user's vocabulary.

When an interface is cluttered, the resultant user code is more complicated. When an interface is defined in the implementor's vocabulary, implementation details will show through, and changing the implementation technique will break user code. Either way, the users lose.

■

Cross references—
FAQ: 20, 70, 72
See Lippman: 8

F A Q

72

Should there be a `get` and a `set` member function for each member datum?

Not necessarily.

Some data members are a legitimate part of an object's interface. Having a `get` or `set` member function for such a datum is appropriate because the datum represents something that is part of the user's vocabulary.

You can tell which data members are a legitimate part of an object's interface by asking a typical user to describe the class in implementation-independent terms; the words used to describe the class form the user's vocabulary.

■

Cross references—
FAQ: 20, 70, 71, 339

Is the real purpose of a class to export attributes?

No, the real purpose of a class is to provide services.

A class is a way to abstract behavior, not just a way to encapsulate bits. A class's interface must make sense from the outside. If a detached user expects services to access an attribute, those services should exist. But remember, the services to access an attribute exist because their existence makes sense in the user's vocabulary (that is, for outside reasons), not because there are bits in the object (that is, not for inside reasons).

You should design a class's interface from the outside in.

■

Cross references—
FAQ: 70, 71, 72
See Stroustrup: 5.1, 12.2

Should you think of OO as data-centric?

No, you should think of OO as behavior-centric.

The data-centric view of OO says that objects are fundamentally buckets of bits and that the primary purpose of a class is to export attributes.

The behavior-centric view of OO sees objects as intelligent agents that export useful services.

The behavior-centric view of OO produces more cost-effective systems that have better reuse potential, are easier to tune for performance, and tend to have fewer defects. The reason for these benefits is simple: behavior-centric systems move common code from a class's users into the class itself, from the many to the few. Coalescing snippets of code that show up in several users reduces maintenance costs (by reducing code bulk) and avoids duplicating defects.

■

Cross references—
FAQ: 38, 59, 60, 61, 71, 73

How should you establish the names of boolean inspector services?

Write an imaginary `if` in user code.

For example, consider a service that tells whether a particular integer is in a set-of-`int`. This is a boolean inspector. It inspects (versus mutates) the set object, and it returns a boolean value.

A naive name for such a service might be `Set::isElemOf(int) const`. However, putting this name in an `if` statement shows that the name gives the wrong connotation, since the user code reads "if my Set is an element of x."

```
if (mySet.isElemOf(x)) ...
```

The proper sentence structure would be "if mySet contains x."

```
if (mySet.contains(x)) ...
```

Note that the names of boolean inspectors should imply the meaning of the true response. For example, File::isOpen() `const` is better than File::status() const.

∎

Cross references—
FAQ: 337, 338
See Stroustrup: 5.2
See Ellis & Stroustrup: 9.3

What does inheritance mean?

In C++, inheritance is closely tied to subtyping, and is used to model the kind-of relationship.

Human beings abstract things in two dimensions: kind-of (classification) and part-of (composition). We say that a Ford Taurus is a kind-of Car, and that a Ford Taurus has parts such as Engine, Tire, and so on. The part-of hierarchy has been used in software design since data structures were invented, but until OO and inheritance, there was no direct way to model the kind-of relationship.

Inheritance and dynamic binding are the two most important features that are missing from object-based programming (also called abstract data types) and found in object-oriented programming.

It is possible to simulate the kind-of relationship in languages that don't support the concept. However, this requires additional effort.

■

Cross references—
FAQ: 15, 16, 19, 77, 78
See Stroustrup: 6.1, 6.2
See Ellis & Stroustrup: 10.1c

How do you express inheritance in C++?

By the : public syntax.

```cpp
#include <iostream.h>

class Vehicle {
public:
  virtual void startEngine() = 0;
  virtual ~Vehicle() { }
};

class V8Engine {
public:
  void start() { cout << "starting V8Engine\n"; }
};

class Car : public Vehicle {
public:                              Car is a kind-of Vehicle
  virtual void startEngine() { engine_.start(); }
protected:
  V8Engine engine_;
};
```

We describe the above relationship in several ways:

- Car **is a kind-of** Vehicle

- Car **is derived from** Vehicle

- Car **is a subclass of** Vehicle

- Car **is a child class of** Vehicle (**not common in the C++ community**)

- Vehicle **is the base class of** Car

- Vehicle **is the parent class of** Car (**not common in the C++ community**)

- Vehicle **is the super-class of** Car (**not common in the C++ community**)

As a consequence of the kind-of relationship, a Car object can be treated as a Vehicle object. For example, since function f(Vehicle&) accepts any kind-of Vehicle, it can be passed a Car, or an object of any other class derived from Vehicle:

```
void f(Vehicle& v)
{
  v.startEngine();
}

main()
{
  Car c;
  f(c);
}
```
→ pass a Car as a Vehicle&

■

Cross references—

FAQ: 15, 76
See Stroustrup: 6.1, 6.2
See Ellis & Stroustrup: 10.1c
See Lippman: 8

What is an abstract base class (ABC)?

A representation of an abstract concept.

Abstract base classes, or ABCs, are a key to real-world OO design. Often, you need an abstraction where several different data structures and algorithms must coexist. In these cases, build an ABC that defines the interface but not the implementation, and write the user code using the interface defined by the ABC. Because ABCs are not complete implementations, the compiler prevents the creation of objects of the ABC. You can only instantiate a concrete derived class.

Technically, an ABC is a class that has one or more pure virtual member functions. A concrete derived class is a class derived from an ABC for which all the pure virtual functions inherited from the ABC have been defined.

■

Cross references—

FAQ: 79, 80, 81, 102, 161, 216
See Stroustrup: 1.4, 6.3
See Ellis & Stroustrup: 10.3
See Lippman: 8.2

FAQ 79

What is meant by abstract concept?

An intangible idea.

For example, vehicle is an abstract concept. If you ask a mechanic if he repairs vehicles, he'd probably reply, "What kind-of vehicles?" While he might repair automobiles and trucks, it's unlikely that he also repairs space shuttles, ocean liners, and bicycles.

The key idea is that the term "vehicle" is an abstract concept; you can't build one until you know what kind-of vehicle to build.

In C++, `Vehicle` is an ABC, and `Bicycle`, `SpaceShuttle`, and so on, are concrete derived classes.

■

Cross references—
FAQ: 78, 81
See Stroustrup: 1.4, 6.3
See Ellis & Stroustrup: 10.3
See Lippman: 8.2

FAQ 80

What is a pure virtual member function?

A member function with no implementation.

A pure virtual member function specifies that a member function will exist on every object of a concrete derived class, even though there is no way to implement this member function in the base class. In a sense, it forces concrete derived classes to provide a definition for this member function.

For example, you may know that all objects of classes derived from `Shape` will have the member function `draw()`. However, because `Shape` is an abstract concept, it does not contain enough information to implement `draw()`. Thus you should make `draw()` a pure virtual member function in `Shape`.

```
class Shape {
public:
  virtual void draw() const = 0;
};
```

"= 0" means pure virtual

This pure virtual function makes Shape an ABC. The const says that invoking the draw() member function won't change the Shape object (that is, the Shape won't move around on the screen, change sizes, and so on). Imagine that the "= 0" is like saying, "the code for this function is at the NULL pointer" (that is, it doesn't exist).

Pure virtual member functions allow users to write code against an interface for which there are several functionally different variants. This means that semantically different objects can be passed to a function if these objects are all under the umbrella of the same abstract base class.

■

Cross references—

FAQ: 78, 79, 81
See Stroustrup: 1.4, 6.3, r.10
See Ellis & Stroustrup: 10.3
See Lippman: 9.1

What is a concrete derived class?

A derived class that has no pure virtual functions.

Because an abstract class cannot be instantiated directly, one or more derived classes are normally defined as implementations of the abstraction provided by the abstract class. A concrete derived class simply provides definitions for all of its inherited pure virtual functions. If you forget to provide a definition for one of the inherited pure virtual functions, and you try to instantiate the class, the compiler will issue an error message.

Suppose an abstract base class B had two pure virtual member functions f() and g(), and if derived class D provided a definition for f() but not for g(), D would also be an ABC. If D2 were derived from D, and you wanted to make D2 concrete, D2 would have to provide a definition for g(), but it wouldn't be required to override D::f().

■

Cross references—

FAQ: 78, 80
See Stroustrup: 6.3, 13.2
See Ellis & Stroustrup: 10.3
See Lippman: 9.1

What do `public:`, `protected:`, **and** `private:` **mean, and how are they different?**

These differentiate between things that aren't secrets (things I'm willing to let anyone know about), family secrets (things I let my kids know about), and personal secrets (things that not even my kids know about).

A `private` member is accessible by members and friends of the class.

A `protected` member is accessible by members and friends of the class, and by members and friends of derived classes (provided they access the base member via a pointer or a reference to their own derived class).

A `public` member is accessible by everyone.

There is no difference between the access rules for data members or member functions. "Members and friends of class x" include member functions of class x, friend functions of class x, and member functions of friend classes of class x.

■

Cross references—

FAQ: 83, 84, 228
See Stroustrup: 5.2, 6.2, 6.6
See Ellis & Stroustrup: 11.1, 11.2, 11.3c, 11.4, 11.5
See Lippman: 5.0

Why can't a derived class access the private members of its base class?

Because the base class intentionally hid some of its implementation details from its derived classes.

Suppose you designed class `Fred` which contained a member datum or member function that was likely to change. Unless derived classes need to access this member, class `Fred` would be wise to declare the member as private, thereby protecting derived classes from rewrites whenever the semantics (or even existence) of the private member changed.

For example, class `Wilma`, below, can access and print `publ_` and `prot_`, but cannot access or print `priv_`:

```
#include <iostream.h>

class Fred {
public:
  Fred() : publ_(1), prot_(2), priv_(3) { }
  int publ_;
protected:
  int prot_;
private:
  int priv_;
};

class Wilma : public Fred {
public:
  void printem()
  {
    cout << publ_ << '\n';      //OK
    cout << prot_ << '\n';      //OK
    #ifdef GENERATE_ERROR
      cout << priv_ << '\n';    //compiler will catch this
    #endif
  }
};

main()
{
  Wilma a;
  a.printem();
}
```

The designer of a base class gives derived classes access to implementation details by declaring them as protected.

■

Cross references—

FAQ: 82, 84
See Stroustrup: 5.2, 6.2, 6.6
See Ellis & Stroustrup: 11.1, 11.2, 11.3c, 11.4, 11.5
See Lippman: 5.0, 5.2, 8.5

How can a base class protect derived classes so that changes to the base class will not affect them?

Define a `protected` interface in addition to the `public` interface.

You can make a class hierarchy more resilient with respect to changes by realizing it has two distinct interfaces for two distinct sets of users:

- Its `public` interface serves unrelated classes
- Its `protected` interface serves derived classes

You must fully specify both interfaces.

For instance, you should make the actual raw data of a class private, and define a set of protected inline member functions for accessing this data. These inline member functions define an interface between the derived classes and the raw bits of the base class.

Now, you can change private data of the base class within reasonable bounds without affecting the derived classes. You will still need to recompile the derived classes after a change to the base class, though.

For example, suppose class `Base` has an `int` data member. `Base` can ensure that derived classes do not rely on the specific data structure by making the data structure private (in this case, a simple `int`), and defining inline protected members for accessing these data. Derived class `Derived` accesses the value using these protected inline services.

```
class Base {
public:
  Base()                          : value_(37) { }
protected:
  void storeValue(int value)      { value_ = value; }
  int  retrieveValue() const      { return value_; }
private:
  int value_;
};

class Derived : public Base {
public:
  void f(int i)                   { storeValue(i); }
};

main()
{
  Derived d;
  d.f(42);
}
```

■

Cross references—

FAQ: 82, 83
See Stroustrup: 5.2, 6.2, 6.6
See Ellis & Stroustrup: 11.1, 11.2, 11.3c, 11.4, 11.5
See Lippman: 5.0, 5.2, 8.5

F A Q

85

Can you convert a derived class pointer into a pointer to its public base class?

Yes, and you don't even need to do a pointer cast.

A publicly derived class is a kind-of its base class. By implication, the upward conversion is perfectly safe, and is quite common. For example, a pointer to a Car is in fact pointing at a Vehicle, since a Car is a kind-of a Vehicle.

```
class Base { };
class Derived : public Base { };

void f(Base* basePointer);

void g(Derived* derivedPointer)
{
   f(derivedPointer);   //perfectly safe; no cast needed
}
```

■

Cross references—

FAQ: 145
See Stroustrup: r.4
See Ellis & Stroustrup: 4.6
See Lippman: 8.6

How can you create a class D that is a kind-of another class B as well as getting the bits of B?

Use public inheritance.

Here is the C++ syntax for public inheritance.

```
class B            { /*bits and/or code go here*/ };
class D : public B { /*more bits and/or code go here*/ };
```

This does two distinct things. First, it provides the kind-of relationship: D is a kind-of B, therefore D supports the same services as B (D might add some new services as well). Second, it shares bits and code: D inherits B's bits (data structures) and code (algorithms).

■

Cross references—
FAQ: 15, 76, 77
See Stroustrup: 6.1, 6.2
See Ellis & Stroustrup: 10.1c
See Lippman: 8.5

How can you create a class X that gets the bits of an existing class Y without making X a kind-of Y?

Use composition, or private inheritance, or protected inheritance.

Here is the C++ syntax for composition:

```
class Y { /*bits and code go here*/ };

class X {
public:
  //typically member functions are declared here
  //they might use Y::f() by calling y_.f()
protected:
  Y y_;    //composition: an X has-a Y
};
```

Here is the C++ syntax for private inheritance:

```
class Y { /*bits and code go here*/ };

class X : private Y {
public:
  //typically member functions are declared here
  //they might use Y::f() by calling Y::f()
};
```

Here is the C++ syntax for protected inheritance:

```
class Y { /*bits and code go here*/ };

class X : protected Y {
public:
  //typically member functions are declared here
  //they might use Y::f() by calling Y::f()
};
```

In all three cases, an X object has a Y object, and users are unaware of any relationship between X and Y. For example, user code will not break if the relationship between X and Y is changed—or even eliminated.

■

Cross references—
FAQ: 14, 449, 450
See Stroustrup: 12.2
See Ellis & Stroustrup: 11.2
See Lippman: 8.5

How can you create a class D that is a kind-of another class B, yet doesn't inherit the bits of B?

F A Q

88

You have to outfox C++.

The only mechanism provided by C++ that defines the kind-of relationship also forces you to inherit the bits of the base class. If the base class's data structures are inappropriate for certain derived classes, you outfox C++ by deferring the definition of the bits to the lower levels of the class hierarchy.

One way to do this is to define an ABC that possesses no (or few) internal data structures, then define the data structures in the concrete derived classes. In this way, the derived classes define the kind-of relationship, but they don't have any bits imposed upon them by the base class.

For example, class Stack can be defined as an ABC with no bits, since there is probably no single data structure that is common to all its derived classes.

```cpp
#include <iostream.h>
#include <stdlib.h>

#include "List.h"    //List<T> template not provided here
#include "Array.h"   //Array<T> template not provided here

class Stack {
public:
  virtual nStack() { }
  virtual void push(int x)   = 0;
  virtual int  pop()         = 0;
  virtual bool empty() const= 0;
};

class StackBasedOnList : public Stack {
public:
  StackBasedOnList(): data_() { }
  virtual void push(int x)   { data_.append(x);              }
  virtual int  pop()         { return data_.removeLast();  }
  virtual bool empty() const{ return data_.length() == 0; }
protected:
  List<int> data_;
};

class StackBasedOnArray : public Stack {
public:
  StackBasedOnArray() : data_(), length_(0) { }
  virtual void push(int x)   { data_[length_++] = x;     }
  virtual int  pop()         { return data_[--length_]; }
  virtual bool empty() const{ return length_ == 0;       }
protected:
  Array<int> data_;
  unsigned   length_;
};
```

```
void
userCode(Stack& s)
{
  s.push(42);
  s.push(42+42);
  cout << "s.pop() == " << s.pop() << '\n';
}

main()
{
  if (rand() % 2) { StackBasedOnList  s; userCode(s); }
  else            { StackBasedOnArray s; userCode(s); }
}
```

What is a virtual member function?

A member function preceded by the keyword `virtual`.

In this context, the keyword `virtual` means that the run-time system will automatically invoke the proper member function when it has been overridden by a derived class (dynamic binding).

Think of `virtual` as meaning "overridable."

■

Cross references—
FAQ: 16, 90, 91, 93
See Stroustrup: 6.2, r.10
See Ellis & Stroustrup: 10.2, 10.7c, 10.8c, 10.9c, 11.6
See Lippman: 8.1, 9.1

When should you define a member function as virtual?

When you expect there will be derived classes that will need to provide their own implementation for the service.

This doesn't require as much clairvoyance as the answer seems to imply. Normally the virtual functions represent specifically architected places where extensibility is supposed to take place.

■

Cross references—

FAQ: 16, 89, 91, 94
See Stroustrup: 6.2, r.10
See Ellis & Stroustrup: 10.2, 10.7c, 10.8c, 10.9c, 11.6
See Lippman: 8.1, 9.1

F A Q

91

How do you override a virtual member function?

Replace the virtual member function's implementation in the derived class.

You can override the member function by declaring the function in the derived class and defining a new implementation.

For example, suppose class Stack has virtual functions push() and pop().

```
class Stack {
public:
              Stack()          : length_(0) { }
  virtual     ~Stack()         { }
  virtual void push(int elem)  { data_[length_++] = elem; }
  virtual int  pop()           { return data_[--length_]; }
          bool empty() const   { return length_ == 0;     }
          bool full()  const   { return length_ == 10;    }
protected:
  int length_;
  int data_[10];
};
```

You can write user code to work with any Stack, including derived classes.

```
void
userCode(Stack& s)
{
  s.push(24);
  s.push(42);
  s.pop();
  s.pop();
}
```

Since push() and pop() are virtual, they can be overridden in a derived class such as VisualStack.

```cpp
#include <iostream.h>

class VisualStack : public Stack {
public:
  VisualStack()
    : Stack() { }
  virtual void push(int elem)
    { cout << "pushing\n"; Stack::push(elem); }
  virtual int  pop()
    { cout << "popping\n"; return Stack::pop(); }
};

main()
{
  Stack s1;
  cout << "main calling userCode(s1)\n";
  userCode(s1);

  VisualStack s2;
  cout << "main calling userCode(s2)\n";
  userCode(s2);
}
```

The output of this program is as follows.

```
main calling userCode(s1)
main calling userCode(s2)
pushing
pushing
popping
popping
```

Note that userCode(s2) invoked the overridden member function defined by VisualStack, even though userCode(Stack&) didn't even know that VisualStack existed.

■

Cross references—

FAQ: 89, 90, 94, 139
See Stroustrup: 6.2, r.10
See Ellis & Stroustrup: 10.2, 10.7c, 10.8c, 10.9c, 11.6
See Lippman: 8.1, 9.1

How much does a virtual function call cost compared to a normal function call?

In theory, the overhead of the dynamic binding part of a virtual function call is very compiler, operating system, and machine dependent. In practice, almost all compilers do it the same way, and the overhead is very small.

Specifically, a virtual function call typically costs 10% to 20% more than a non-virtual function call. The overhead gets smaller if there are several parameters, since the dynamic binding part of a virtual function call has constant cost. In practice, the overhead for the linkage of a function call is usually a very small percentage of the cost of the work that gets done, so the cost for a virtual function call is about the same as a normal function call.

For example, if a system or application spends 5% of its CPU utilization performing the linkage for function calls, and 25% of those calls are converted to virtual function calls, the additional overhead will be 10% of 25% of 5%, or around one-tenth of one percent overall.

If you can afford a normal function call, you can almost always afford a virtual function call.

■

Cross references—
FAQ: 16, 89, 93, 94, 349
See Stroustrup: 1.5
See Ellis & Stroustrup: 7.4
See Lippman: 10.3

What is dynamic binding?

The run-time selection of the right server code.

Given a kind-of relationship between base class Stack and derived class VisualStack, a Stack& may actually refer to a VisualStack object. Therefore, the type of the object and the type of the reference may be different.

When a virtual function is invoked, the code that gets called is selected based on the type of the object, rather than being selected based on the type of the reference (this is called dynamic binding, because the binding between the function call and code to be executed is resolved at run-time). In contrast, when a non-virtual function is invoked, the code that gets called is selected based on the type of the pointer (this is called static binding, because the call is resolved at compile-time).

Continuing from the earlier example, each time userCode(Stack& s) is called, s could refer to a different object of a different type: s might refer to a Stack object, a VisualStack object, or an object of any other class derived from Stack. Yet userCode(Stack&) always selects the right push() and pop() code, because it binds to that code dynamically.

■

Cross references—
FAQ: 16, 89, 92
See Stroustrup: 6.2, r.10
See Ellis & Stroustrup: 10.2, 10.7c, 10.8c, 10.9c, 11.6
See Lippman: 8.4

F A Q
94

What is the advantage of dynamic binding?

It decouples the user's service request from the implementation provided.

The user code specifies what service it needs without specifying how the service will be implemented. After all, the user does not care how the service is provided, just that it is provided.

Also, the derived class can substitute a different algorithm in place of the one supplied by the base class without affecting the base class or the user code.

Finally, and perhaps most importantly, the user code does not need to know about the existence of classes derived from the base class. Continuing from the earlier example, when userCode(Stack&) is written and compiled, the user does not need to know what kind of Stack is passed in. It might be a Stack, a VisualStack, or any other class derived from Stack.

The compiler effectively looks into the future and predicts all the possible derived classes that will ever be created. It then generates code such that the right override of any virtual functions will always be executed.

■

Cross references—

FAQ: 16, 89, 90, 91, 95
See Stroustrup: 6.2, r.10
See Ellis & Stroustrup: 10.2, 10.7c, 10.8c, 10.9c, 11.6
See Lippman: 8.4

How does dynamic binding change the way you program?

You must learn to program in terms of what you want done, not how to do it.

If you program in terms of what you want done without specifying how to do it, then you benefit because in the future servers will provide new and better implementations, and you get to use them without having to change your code.

For example, if your user code is looking for an item stored in a binary tree, then you have two options. First, you can traverse the binary tree yourself. This mixes the what (find item) with the how (traversing a binary tree). Second, you can ask the binary tree object to find the item for you (this separates the what from the how).

In the second scenario, you can take advantage of new algorithms and implementations without changing the user code. In the first case, you cannot take advantage of new algorithms and implementations without changing the user code because you have hard wired the traversal algorithm into the user code.

If you are developing user code, you must demand that the objects provided to you have an interface that provides services rather than exposing implementation techniques.

If you are developing server code, you must create an interface that provides high level services to user code rather than forcing users to do everything themselves by exposing your implementation technique.

■

Cross references—

FAQ: 16, 89, 90, 91, 94
See Stroustrup: 6.2, r.10
See Ellis & Stroustrup: 10.2, 10.7c, 10.8c, 10.9c, 11.6
See Lippman: 8.4

How does C++ perform static typing while supporting dynamic binding?

Dynamic binding causes functions to be called through a pointer; static typing ensures there's good code on the other end of such a pointer.

Given a reference (or pointer) to an object, there are two distinct types in question: the static type of the reference, and the dynamic type of the referent (that is, the object). In other words, the object may be an instance of a class that is derived from the class of the reference. Non-virtual (statically bound) member functions are selected based upon the (statically known) type of the reference. Virtual (dynamically bound) member functions are selected based on the (dynamically known) type of the object.

The legality of the call is checked based on the (statically known) type of the reference or pointer. This is safe because the referent must be "at least as derived as" the type of the reference. This gives us the following type safety guarantee: if the class of the reference has the indicated service, then the class of the referent will as well.

■

Cross references—
FAQ: 16, 89, 91, 93, 94, 152
See Stroustrup: 6.2, r.10
See Ellis & Stroustrup: 10.2, 10.7c, 10.8c, 10.9c, 11.6
See Lippman: 8.4

Can destructors be virtual?

Yes. In fact, many should be virtual.

Virtual destructors are extremely valuable when each derived class has unique cleanup code.

A practical, easy-to-remember guideline is: if a class has any virtuals, it should have a virtual destructor. Rationale: if a class has no virtual functions, chances are the class designer wasn't planning on the class being used as a base class, so a virtual destructor is unnecessary. Besides, on most compilers there is no additional per-object space cost after the first virtual function, so there is very little reason not to make the destructor virtual if the class already has at least one virtual function.

Note that the above guideline is not precise enough for every circumstance, but the precise rule is much harder to remember: if any derived classes (or data members and/or base classes of, derived classes, or base classes of data members, or members of base classes, or bases of bases of members of bases, and so on) has (or will ever have) a nontrivial destructor, and if anyone anywhere deletes (or will ever delete) a derived class object via a base class pointer, then the base class's destructor needs to be virtual.

■

Cross references—

FAQ: 16, 89, 91, 93, 98, 103, 170
See Stroustrup: 6.2, r.10, r.12
See Ellis & Stroustrup: 10.2, 10.7c, 10.8c, 10.9c, 11.6
See Lippman: 9.1

**FAQ
98**

What is the purpose of a virtual destructor?

To tell the compiler to use dynamic binding for calling the destructor.

A destructor will be called whenever an object gets deleted, however there are some cases when the user code doesn't know *which* destructor should be called. For example, in the following situation, while compiling `unawareOfDerived(Base*)`, the compiler doesn't even know that `Derived` exists, much less that the pointer `base` may actually be pointing at a `Derived`.

```
#include <iostream.h>

class Base {
public:
  ~Base() { cout << "Base destructor\n"; }
};

void
unawareOfDerived(Base* base)
{
  delete base;
}

class Derived : public Base {
public:
  ~Derived() { cout << "Derived destructor\n"; }
};
```

```
main()
{
  Base* base = new Derived;
  unawareOfDerived(base);
}
```

Because Base::~Base() is non-virtual, the Derived destructor will not run. This could be a very serious error, especially if the Derived destructor is supposed to release some precious resource such as closing a shared file or unlocking a semaphore.

The solution is to put the virtual keyword in front of Base's destructor. Once that is done, the compiler will dynamically bind to the destructor, thus the right destructor will always be called.

■

Cross references—
FAQ: 16, 89, 90, 91, 97, 103, 170, 302
See Stroustrup: 6.2, r.10, r.12
See Ellis & Stroustrup: 10.2, 10.7c, 10.8c, 10.9c, 11.6
See Lippman: 9.1

What is a virtual constructor?

F A Q
99

A virtual constructor is an idiom that allows you to create an object without specifying the exact type of the object.

For example, you can provide a base class with a virtual createCopy() const member function (for creating a new object of the same class and for copying the state of the object, just like the copy constructor would do), or a virtual createSimilar() const member function (for creating a new object of the same class, just like the default constructor would do).

The following is an example of this idiom.

```
#include <iostream.h>

class Shape {
public:
           Shape()                        { }
  virtual ~Shape()                        { }
  virtual void draw() const       = 0;
  virtual Shape* createCopy() const    = 0;
  virtual Shape* createSimilar() const = 0;
};
```

```
class Circle : public Shape {
public:
  Circle(int radius=0)
    : Shape(), radius_(radius) { }
  virtual void draw() const
    { cout << "Circle: radius=" << radius_ << '\n'; }
  virtual Shape* createSimilar() const
    { return new Circle(); }
  virtual Shape* createCopy() const
    { return new Circle(*this); }
protected:
  int radius_;
};
```

In `Circle::createSimilar() const` and `Circle::createCopy() const`, the kind-of relationship allows the conversion from a `Circle*` to a `Shape*`. In `Circle::createCopy() const`, the expression `new Circle(*this)` calls `Circle`'s copy constructor, since `*this` has type `const Circle&` inside a `const` member function of class `Circle`.

Users can use `createCopy` and/or `createSimilar` as if they were virtual constructors. An example follows.

```
void
userCode(Shape& s)
{
  cout << "userCode() number 1: ";
  s.draw();

  Shape* copy = s.createCopy();
  cout << "userCode() number 2: ";
  copy->draw();
  delete copy;

  Shape* similar = s.createSimilar();
  cout << "userCode() number 3: ";
  similar->draw();
  delete similar;
}

main()
{
  Circle c = Circle(42);
  cout << "main() number 1: ";
  c.draw();
  userCode(c);
}
```

The output of this program is as follows.

```
main() number 1: Circle: radius=42
userCode() number 1: Circle: radius=42
userCode() number 2: Circle: radius=42
userCode() number 3: Circle: radius=0
```

The reason constructors can't be virtual is simple. A constructor turns raw bits into a living object. Until there is a living recipient against which to invoke a member function, the member function couldn't possibly work correctly. Thinking of constructors as member functions attached to an already-existing object is the wrong mental model; instead think of them as factories that churn out objects.

■

Cross references—
FAQ: 16, 54, 89, 90, 93, 168
See Stroustrup: 6.2, 6.7, r.10
See Ellis & Stroustrup: 10.2, 10.7c, 10.8c, 10.9c, 11.6
See Lippman: 10.2

What syntax should be used when a constructor or destructor needs to call a virtual function in its object?

F A Q
100

Use the scope operator, ::.

If a constructor or a destructor of class `Base` calls a virtual function `this->f()`, call it via `Base::f()` rather than merely `f()`. In our experience, this guideline reduces the probability that misunderstandings will introduce subtle defects, since it forces developers to explicitly state what the compiler is obliged to do anyway.

In particular, when a constructor invokes a virtual member function that is attached to `this` object, the language guarantees that the member function that gets invoked will be the one associated with the class of the constructor, even if the object being constructed will eventually be an object of a derived class that has its own version of the virtual function. An analogous statement can be made for calling a virtual function from a destructor.

```
#include <iostream.h>

class Base {
public:
  Base()
    {
      cout << " Base::Base() calling f()\n";
      f();
    }                    ──────►  this should be changed to Base::f()
  virtual void f()
    { cout << "  Base::f()\n"; }
  virtual ~Base()
    { }
};

class Derived : public Base {
public:
  Derived()
    : Base()
    {
      cout << " Derived::Derived() calling f()\n";
      f();
    }                    ──────►  this should be changed to Derived::f()
  virtual void f()
    { cout << "  Derived::f()\n"; }
};

main()
{
  cout << "Creating a Derived:\n";
  Derived d;
}
```

The initialization list of Derived::Derived() calls Base::Base(), even
if you don't explicitly specify Base() in the initialization list. During
Base::Base(), the object is merely a Base, even though it will eventually
be a Derived. This is why Base::f() is called from the body of
Base::Base(). During the body of Derived::Derived(), however,
Derived::f() is called. The output of this program is as follows.

```
Creating a Derived:
 Base::Base() calling f()
  Base::f()
 Derived::Derived() calling f()
  Derived::f()
```

This language rule helps ensure that member objects of Derived get constructed before they get used (for example, if Base::Base() called Derived::f(), the member objects of Derived could get used by Derived::f() before they were constructed). Nonetheless, we have found that developers are often somewhat surprised by this behavior, therefore we recommend that such calls should be explicitly qualified with the scope operator, ::.

■

Cross references—
FAQ: 16, 89, 93, 168, 170
See Stroustrup: 6.2, r.10
See Ellis & Stroustrup: 10.2, 10.7c, 10.8c, 10.9c, 11.6

F A Q
101

Should you use the scope operator :: when invoking virtual member functions?

Only from derived classes, constructors, or destructors.

The purpose of the scope operator is to bypass the dynamic binding mechanism. Because dynamic binding is so important to users, user code should generally avoid using ::. For example, the following prints Base::f() even though the object is really a Derived.

```
#include <iostream.h>

class Base {
public:
  virtual void f()      { cout << "Base::f()\n"; }
  virtual ~Base()       { }
};

class Derived : public Base {
public:
  virtual void f()      { cout << "Derived::f()\n"; }
};

main()
{
  Derived d;
  d.Base::f();
}
```

use of "::" in user code: bad form

■

Cross references—

FAQ: 100, 102
See Lippman: 9.1

Can a pure virtual function be defined in the same class that declares it?

Yes, but new C++ programmers don't usually understand what it means, so be cautious if your organization rotates developers.

If your goal is to create a member function that you intend will be invoked only by derived classes (such as sharing common code in the abstract base class), create a `protected` non-virtual function instead of using this feature. If your goal is to make something that may be callable from user code, create a distinctly named service so users aren't forced to use the scope operator, `::`.

The exception to this guideline is a pure virtual destructor in an ABC.

■

Cross references—

FAQ: 16, 80, 89, 91, 101, 104
See Stroustrup: 6.2, 6.3, r.10
See Ellis & Stroustrup: 10.2, 10.3, 10.7c, 10.8c, 10.9c, 11.6
See Lippman: 9.1

How should you declare a virtual destructor that has no code?

Make it an inline virtual function.

An example follows.

```
#include <iostream.h>

class Base {
public:
  virtual void f()        { cout << "Base::f()\n"; }
  virtual void g()        { cout << "Base::g()\n"; }
  virtual ~Base()         { }
};
```

```
class Derived : public Base {
public:
  virtual void f()        { cout << "Derived::f()\n";  }
};

main()
{
  Base    b;  b.f();  b.g();   //Base is not an ABC
  Derived d;  d.f();  d.g();
}
```

The reason `Base::~Base()` is inline is to avoid an unnecessary function call when `Derived::~Derived()` automatically calls `Base::~Base()`. In this case, `Derived::~Derived()` is synthesized by the compiler.

■

Cross references—
FAQ: 16, 89, 97, 98, 170, 178, 196, 350
See Stroustrup: 6.2, r.10, r.12
See Ellis & Stroustrup: 10.2, 10.7c, 10.8c, 10.9c, 11.6
See Lippman: 9.1

F A Q
104

Can an ABC have a pure virtual destructor?

Yes, provided the ABC gives an explicit definition elsewhere.

An example follows.

```
class Base {
public:
  Base() { }
  virtual ~Base() = 0;
};

inline Base::~Base() { }
```
⟶ explicit definition required!
```
class Derived : public Base {
public:
  Derived() : Base() { }
};

main()
{
  Derived d;
}
```

Leaving out a definition for `Base::~Base()` will cause a linker error, because `Derived::~Derived()` automatically calls `Base::~Base()`. In this case, `Derived::~Derived()` is synthesized by the compiler.

Depending on the compiler, there may be a marginal performance benefit in using a pure virtual destructor with an explicit inline definition versus the inline virtual technique. Calls to inline virtual functions can be inlined if the compiler is able to statically bind to the class. However, the compiler may also make an outlined copy of an inline virtual function (for any other cases where it isn't able to statically bind to the call). Although in theory destructors of ABCs don't have the above limitations, in practice not all compilers produce optimal code when using the inline virtual technique.

■

Cross references—

FAQ: 103, 150, 178, 196

FAQ

105

What is an advertised requirement?

An advertised requirement is a condition that the user of a service must comply with before the service can be used. Some people use the term pre-condition instead of the term advertised requirement.

■

Cross references—
FAQ: 106, 107

FAQ

106

What is an advertised promise?

An advertised promise is a guarantee that a service makes to its users. Some people use the term post-condition instead of the term advertised promise.

■

Cross references—
FAQ: 105, 107

FAQ 107

How are advertised promises related to advertised requirements?

When a user fails to fulfill the advertised requirements of a service, that service usually fails to fulfill its advertised promises.

For example, part of the advertised promise for `stack.pop()` is that the number of elements will decrease by one. If, however, `stack.empty()` returns `true`, `stack.pop()` cannot fulfill this promise. Therefore the advertised requirements for `stack.pop()` will include `!stack.empty()`.

When users fail to fulfill the advertised requirements, services normally throw exceptions. It is also legal, although often less desirable, for services to respond more severely to users who fail to fulfill the requirements. For example, if `Stack::pop()` were invoked in a performance-critical path of the system, testing the advertised requirement might prove to be too expensive, in which case `Stack::pop()` might advertise, "If the `Stack` is `empty()`, arbitrarily disastrous things might happen."

∎

Cross references—
FAQ: 105, 106, 245, 247

FAQ 108

How do you express the advertised requirements and advertised promises of the member functions?

With disciplined and consistent use of comments in the class declaration.

- `//PURPOSE`: tells users the overall purpose of the service.

- `//REQUIRE`: tells users the advertised requirements. These must make sense to users, therefore the text in the `//REQUIRE`: section may only refer to parameters and (`const`) `public` services.

- `//PROMISE`: tells users the advertised promises. These must make sense to users, therefore the text in the `//PROMISE`: section may only refer to parameters and (`const`) `public` services. `INITIAL(expr)` is the value of the expression `expr` before the service is invoked. This is useful in the `//PROMISE`: section, where other, undecorated expressions are implicitly evaluated after the service is finished.

- `RESULT` is a useful name for the service's return value. This is also useful in the `//PROMISE`: section.

```
class Stack {
public:

  Stack();
    //PURPOSE: initializes a Stack
    //REQUIRE: nothing
    //PROMISE: numElems() == 0

  unsigned numElems() const;
    //PURPOSE: returns the number of elements on this Stack
    //REQUIRE: nothing
    //PROMISE: RESULT >= 0 and RESULT <= 10

  int top() const;
    //PURPOSE: returns the top element of this Stack
    //REQUIRE: numElems() != 0
    //PROMISE: nothing

  void push(int elem);
    //PURPOSE: pushes "elem" onto the end of this Stack
    //REQUIRE: numElems() < 10
    //PROMISE: numElems() == INITIAL(numElems()) + 1
    //PROMISE: top() == elem

  int pop();
    //PURPOSE: pops and returns the top element from this
    //REQUIRE: numElems() != 0
    //PROMISE: numElems() == INITIAL(numElems()) - 1
    //PROMISE: RESULT == INITIAL(top())

protected:
  int data_[10];
  unsigned numElems_;
};

inline
Stack::Stack()
  : numElems_(0)
{
  //intentionally left blank
}

inline
unsigned
Stack::numElems() const
{
  return numElems_;
}
```

```
inline
int
Stack::top() const
{
  if (numElems_ == 0)
    throw "Empty";
  return data_[numElems_-1];
}

inline
void
Stack::push(int elem)
{
  if (numElems_ == 10)
    throw "Full";
  data_[numElems_++] = elem;
}

inline
int
Stack::pop()
{
  if (numElems_ == 0)
    throw "Empty";
  return data_[--numElems_];
}

main()
{
  Stack s;
  s.push(42);
  int elem = s.pop();
}
```

Keeping a class's specification in the header (.h) file makes it easier for developers to find the specification and keep it synchronized with the code when changes are needed.

■

Cross references—
FAQ: 105, 106, 115

What's the difference between a big change and a little change?

Big changes break existing user code; little changes do not.

Developers are often surprised at the enormous ripple effect caused by a few interface changes. If too many non-substitutable (non-backward compatible) interface changes are made to primitive objects, organizations can spend more time adjusting their old code than writing new code. This is especially true for organizations that are building large, complicated systems or applications.

Developers should therefore be somewhat cautious of the difference between a substitutable change and a change that will break existing user code.

■

Cross reference—
FAQ: 110

How do developers determine if a proposed change will be big or little?

Specification.

With proper specification, maintenance programmers can easily distinguish between big or little changes. Ill-specified systems typically suffer from "change phobia": if anyone even contemplates changing *anything*, everyone starts sending out their résumés for fear that the system will collapse. Unfortunately, changes often *do* make the world fall apart in ill-specified systems. It's called maintenance cost, and it eats software companies alive.

Did somebody say, "Inertia"?

■

Cross references—
FAQ: 110, 111

What are the properties of a little (or "substitutable") change in a specification?

Require no more, promise no less.

A new specification is substitutable with respect to the old specification if and only if two conditions are met. First, any user who fulfilled the old advertised requirements still fulfills the new ones. Second, any service that fulfills the new advertised promises also would have fulfilled the old ones. In other words, existing user code will need to be adjusted if the replacement class requires users to do more, or promises less than the original class did.

For example, Mac agrees to mow Lonnie's lawn for $10. Mac could substitute his friend, Pepper, if the requirements went down (say $5), or if the promises went up (to also weed the garden, for instance). However, Lonnie would be justifiably upset if Pepper required more (say $20) or promised less (to only mowing half the lawn, for instance).

In the following example, class Version1 and Version2 represent subsequent versions of some class. Version2 is substitutable for Version1 since Version2 requires no more and promises no less than Version1 (in fact, Version2 requires less and promises more).

```
class Version1 {
public:
  int f(int x);
    //REQUIRE: x must be odd
    //PROMISE: RESULT will be even
};

class Version2 {
public:
  int f(int x);
    //REQUIRE: x can be anything
    //PROMISE: RESULT will be 8
};
```

Note that *every* service for the new version must require no more, and promise no less than the equivalent service in the old version. If even one service is changed such that it requires more or promises less, the entire class is not substitutable.

■

Cross reference—

FAQ: 112

How do you know if the implementation of a service fulfills its specification?

The implementation requires no more than the advertised requirements of its specification, and delivers no less than the advertised promises of its specification.

The implementation of a service doesn't have to be as picky as its advertised requirements. Also, a service can do more than the minimum specified by its advertised promises. In the following example, the actual behavior of `Fred::f()` is different from its advertisement, but in a way that is substitutable and, therefore, won't surprise users.

```cpp
class Fred {
public:
  int f(int i);
    //REQUIRE: i must be odd (if i is even, we don't
    //         guarantee to fulfill the PROMISE)
    //PROMISE: RESULT will be even
};

int
Fred::f(int i)
{
  if (i % 2 == 0) {
    //we COULD throw an exception here but we don't HAVE to
  }

  //we're allowed to return ANY even number,
  //but we can do something very specific if we want to...
  return 8;
}

main()
{
  Fred fred;
  int result = fred.f(37);
  //we're allowed to assume that "result" is even...
}
```

We say that a specification is adaptable when it is vague enough that an implementation may actually require less than its advertised requirements or when an implementation may actually deliver more than its advertised promises.

We will see that adaptable specifications are common in base classes, since they give extra latitude to derived classes.

■

Cross references—

FAQ: 111, 120

Should users of a service rely on what the code actually does, or on the specification?

The specification!

Many software organizations systematically fail to observe this critical guideline. Developers in these organizations are trained to rely on what the code does instead of what it promises to do.

Users of a service must rely only on the service's specification, not the implementation of that specification. In fact, there are only a few times when users legitimately need to look at the source code to find out what a service actually does (such as when you are inspecting the code to ensure it fulfills its promise).

In the following example, the specification of `Version2::f()` didn't change from `Version1::f()`, even though its actual implementation is different. Any users who relied only on what the member function promised to do wouldn't be hurt by the new version; but users who relied on what the code actually did would be broken.

```cpp
class Version1 {
public:
  int f();   //PROMISE: RESULT will be even
};

class Version2 {
public:
  int f();   //PROMISE: RESULT will be even
};

int Version1::f() { return 4; }
int Version2::f() { return 8; }
```

Never assume that a service will always do what the code currently does. The code will change; only the specification is stable.

■

Cross references—

FAQ: 114, 121

What are the advantages of relying on the specification rather than the implementation?

Time, specifiability, flexibility, fixability, extensibility, and understandability.

Time: It is far easier to read the service's specification than to reverse-engineer its actual behavior.

Specifiability: If a specification is insufficient or absent, the class is broken and must be fixed. By forcing users to rely on the specification rather than the code, users will report insufficient specification as a serious error, thus specifications will get developed early in the development life cycle.

Flexibility: The code of a service may be (and generally will be) modified. When such modifications occur, user code that relied only on the specification won't break, assuming the new behavior is compatible with the old specification. However, if user code depends on how the service was implemented, that user code may break when legitimate modifications are made.

Fixability: The definition of a defect is, "The service doesn't fulfill its specification." The right course of action is usually to make the service do what it is supposed to do, rather than to back-patch the specification to reflect the erroneous implementation. If some users are relying on the actual code, it's hard to tell whether it would be better (that is, less damaging) to fix the code to match the specification, or to fix the specification to match the code.

Extensibility: Adaptable specifications give latitude to derived classes. If users rely on the code of the base class, users may break when supplied with a derived class.

Understandability: By providing accurate specifications, the system's behavior can be more easily understood. In systems that don't use complete and consistent specifications, the long-term result is an over-reliance on those rare individuals, the system experts, who can understand the entire system at once. For example, to repair a certain defect, either part X or part Y must be modified. Without specification of what these parts are supposed to do, only the system expert will be able to determine whether anyone else in the world is going to break if X or Y are changed. Specifications enable average developers to make more of these decisions. From a business perspective, this mitigates risk in cases where a system expert gets run over by a truck.

Write code to fulfill a specification, not the other way around.

■

Cross reference—

FAQ: 113

Is it possible to keep the specification synchronized with the code?

Challenging, but doable.

On projects ranging from very small (10K lines of OO/C++) to very large systems (millions of lines of OO/C++) our experience has shown that this is a solvable problem. In fact, the larger the system, the more important it is to separate specification from implementation.

Since specifications describe behavior in terms that are observable to the user, rather than in terms of the implementation, specifications tend to stabilize fairly early in the product life cycle. Compared to the previous technology, where the specification was the implementation, our approach vastly reduces the frequency of specification changes.

■

Cross reference—

FAQ: 108

What is proper inheritance?

When the advertised behavior of the derived class is substitutable for that of the base class.

Proper inheritance and substitutable behavior can be guaranteed when the specifications of the derived class services require no more and promise no less than the specifications of the corresponding services in the base class(es). The derived class can also add new services; the specification for these new services can require as much or promise as little as they like, since no corresponding services exist in any base class with which the new services can be compared.

In the following example, the specification for `Derived::f()` requires no more (in fact, it imposes a weaker requirement) and promises no less (in fact, it makes a stronger promise) than the specification of `Base::f()`.

```
#include <iostream.h>

class Base {
public:
  virtual int f(int x);
    //REQUIRE: x must be odd
    //PROMISE: RESULT will be even
  virtual ~Base() { }
};

class Derived : public Base {
public:
  virtual int f(int x);
    //REQUIRE: x can be any integer
    //PROMISE: RESULT will be 8
};
```

```
int
Base::f(int x)
{
  if (x % 2 == 0)
    throw "Even!";
  return x + 1;
}

int
Derived::f(int x)
{
  return 8;
}

void
userCode(Base& base)
{
  //we should only pass odd numbers, since base may
  //actually be a Base...
  int result = base.f(37);

  //we expect result to be even:
  if (result % 2 == 1)
    cerr << "PANIC: call the hotline at 1-800-BIG-BUGS\n";
}

main()
{
  Base b;      userCode(b);
  Derived d;   userCode(d);
}
```

Note that every service of the derived class must have substitutable behavior with respect to the corresponding specification in the base class(es). If even one derived class service specifies stronger requirements or weaker promises than the corresponding specification in the appropriate base class, the inheritance relationship is improper.

The formal name for this rule is contravariance, but we usually call it substitutability.

■

Cross references—

FAQ: 111, 117, 118, 121

What are the benefits of proper inheritance?

Substitutablility and extensibility.

Substitutability: An object of a properly derived class can be freely and safely substituted for an object of its base class. For example, suppose a user defines a function userCode(Base& base). If class Derived properly inherits from class Base, userCode(Base& base) will work correctly when an object of class Derived is passed instead of an object of class Base. In contrast, there is no guarantee that userCode(Base& base) will work correctly when it is passed an object of a class that was produced by improper inheritance.

Extensibility: The properly derived class can be freely and safely used in place of its base class even if the properly derived class is created months or years after the user code was defined. It's easy to extend a system's functionality when you add properly derived classes that contain enhanced functionality. These guarantees cannot be made when improper inheritance is used.

Note that these guarantees only work when the user code relies on the specification of the base class rather than the (possibly more specific) implementation of the base class.

■

Cross references—
FAQ: 116, 118, 121

What is improper inheritance?

A design error that creates a mess.

Improper inheritance occurs when the derived class is not substitutable with respect to its base class(es). That is, when the specification of one or more inherited services either requires more or promises less than the corresponding specification in the base class.

One symptom of improper inheritance is when the user code uses dynamic typing (that is, run-time type checks, capability queries, and down casting) and treats objects of different derived classes in different ways (for example, to avoid using some services on some derived classes).

Improper inheritance imposes the following costs: more complex user code (it is littered with run-time type checks and expensive decision logic), increased maintenance costs (every time a change is made, all the run-time type checks in the user code must be re-analyzed to ensure nothing will break), and reduced extensibility (every time a new derived class is added to the system, all the run-time type checks in the user code must be re-analyzed to ensure nothing will break).

Most of the benefits of OO technology vanish when improper inheritance is employed. In C++, public inheritance should be tied closely to subtyping, which means public inheritance has a strong semantic meaning. When public inheritance is used improperly, the software usually ends up being brittle, over budget, and delivered late.

■

Cross references—
FAQ: 116, 119, 125

Isn't the difference between proper and improper inheritance obvious?

Apparently not.

The single largest source of design errors is improper inheritance. This seems to be because developers base inheritance relationships on their intuition rather than the objective criteria of substitutability.

The following inheritance relationships are improper due to the behaviors of the derived class either requiring more or promising less.

- A `Stack` **is not a kind-of** `List` (**assuming** `List` **provides more services than** `Stack`).

- A `ListOfApples` **is not a kind-of** `ListOfFruit` (**assuming that any type of** `Fruit` **can be put into a** `ListOfFruit`).

The following inheritance relationships may or may not be proper inheritance depending on the specified behavior of the base class and the derived class.

- A Circle **may not be a kind-of** Ellipse.

- An Ostrich **may not be a kind-of** Bird.

- An Integer **may not be a kind-of** RationalNumber.

These examples are explained in Chapter 11.

■

Cross references—
FAQ: 116, 117, 118, 125, 129, 131, 134

What is contravariance?

The glue that holds OO technology together.

Contravariance is good.

Contravariance is just a fancy way of saying that a derived class shouldn't shock users of the base class. It amounts to the same thing as substitutability.

Just remember: require no more, promise no less.

■

Cross reference—
FAQ: 116

F A Q
120

Is substitutability tied to what the actual code does, or the specification?

The specification.

The specification of an overridden service must require no more and promise no less than the specification of the base class. It must also correctly implement whatever specification it provides. However, when the base class gives an adaptable specification, the code of the override doesn't necessarily have to do the same as the code of the base class.

F A Q
121

In the example below, Base::f() provides an adaptable specification: the code does more than the strict minimum guaranteed by the specification. The code of the derived class isn't substitutable with respect to the implementation of the base class, but it is substitutable with respect to the specification of the base class. Since the user code, userCode(Base& base), relies only on the specification of Base::f() rather than the more specific implementation, the user code won't break when it is passed a Derived object. Conversely, if the user code had relied on the implementation of Base::f(), it would break when passed a Derived object (it would also break if a legitimate, substitutable modification was made to Base::f(), such as returning 42).

```cpp
#include <iostream.h>

class Base {
public:
  virtual int f();
    //PROMISE: RESULT will be even
  virtual ~Base() { }
};

class Derived : public Base {
public:
  virtual int f();
    //PROMISE: RESULT will be 8
};

int
Base::f()
{
  //we're allowed to return ANY even number...
  return 4;
}

int
Derived::f()
{
  //we MUST return 8...
  return 8;
}
```

```
void
userCode(Base& base)
{
  int result = base.f();

  //we are ONLY allowed to expect result will be even.
  //in particular, we must NOT assume it is 4.
  if (result % 2 == 1)
    cerr << "PANIC: call the hotline at 1-800-BIG-BUGS\n";
}

main()
{
  Base b;      userCode(b);
  Derived d;   userCode(d);
}
```

Remember: never assume that a class will always be implemented as it is currently implemented.

■

Cross reference—

FAQ: 113

Should you revoke or hide a public member function that a class inherits through `public` **inheritance?**

F A Q
122

No.

Never.

Too often, programmers try to use inheritance even when it doesn't fit the constraints of substitutability. Typically this means creating a derived class, then fixing whatever is wrong, usually by trying to hide one or more inherited `public` member functions.

Revoking an inherited `public` service is evil.

■

Cross references—

FAQ: 15, 76, 89, 91
See Stroustrup: 6.2, 12.2, 12.3, 12.4, 12.5
See Ellis & Stroustrup: 10.1c, 10.2, 10.7c
See Lippman: 8.2, 8.4, 8.5

FAQ 123

What is specialization?

A major source of confusion and design errors.

Some people assume that proper inheritance can be determined by the vague concept of specialization. For example, if `Derived` is a special `Base`, some people assume that `Derived` can properly be derived from `Base`. While this simple rule works some of the time, it is incorrect often enough to be misleading.

One problem with using the concept of specialization is that it is ambiguous. Does it mean "better than" (`JetPlane` is a specialized `Plane`), or "more skilled" (`Doctor` is a specialized `Person`), or "subset of" (`Circle` is a specialized `Ellipse`), or "more specific" (`Unix` is a specialized `Operating System`), or "restricted" (a `Bag` that can only contain `Apples` is a specialized `Bag` that can contain `Fruit`)?

Not only is it ambiguous, but it is, in certain cases, completely incorrect. In particular, specialization does not imply that `Derived` must support all the operations defined by `Base`, as is necessary for proper inheritance.

Forget specialization and learn about substitutability.

■

Cross references—

FAQ: 15, 76, 120, 129
See Stroustrup: 6.2, 12.2, 12.3, 12.4, 12.5
See Ellis & Stroustrup: 10.1c, 10.2, 10.7c
See Lippman: 8.2, 8.4, 8.5

FAQ 124

What do subsets have to do with proper inheritance?

Nothing.

The set of circles is a subset of the set of all ellipses, yet circles can't deform themselves asymmetrically, which may be a property (service) guaranteed by class `Ellipse`.

The set of ostriches is a subset of the set of all birds, yet ostriches cannot fly, which may be a property (service) guaranteed by class `Bird`.

The root problem with the subsets-mean-subtypes idea is that subsets deal with values, where objects normally have mutative services.

Forget subsets and learn about substitutability.

■

Cross references—
FAQ: 120, 125, 129

Is Ostrich **a kind-of** Bird?

Not if all kinds-of birds can fly!

Suppose we have a class Bird with member functions altitude() and fly(), where fly() promises that the bird's altitude() will be bigger than zero.

```
class Bird {
public:

  int altitude() const;
    //PROMISE: returns this Bird's current altitude

  virtual void fly();
    //PROMISE: altitude() > 0

  virtual ~Bird() { }
};
```

Subsequently, 100,000 lines of user code are written based on this set of promises.

At some point, someone wants to create an Ostrich class, with Ostrich being a kind-of Bird. Unfortunately, ostriches can't fly (that is, the altitude of an ostrich remains at zero when it tries to fly).

Despite its intuitive appeal, and regardless of how many other services are inheritable, deriving Ostrich from Bird will cause problems. Those problems stem from the inherent incompatibility of the following statements.

1. **The altitude of every Bird will be non-zero when it flies.**

2. **Ostrich is a kind-of Bird.**

3. **The altitude of an Ostrich remains zero after it flies.**

At least one of those statements *must* be false; they cannot be simultaneously satisfied. We'll examine the impact of invalidating each of the three statements. Note that there is no correct solution; you must choose whichever is best (or perhaps least bad) for your situation.

- **If you wish to maintain statements 2 and 3, you are obliged to invalidate statement 1: you must change the behavior of Bird. In particular, it is no longer the case that the altitude of every Bird is non-zero when it flies. Unfortunately, this breaks existing user code that relies on the original behavior.**

- **If you wish to maintain statements 1 and 3, you are obliged to invalidate statement 2: Ostrich cannot be a kind-of Bird. While ostrich is a type of bird in the biological sense, an Ostrich is not a type of Bird_That_Can_Fly, which is what class Bird promises.**

- **If you wish to maintain statements 1 and 2, you are obliged to invalidate statement 3: the altitude of an Ostrich must be non-zero after it flies. To make this option more palatable, one can imagine that an Ostrich uses some artificial means to achieve its increase in altitude (stairs, a jet pack, plane tickets, or something like that).**

Remember, do not confuse kind-of with subset. Even though the set of ostriches is a subset of the set of birds (every ostrich is in the set of birds), this does not imply that Ostrich is a kind-of Bird. The kind-of relation has to do with services, not just subsets. When you evaluate a potential inheritance relationship, your primary criterion should be substitutability, not subsets.

■

Cross references—
FAQ: 120, 124

Can an overridden virtual function throw an exception?

FAQ
126

Only if the base class says it might.

It's legal for a dynamically bound override to throw an exception if, and only if, the specification of the service in the base class does not prohibit an exception from being thrown. Without such an adaptable specification in the base class, throwing an exception in an override is like false advertising. For example, consider a used-car salesman selling you a kind-of car that blows up (that is, throws an exception) when you turn on the ignition switch. Ralph Nader would correctly say that such a vehicle isn't a kind-of car.

Also, consider the Ostrich-kind-of-Bird dilemma. Suppose Bird::fly() promises to never throw an exception, as follows.

```
#include <iostream.h>

class Bird {
public:
  Bird()                            : altitude_(0) { }
  virtual ~Bird()                   { }
  int altitude() const              { return altitude_; }
  virtual void fly()                { altitude_ = 100; }
    //PROMISE: altitude() > 0; never throws an exception.
protected:
  int altitude_;
};
```

Suppose Ostrich::fly() is defined to throw an exception, as follows.

```
class Ostrich : public Bird {
public:
  virtual void fly()                { throw "gotchya!"; }
    //PROMISE: throws an exception despite what Bird says
```

        └──▶ Violates base class promise; bad form!

```
};
```

Defining `Ostrich::fly()` to throw an exception breaks the following user code that (legitimately) relied on the promise made by `Bird::fly()`.

```
void
userCode(Bird& bird)
{
  bird.fly();
            ┌──────► the spec says this will NOT throw an exception, yet it might!
}

main()
{
  Ostrich fred;
  try {
    userCode(fred);
    cout << "Bird::fly() spec says we SHOULD get here\n";
  }
  catch (const char* msg) {
    cout << "we ACTUALLY get here; msg=" << msg << endl;
  }
}
```

For an exception to this guideline, see FAQ-263.

■

Cross references—
FAQ: 125, 157, 263

Can an overridden virtual function be a no-op?

Only if the base class says it might.

It's legal for an overridden virtual function to do nothing if, and only if, the specification of the service in the base class tells users that it might do nothing. Without such an adaptable specification in the base class, doing nothing is like false advertising. For example, consider a used-car salesman selling you a kind-of car where applying the brakes is a no-op (that is, the brake lines have been cut). Ralph Nader would correctly say that such a vehicle isn't a kind-of car.

Consider the Ostrich-kind-of-Bird dilemma. Suppose Bird::fly() promises that the altitude of the Bird will be strictly positive.

```cpp
#include <iostream.h>

class Bird {
public:
  Bird()                      : altitude_(0) { }
  virtual ~Bird()             { }
  int altitude() const        { return altitude_; }
  virtual void fly()          { altitude_ = 100; }
    //PROMISE: altitude() > 0
protected:
  int altitude_;
};
```

Suppose Ostrich::fly() is defined as a no-op, as follows.

```cpp
class Ostrich : public Bird {
public:
  virtual void fly()          { /*no-op*/ }
    //PROMISE: altitude() will still be zero

};
```

⌐─────▶ volates base class promise; bad form!

Unfortunately this breaks user code that (legitimately) relied on the promise made by Bird::fly().

```cpp
void
userCode(Bird& bird)
{
  bird.fly();

  if (bird.altitude() <= 0)
    cerr << "Error! Call the hotline at 1-800-BAD-BUGS\n";
}

main()
{
  Ostrich fred;
  userCode(fred);
}
```

Note that decorating the Ostrich class with a comment ("I can't fly") isn't good enough, since many users won't even be aware that they're dealing with an Ostrich.

Trying to make this safe with a canYouFly() query will still break existing user code, because calls to bird.fly() will need to be patched with a test, "if you can fly then fly." Note also that these "capability queries" prohibit extensibility.

Cross reference—
FAQ: 125

FAQ
128

Why does C++ make it so hard to fix the Ostrich-**kind-of**-Bird dilemma?

The problem is a bad domain analysis; it has nothing to do with C++.

The problem of whether or not Ostrich is a kind-of Bird is not a failure of the C++ language, nor is it a failure of object-oriented technology. It is a failure of domain analysis. The domain analysis incorrectly concluded something about the problem domain: that the altitude of all kinds-of birds will be strictly positive when they fly.

Stable OO software depends on both an accurate understanding of the problem domain and properly encoding that problem domain knowledge in the class relationships.

Cross references—
FAQ: 41, 125

FAQ
129

Is Circle **a kind-of** Ellipse?

Probably not.

The answer depends on what class Ellipse promises to do. Circle can be a kind-of Ellipse only if Circle supports all of the services defined by Ellipse.

Suppose, Ellipse has a setSize(x,y) member function that sets the width and height of the Ellipse. In this case, a Circle cannot be a kind-of

Ellipse because Circle cannot be resized asymmetrically (unless a Circle isn't necessarily circular!).

```cpp
#include <iostream.h>

class Ellipse {
public:
  Ellipse(float x, float y)
    : width_(x), height_(y) { }
  virtual ~Ellipse()
    { }
  virtual void setSize(float x, float y)
    { width_ = x; height_ = y; }
  float width() const
    { return width_; }
  float height() const
    { return height_; }
protected:
  float width_, height_;
};

void
userCode(Ellipse& ellipse)
{
  //set the dimensions of the Ellipse to 10x20
  ellipse.setSize(10, 20);
}

class Circle : public Ellipse {
public:
  Circle(float initRadius)
    : Ellipse(initRadius, initRadius) { }
  //what should we do with "setSize(float x, float y);"?
};

main()
{
  Circle c(10);
  cout << "initial Circle dimensions = "
       << c.width() << "x" << c.height() << "\n";

  userCode(c);
  cout << "final Circle dimensions = "
       << c.width() << "x" << c.height() << '\n';
}
```

The output of this program is:

```
initial Circle dimensions: 10x10
final Circle dimensions: 10x20
```

A 10 x 20 circle is a strange-looking circle!

■

Cross references—
FAQ: 15, 76, 130
See Stroustrup: 6.2, 12.2, 12.3, 12.4, 12.5
See Ellis & Stroustrup: 10.1c, 10.2, 10.7c
See Lippman: 8.2, 8.4, 8.5

FAQ
130

What can be done about the asymmetric-circle dilemma?

Admit that you can't have it all.

Despite its intuitive appeal, and regardless of how many other services are inheritable, deriving Circle from Ellipse will cause problems. Those problems stem from the inherent incompatibility of the following statements.

    1. Every Ellipse can be stretched asymmetrically.

    2. Circle is a kind-of Ellipse.

    3. A Circle cannot be stretched asymmetrically.

At least one of those statements *must* be false. In other words, we have exactly the same options as with the Ostrich-kind-of-Bird dilemma. Hmmm. Do we detect a pattern here? The three options follow.

- If you are willing to invalidate statement 1, you must either remove Ellipse::setSize(x,y), or give it an adaptable specification such as "this may or may not do something." Either way, the change may break existing user code.

- If you are willing to invalidate statement 2, then you won't be able to pass a Circle as a kind-of Ellipse.

- If you are willing to invalidate statement 3, Circle must be able to stretch asymmetrically; not very satisfying.

The basic problem is that Ellipse is too strong: Ellipse has such powerful services that Circle couldn't possibly be substitutable. We must either weaken Ellipse, strengthen Circle, or admit that a Circle isn't a kind-of Ellipse. Ultimately the situation occurred as a result of an inadequate domain analysis: either we did not clearly understand what we needed in class Ellipse, or we did not understand the consequences of trying to define Circle as a kind-of Ellipse. Remember, do not confuse kind-of with specialization. Because a circle is a specialized ellipse (circles are ellipses that have an extra symmetry constraint) does not imply that Circle is a kind-of Ellipse. The kind-of relation has to do with services, not just specialization. When evaluating a potential inheritance relationship, your primary criterion should be substitutability, not specialization.

Note that if you redefine Circle::setSize(x,y) so that it throws an exception, it would break user code unless the specification of Ellipse::setSize(x,y) allows exceptions to be thrown. If you redefine Circle::setSize(x,y) so that it is a no-op, it would break user code unless the specification of Ellipse::setSize(x,y) says "this service might do nothing."

There are many other ways to illustrate this basic issue. Integer, for example, is not a kind-of RationalNumber if RationalNumber has a divide-self-by-two service (unless the divide-self-by-two service has an adaptable specification, such as, "after multiplying the result by two, you may not get the original number back").

What convinces us of the importance of this issue is how often we have seen it come up in real-life training and consulting sessions.

■

Cross references—
FAQ: 120, 125, 126, 127, 128, 129
See Stroustrup: 6.2, 12.2, 12.3, 12.4, 12.5
See Ellis & Stroustrup: 10.1c, 10.2, 10.7c
See Lippman: 8.2, 8.4, 8.5

F A Q
131

Is Stack **a kind-of** List?

No, assuming class List provides services that class Stack doesn't want to support.

The Stack-kind-of List question is often motivated by a desire to use inheritance as a mechanism to reuse the bits and code from class List (for example, if List was a linked list). However, even if List is an abstract class, its users will want it to supply services that aren't natural for a Stack. For example, the interface to a typical Stack class might look like the following (some or all may be virtual).

```
template<class T>
class Stack {
public:
  void push(const T& item); //push another item onto this
  T    pop();               //remove the top item from this
  T    top() const;         //peek at the top item of this
  int  numElems() const;    //returns number of items
};
```

In contrast, the interface of a typical List class might look like the following (some or all may be virtual).

```
template<class T>
class List {
public:
  void      prepend(const T& item);
  void      append(const T& item);
  void      removeFirst();
  void      removeLast();
  void      insertAtPosition(const T& item, unsigned pos);
  void      removeAtPosition(unsigned pos);
  T&        operator[] (unsigned index);
  const T&  operator[] (unsigned index) const;
  unsigned  length() const;
  void      setLength(unsigned newLength);
  unsigned  countMatches(const T& itemToMatch) const;
  unsigned  findPositionOfMatch(const T& item) const;
};
```

If Stack were to inherit from List, Stack would need to support all of the services supplied by List, including services to access, insert, and/or remove elements at an arbitrary offset or position.

Remember, do not confuse kind-of and code reuse. Just because Stack may use the bits and code from List does not imply that Stack is a kind-of List. The kind-of relation has to do with services, not just code reuse.

When evaluating a potential inheritance relationship, your primary criterion should be substitutability, not code reuse.

■

Cross references—

FAQ: 15, 76, 120
See Stroustrup: 6.2, 12.2, 12.3, 12.4, 12.5
See Ellis & Stroustrup: 10.1c, 10.2, 10.7c

Can you achieve code reuse without using inheritance?

Yes; use composition.

In fact, code reuse is typically achieved by composition, since inheritance relationships which generate a lot of code reuse are often improper inheritance relationships. Attempting to derive `Stack` from `List` is an example of using improper inheritance to achieve code reuse.

In the following example, a `Stack` object is a composite built from a `List` object. Thus, class `Stack` is reusing the code from class `List` via composition.

```
template<class T>
class List {
public:
   void      prepend(const T& item);
   void      append(const T& item);
   void      removeFirst();
   void      removeLast();
   void      insertAtPosition(const T& item, unsigned pos);
   void      removeAtPosition(unsigned pos);
   T&        operator[] (unsigned index);
   const T&  operator[] (unsigned index) const;
   unsigned length() const;
   void      setLength(unsigned newLength);
   unsigned countMatches(const T& itemToMatch) const;
   unsigned findPositionOfMatch(const T& item) const;
protected:
   //implementation intentionally omitted
};

template<class T>
class Stack {
public:
   void push(const T& x) { list_.append(x); }
   T    pop()            { return list_.removeLast(); }
   T    top() const      { return list_[list_.length()-1]; }
   int  numElems() const { return list_.length(); }
```

```
protected:
  List<T> list_;
};
```

■

Cross reference—
FAQ: 131

Is container-of-thing a kind-of container-of-anything?

No, even if thing is a kind-of anything.

This design error is, unfortunately, both common and disastrous.

Despite its intuitive appeal, container-of-thing is not a kind-of container-of-anything. You can put anything in a container-of-anything, but you can put only things in a container-of-thing. Therefore, container-of-thing is strictly less powerful than container-of-anything.

This is often surprising to people new to OO (as well as those who are new to the school of proper inheritance). The reason it is surprising is that intuitive notions of the kind-of relationship are muddy. Too often, developers think the kind-of relationship as a glorified subset.

■

Cross references—
FAQ: 120, 124, 134, 135

Is bag-of-apple a kind-of bag-of-fruit (assuming bag-of-fruit lets you insert any kind-of fruit)?

NO!

This is a specific example of the general guideline presented in the previous FAQ.

In the following, Fruit is an ABC, and Apple and Banana are concrete kinds-of Fruit:

```
#include <iostream.h>

class Fruit {
public:
```

```
   virtual void printClassName() = 0;
   virtual    ~Fruit() { }
};

class Apple : public Fruit {
public:
   virtual void printClassName()    { cout << "Apple\n"; }
};

class Banana : public Fruit {
public:
   virtual void printClassName()    { cout << "Banana\n"; }
};
```

The `BagOfFruit` class, following, allows insertion and removal of objects of any kind-of `Fruit`.

```
class Full  { };
class Empty { };

class BagOfFruit {
public:
   BagOfFruit()
     : numElems_(0) { }
   unsigned numElems() const
     { return numElems_; }
   void insert(Fruit& f)
     { if (numElems_ == numElemsMax_) throw Full();
       data_[numElems_++] = &f; }
   Fruit& remove()
     { if (numElems_ == 0) throw Empty();
       return *data_[--numElems_]; }
protected:
   enum      { numElemsMax_ = 20 };
   unsigned  numElems_;
   Fruit*    data_[numElemsMax_];
};
```

The `BagOfApple` class, following, claims to be a kind-of `BagOfFruit`, however `BagOfFruit` is not substitutable for `BagOfApple`. There are several other things wrong with this class as well; it uses a reference cast, and it hides `BagOfFruit::remove()` and `BagOfFruit::insert(Fruit&)`.

```
class BagOfApple : public BagOfFruit {
public:                                        Improper inheritance
  BagOfApple()  : BagOfFruit() { }
  void insert(Apple& a) { BagOfFruit::insert(a); }
  Apple& remove() { return (Apple&) BagOfFruit::remove(); }
};
```

You can write polymorphic functions to insert any piece of Fruit into a BagOfFruit.

```
void
insertFruitIntoBag(BagOfFruit& bag, Fruit& fruit)
{
  bag.insert(fruit);
}
```

Unfortunately, nonsensical combinations of kinds-of bags and kinds-of fruit can also be passed to insertFruitIntoBag().

```
main()
{
  BagOfApple bagOfApple;
  Banana banana;
  insertFruitIntoBag(bagOfApple, banana);

  cout << "Removing an Apple from bagOfApple: ";
  Apple& a2 = bagOfApple.remove();
  a2.printClassName();
}
```

The output of this program follows.

```
Removing an Apple from bagOfApple: Banana
```

You could blame the pointer (reference) cast in the remove() service, but the real culprit is improper inheritance. Inheritance must be evaluated using something rigorous such as substitutability, because intuition is often muddy (in other words, wrong).

■

Cross references—

FAQ: 133, 139, 143, 324

Is parking-lot-for-cars a kind-of parking-lot-for-arbitrary-vehicles (assuming parking-lot-for-vehicles lets you park any kind-of vehicle)?

NO!

This is another specific example of the general guideline presented earlier. In the following, `Vehicle` is an ABC, and `Car` and `NuclearSubmarine` are concrete kinds-of `Vehicle`.

```cpp
#include <iostream.h>

class Vehicle {
public:
  virtual ~Vehicle() { }
};

class Car : public Vehicle {
public:
  virtual void startEngine()
    { cout << "starting a Car...\n"; }
};

class NuclearSubmarine : public Vehicle {
public:
  virtual void launchMissile()
    { cout << "starting a War...\n"; }
};
```

If a container of `Car` was a kind-of container of `Vehicle`, someone might put a `NuclearSubmarine` inside the container of `Car`, then remove that `NuclearSubmarine` thinking it was a `Car`.

This is an egregious error. When the `startEngine()` service is called, the `launchMissile()` may actually be executed (depending on the compiler and implementation). Thus, starting the car's engine might inadvertently start World War III! See the previous FAQ to see the user code that might cause this to happen.

The root problem is bad inheritance. You can't patch up a bad design with a little extra inheritance. Throwing more inheritance at an already defective design will usually make it worse. If the design is broken, the design needs to be fixed; don't try to patch around it with clever coding tricks.

■

Cross references—

FAQ: 133, 134

Is array-of `Derived` a kind-of array-of `Base`?

NO! (although the compiler doesn't detect this error).

This is another specific example of the general guideline presented earlier. For example, suppose class Base has one integer, plus whatever compiler-specific overhead is used to implement virtual functions (usually a single pointer).

```
#include <iostream.h>

class Base {
public:
  Base() : i_(42*42) { }
  virtual ~Base() { }
  virtual void service()
    { cout << "Base::service()\n" << flush; }
protected:
  int i_;
};
```

Suppose class `Derived` has another integer, `j_`, on top of whatever it inherits from `Base`.

```
class Derived : public Base {
public:
  Derived() : Base(), j_(42*42*42) { }
  virtual void service()
    { cout << "Derived::service()\n" << flush; }
protected:
  int j_;
};
```

Making a `Base` pointer refer to the first element in an array-of `Derived` objects is OK, provided users never perform pointer arithmetic (such as applying the subscript operator) to that `Base` pointer. Subscripting into the array using the `Base` pointer is wrong since it will use `sizeof(Base)` for the pointer arithmetic rather than `sizeof(Derived)`. Thus, subscripting into the array using the Base pointer may not refer to the correct Derived object.

This underscores the advantage of using an array-like class instead of using a C++ array. The preceding problem would have been properly trapped as an error if an Array<Derived> had been used rather than a Derived[], where Array<Derived> is an array-like class. For example, attempting to pass an Array<Derived> to f(Array<Base>& a) will cause a compile-time error.

For the following example, assume an imaginary machine where sizeof(Base) is 8 and sizeof(Derived) is 12. In this case, b[1] would be somewhere inside the belly of d[0]! In any event, it probably wouldn't be the same as d[1].

```
void
useSubscript(Base* b)
{
  cout << "b[0].service(): " << flush;  b[0].service();
  cout << "b[1].service(): " << flush;  b[1].service();
}                                                        BOOM

main()
{
  Derived d[10];
  useSubscript(d);
}
```

This is horrendously evil; it will probably eat your customer alive. The very best you can hope for is an immediate system crash.

The fundamental problem is that a pointer to the first of an array-of things has exactly the same type as a pointer to a single thing. This was inherited from C.

■

Cross references—

FAQ: 15, 76, 133, 137, 275, 276, 308
See Stroustrup: 6.2, 12.2, 12.3, 12.4, 12.5
See Ellis & Stroustrup: 10.1c, 10.2, 10.7c
See Lippman: 9.3

FAQ 137

Does the fact that an array-of Derived can be passed as an array-of Base mean that arrays are bad?

Arrays are dangerous; use templatized container classes instead.

Compared to a C++ array, a user-defined array-like class catches more errors at compile-time so you don't have to rely as heavily on run-time testing. For example, attempting to pass an Array<Derived> as an Array<Base> would be caught at compile-time.

Cross references—

FAQ: 85, 134, 136, 138, 145, 275, 276
See Stroustrup: 6.2, 12.2, 12.3, 12.4, 12.5
See Ellis & Stroustrup: 10.2, 10.1c, 10.7c
See Lippman: 9.3

FAQ 138

How do templates help prevent an array-of Derived from being passed as an array-of Base?

Templates allow the compiler to distinguish between a pointer to a thing and a reference to an array-of things.

Unless you explicitly say otherwise, the compiler doesn't assume a kind-of relationship exists between templates. For example, the following class template Array, provides a fixed length, array-like abstraction.

```
template<class T>
class Array {
public:
  Array()                                      {                     }
  const T& operator[] (unsigned i) const { return data_[i]; }
  T&       operator[] (unsigned i)       { return data_[i]; }
  unsigned length() const                { return length_;  }
protected:
  enum  { length_ = 10 };
  T     data_[length_];
};
```

Class Derived is derived from class Base.

```
#include <iostream.h>

class Base {
public:
  virtual ~Base() { }
  virtual void service() { cout << "Base::service()\n"; }
};

class Derived : public Base {
public:
  virtual void service() { cout << "Derived::service()\n"; }
};
```

When we used C++ arrays, the compiler wasn't able to detect the error of passing an array-of Derived as if it were a kind-of array-of Base. Now that we are using templates, the compiler will detect this error.

```
void
useSubscript(Array<Base>& array)
{
  cout << "array[0].service(): ";   array[0].service();
  cout << "array[1].service(): ";   array[1].service();
}                                                       ──────▶ OK
main()
{
  Array<Base> arrayOfBase;
  useSubscript(arrayOfBase);

  #ifdef GENERATE_ERROR
    Array<Derived> arrayOfDerived;
    useSubscript(arrayOfDerived);
  #endif                            ──────▶ caught at compile-time

}
```

■

Cross reference—

FAQ: 136

See Lippman: 9.3

What is the difference between overloaded functions and overridden functions?

- Overloading has the same scope, same name, different signatures, virtual not required.

- Overriding has different scopes, same name, same signatures, virtual required.

We use the term "signature" to designate the combination of a function's name, the types and order of its parameters, and, if the function is a non-static member function, its const and/or volatile qualifiers.

Overloading occurs when two or more functions are in the same scope (for example, both in the same class or both at file scope) and have the same name but have different signatures. Overriding occurs when a class and one of its derived classes both define a member function with the same signature, and that member function is declared to be virtual in the base class.

In the following example Base::f(int) and Base::f(float) overload each other, while Derived::g() overrides Base::g().

```
#include <iostream.h>

class Base {
public:
  virtual ~Base()         { }
  virtual void f(int x)    { cout << "Base::f(int)\n";   }
  virtual void f(float x) { cout << "Base::f(float)\n"; }
  virtual void g()         { cout << "Base::g()\n";       }
};
```

```
class Derived : public Base {
public:
  virtual void g()            { cout << "Derived::g()\n"; }
};

main()
{
  Derived d;
  Base* bp = &d;              //OK: Derived is kind-of Base
  bp->f(42);
  bp->f(3.14f);
  bp->g();
}
```

The output of this program follows.

```
Base::f(int)
Base::f(float)
Derived::g()
```

■

Cross references—
FAQ: 16, 89, 91, 140
See Stroustrup: 6.2, r.10
See Ellis & Stroustrup: 10.2, 10.7c, 10.8c, 10.9c, 11.6, 13.1

F A Q
140

What is the hiding rule?

A member of a derived class hides any member of a base class that has the same name as the derived class member.

There are two common situations when the hiding rule shows up. First, when a base class and a derived class declare member functions with different signatures but with the same name, then the base class member function is hidden. Second, when a base class declares a non-virtual member function, and a derived class declares a member function with the same signature, then the base class member function is hidden.

In the following example Derived::f(float) is a normal override of virtual member function Base::f(float). However Derived::g(int) hides (rather than overloads) Base::g(float) and Derived::h(float) hides (rather than overrides) Base::h(float).

```
#include <iostream.h>
class Base {
public:
  virtual ~Base()          { }
  virtual void f(float x) { cout << "Base::f(float)\n"; }
  virtual void g(float x) { cout << "Base::g(float)\n"; }
          void h(float x) { cout << "Base::h(float)\n"; }

};

class Derived : public Base {
public:
  virtual void f(float x) { cout << "Derived::f(float)\n"; }
  virtual void g(int x)   { cout << "Derived::g(int)\n";   }
          void h(float x) { cout << "Derived::h(float)\n"; }
};
```

Because `Base::g(float)` is hidden, `dp->g(3.14f)` will invoke `Derived::g(int)` (3.14 is converted to an `int`). Because `Base::h(float)` is not overridden, `bp->h(3.14f)` will invoke the member function associated with the pointer rather than the member function associated with the object. These behaviors will surprise users, since users normally expect behavior to depend on the type of the object rather than on the type of the pointer used to access that object.

```
main()
{
  Derived d;
  Base* bp = &d;   //OK: Derived is kind-of Base
  Derived* dp = &d;

  //Good: behavior depends solely on type of the object:
  bp->f(3.14f);    //calls Derived::f(float)
  dp->f(3.14f);    //calls Derived::f(float)

  //Bad: behavior depends on type of the pointer:
  bp->g(3.14f);    //calls Base::g(float)
  dp->g(3.14f);    //calls Derived::g(int) (surprise!)

  //Bad: behavior depends on type of the pointer:
  bp->h(3.14f);    //calls Base::h(float) (surprise!)
  dp->h(3.14f);    //calls Derived::h(float)
}
```

The output of this program follows.

```
Derived::f(float)
Derived::f(float)
Base::g(float)
Derived::g(int)
Base::h(float)
Derived::h(float)
```

The hiding rule may not seem intuitive, but it prevents worse errors, especially in the case of assignment operators. If, for example, the hiding rule were removed, it would be legal to assign a Circle to a Square (the Shape part of the Square would be assigned).

■

Cross references—
FAQ: 16, 89, 91, 139, 141
See Stroustrup: 6.2, r.10
See Ellis & Stroustrup: 10.2, 10.7c, 10.8c, 10.9c, 11.6, 13.1

F A Q
141

How do you get around the hiding rule?

Very carefully.

Hiding an inherited public member function is considered immoral and should be avoided whenever possible. When it cannot be avoided, you must be careful not to surprise the class's users. In particular, when a Base* can be used to call a member function on a Derived object, calling via a Derived* shouldn't alter the observable behavior.

In the case of redefining a non-virtual member function, as in Base::h(float) from the previous FAQ, the simplest way to avoid surprising users is to use the virtual keyword when declaring the base class member function. In those rare cases where the base class function cannot be virtual, you must ensure that the observable behavior of the derived class function is identical to that of the base class.

For example, an experienced C++ programmer might use a non-virtual member function to avoid the (small) overhead of a virtual function call, yet might also redefine that member function in a derived class to make better use of the derived class's resources. To avoid surprising users, there must not be any differences in the observable behavior of the two functions.

Note: These relationships are somewhat subtle; if the code will be maintained by less experienced programmers, you should probably use a normal, virtual function instead.

In the case when a base class and a derived class declare member functions with the same name but different signatures, as in Base::g(float) and Derived::g(int) from the previous FAQ, the hidden member function should be redefined in the derived class. In order to share code and ensure the observable behavior is the same, the redefined function will typically call the base class function. The base class function must be redefined even if it is non-virtual; this is one of the situations where it is necessary to redefine an inherited non-virtual function.

The following shows how these guidelines can be applied to the example from the previous FAQ. The behavior now depends on the type of the object rather than on the type of the pointer used to access that object.

```
#include <iostream.h>

class Base {
public:
  virtual ~Base()          { }
  virtual void f(float x) { cout << "Base::f(float)\n"; }
  virtual void g(float x) { cout << "Base::g(float)\n"; }
  virtual void h(float x) { cout << "Base::h(float)\n"; }
};
```
    ➤ h (float) is now virtual
```
class Derived : public Base {
public:
  virtual void f(float x) { cout << "Derived::f(float)\n"; }
  virtual void g(int x)   { cout << "Derived::g(int)\n";   }

  //redefine Base::g(float); Derived::g is now overloaded
  virtual void g(float x) { Base::g(x); }

  //since Base::h(float) is virtual, this is now an override
  virtual void h(float x) { cout << "Derived::h(float)\n"; }
};
```

```
main()
{
  Derived d;
  Base* bp = &d;    //OK: Derived is kind-of Base
  Derived* dp = &d;

  //Good: behavior depends solely on type of the object:
  bp->f(3.14f);    //calls Derived::f(float)
  dp->f(3.14f);    //calls Derived::f(float)

  //Good: behavior depends solely on type of the object:
  bp->g(3.14f);    //calls Derived::g(float)
  dp->g(3.14f);    //calls Derived::g(float)

  //Good: behavior depends solely on type of the object:
  bp->h(3.14f);    //calls Derived::h(float)
  dp->h(3.14f);    //calls Derived::h(float)
}
```

The output of this program follows.

```
Derived::f(float)
Derived::f(float)
Derived::g(float)
Derived::g(float)
Derived::h(float)
Derived::h(float)
```

These guidelines apply only to public inheritance; hiding base class member functions is fine for private or protected inheritance.

■

Cross references—

FAQ: 16, 89, 91, 139, 140
See Stroustrup: 6.2, r.10
See Ellis & Stroustrup: 10.2, 10.7c, 10.8c, 10.9c, 11.6, 13.1

FAQ
142

Can a derived class redefine some-but-not-all of a set of overloaded member functions inherited from the base class?

It's legal, but it's not moral.

If you redefine some-but-not-all of a set of overloaded member functions inherited from the base class, the redefined member functions will hide all the inherited overloads. The work-around is to redefine all of them, usually with simple call-throughs to the base class's member functions.

For example, if class Derived wants to redefine f(int), it should also redefine f(float) to avoid the hiding rule. To share code, Derived::f(float) can simply call Base::f(float).

```
#include <iostream.h>

class Base {
public:
  virtual ~Base()        { }
  virtual void f(int x)   { cout << "Base::f(int)\n";   }
  virtual void f(float x) { cout << "Base::f(float)\n"; }
};

class Derived : public Base {
public:

  //suppose Derived wants to override f(int):
  virtual void f(int x)   { cout << "Derived::f(int)\n"; }

  //the hiding rule forces us to redefine f(float):
  virtual void f(float x) { Base::f(x); }
};

main()
{
  Derived d;
  Base* bp = &d;    //OK: Derived is kind-of Base
  Derived* dp = &d;

  //Good: behavior depends solely on type of the object:
  bp->f(42);        //calls Derived::f(int)
  dp->f(42);        //calls Derived::f(int)

  //Good: behavior depends solely on type of the object:
  bp->f(3.14f);     //calls Derived::f(float)
  dp->f(3.14f);     //calls Derived::f(float)
}
```

The output of this program follows.

```
Derived::f(int)
Derived::f(int)
Derived::f(float)
Derived::f(float)
```

Note that class Derived should redefine f(float) even if Base::f(float) was non-virtual. This is one of the rare circumstances where it is necessary for a derived class to redefine a non-virtual function.

This guideline applies only to public inheritance; hiding base class member functions is fine for private or protected inheritance.

■

Cross references—

FAQ: 140, 142, 449

Can virtual functions be overloaded?

Yes, but it's often easier to use non-virtual overloads that call non-overloaded virtuals.

As was discussed above, when you overload virtuals, the hiding rule forces derived classes to redefine more functions than necessary. In these situations, it is often easier if the overloads are non-virtuals that call virtuals that aren't overloaded. These non-overloaded virtuals are normally protected:.

The code below shows how to apply this guideline to the situation in the previous FAQ where Base::f(int) and Base::f(float) were overloaded virtuals. These functions are now non-virtuals that call non-overloaded virtuals f_i(int) and f_f(float). In class Derived, the behavior of f(int) is changed by overriding Base::f_i(int); redefining f(int) itself would be wrong, since it would hide Base::f(float).

```
#include <iostream.h>

class Base {
public:
  virtual ~Base() { }

  //the non-virtual overloads call non-overloaded virtuals:
  void f(int x)   { f_i(x); }
  void f(float x) { f_f(x); }

protected:
  //the real work is done by the non-overloaded virtuals:
  virtual void f_i(int x)   { cout << "Base::f(int)\n"; }
  virtual void f_f(float x) { cout << "Base::f(float)\n"; }
};
```

```
class Derived : public Base {
public:
  //Derived doesn't redefine either f(int) or f(float)

protected:
  //f(int)'s behavior is changed by overriding f_i(int):
  virtual void f_i(int x) { cout << "Derived::f(int)\n"; }
};

main()
{
  Derived d;
  Base* bp = &d;    //OK: Derived is kind-of Base
  Derived* dp = &d;

  //Good: behavior depends solely on type of the object:
  bp->f(42);        //calls Derived::f(int)
  dp->f(42);        //calls Derived::f(int)

  //Good: behavior depends solely on type of the object:
  bp->f(3.14f);     //calls Base::f(float)
  dp->f(3.14f);     //calls Base::f(float)
}
```

The output of this program follows.

```
Derived::f(int)
Derived::f(int)
Base::f(float)
Base::f(float)
```

The other way to get around the hiding rule (see the previous FAQ) requires the developer of every derived class to understand the hiding rule, since the hiding rule is managed by extra code in every derived class. The guideline presented here only requires the base class developer to understand the hiding rule, since the code to manage the hiding rule is only in the base class. Since base classes are normally developed by the more sophisticated developers, the guideline presented here usually provides the right trade-off.

Note that this guideline does not imply any performance overhead, since the overloaded public member functions are inline non-virtuals.

As before, this guideline applies only to `public` inheritance; hiding base class member functions is fine for `private` or `protected` inheritance.

■

Cross references—
FAQ: 140, 141

Can an overridden member function use a different default parameter than the one specified in the base class?

It's legal, but it's not moral.

If a base class has a virtual function with a default parameter, overrides of that virtual function should specify exactly the same value for the default parameter.

Default parameters are chosen based on the type of the pointer, not on the type of the pointed-to object. That is, they are chosen using static information (type of the pointer) rather than dynamic information (type of the object). Having a different default parameter in an override would cause different behaviors when the same member function is applied to the same object using pointers of different types. This would be confusing.

```
#include <iostream.h>

class Base {
public:
  virtual ~Base() { }
  virtual void f(int i=5)
    { cout << "Base::f(int i); i=" << i << "\n"; }
};

class Derived : public Base {
public:
  virtual void f(int i=7)    //BAD FORM: different default
    { cout << "Derived::f(int i); i=" << i << "\n"; }
};
```

```
main()
{
  Derived d;
  Base*    bp = &d;
  Derived* dp = &d;
  bp->f();
  dp->f();
}
```

Despite the fact that bp->f() and dp->f() apply the same virtual function to the same object, the behavior is different. The output of this program follows.

```
Derived::f(int i); i=5
Derived::f(int i); i=7
```

Thus bp->f() gets the default parameter from Base::f(int) but gets the code from Derived::f(int). Since this is confusing, the value of a default parameter in an override should be the same as the value of the corresponding default parameter in the base class.

Why does the compiler complain when you try to convert a Derived** **to a** Base**?**

FAQ
145

It's trying to help you.

If class Derived publicly inherits from class Base, C++ lets you convert a Derived* to a Base* because Derived is a kind-of Base. However, trying to convert a Derived** to a Base** is incorrect, and is flagged as a compile-time error. Just because there is a kind-of relationship between Derived and Base does not mean there is a kind-of relationship between Derived* and Base*.

For example, suppose classes Car and NuclearSubmarine are derived from class Vehicle.

```
class Vehicle {
public:
  virtual ~Vehicle() { }
};
```

```
class Car : public Vehicle {
public:
  virtual void startRadio();   //play some tunes
};

class NuclearSubmarine : public Vehicle {
public:
  virtual void startWar();     //launch some missiles
};

main()
{
  NuclearSubmarine sub;
  NuclearSubmarine* p1 = &sub;
  Car* p2;

  Vehicle** vp1 = &p1;   //illegal in C++ (fortunately)
  Vehicle** vp2 = &p2;   //illegal in C++ (fortunately)

  //if the previous two lines were legal, you could
  //silently make a Car* point at an NuclearSubmarine:
  *vp2 = *vp1;

  p2->startRadio();      //if *p2 was a NuclearSubmarine,
}                        //this would do the wrong thing
```

If C++ allowed you to convert a Derived** to a Base**, the statement p2->startRadio() could have started World War III instead of starting a car's radio! The only way to convert a Derived** to a Base** is with an explicit pointer cast (but please don't use pointer casts).

∎

Cross references—

FAQ: 85
See Stroustrup: r.4
See Ellis & Stroustrup: 4.6

What is incremental programming?

Programming through a series of enhancements.

Incremental programming is based on two observations: many things in the real world share common characteristics, and most new software can be created by incrementally enhancing an existing piece of software.

Based on these observations, you start by looking for the common characteristics of two things, make a base class containing these common characteristics, and then make derived classes representing the differences. Then, when you need a new class, you start by finding an existing class that has the right basic properties, inherit from that existing class, and incrementally enhance the derived class to provide the necessary value-add.

A derived class inherits both the representation (bits) and the mechanism (code) from the base class. Virtual functions allow derived classes to selectively override some or all of the inherited mechanism (for example, replace or enhance the selected algorithms).

This simple ability is surprisingly powerful.

■

Cross references—
FAQ: 15, 16, 17, 76, 89, 90, 91
See Stroustrup: 6.2, 12.2, 12.3, 12.4, 12.5
See Ellis & Stroustrup: 10.1c, 10.2, 10.7c
See Lippman: 10.1, 10.2, 10.3

F A Q
146

What are the variations of incremental programming?

Mechanism replacement and interface augmentation.

The following `Stack` class will serve as the basis for both forms of incremental programming. For simplicity, the class doesn't perform any error detection.

F A Q
147

```
class Stack {
public:
                    Stack()       : len_(0) { }
    virtual     ~Stack()        { }
    virtual void push(int x) { data_[len_++] = x; }
    virtual int  pop()        { return data_[--len_]; }
    virtual int  top() const { return data_[len_-1]; }

protected:
    enum { lenMax_ = 10 };
    int len_;
    int data_[lenMax_];
};
```

In the first form of incremental programming, mechanism replacement, some or all of the base class's services are overridden. Class InstrumentedStack, shown below, maintains statistics regarding the number of times the services push(int) and pop() are invoked. The code in the base class is used to manipulate the underlying data structure.

```
class InstrumentedStack : public Stack {
public:
    InstrumentedStack() : Stack(), pushes_(0), pops_(0) { }
    virtual void push(int x) { ++pushes_; Stack::push(x); }
    virtual int  pop()        { ++pops_; return Stack::pop(); }

protected:
    int pushes_, pops_;
};
```

In the second form of incremental programming, interface augmentation, the derived class adds new services to extend the suite of services defined by the base class. The derived class generally overrides very few, if any, of the base class services. In this example, class PrintableStack adds the operation print(), which prints the elements stored on the stack.

```
#include <iostream.h>

class PrintableStack : public Stack {
public:
    void print();
};
```

```
void
PrintableStack::print()
{
   for (int i = 0; i < len_; ++i)
     cout << data_[i] << ' ';
}

main()
{
   InstrumentedStack a;
   PrintableStack     b;
   a.push(42);   a.push(42+42);   a.push(42+42+42);   a.pop();
   b.push(42);   b.push(42+42);   b.push(42+42+42);   b.pop();
   b.print();
}
```

What should you do when you make a non-substitutable change in the semantics of a service?

Change the name of the service (rather than subtly breaking user code, break it violently).

Suppose class Bird has a fly() service that makes a strong promise, such as "the bird's altitude() will be strictly positive." Suppose the revised Bird::fly() service weakens this guarantee by promising "the bird's altitude() won't be negative."

```
class Bird {
public:

   int altitude() const;
     //PROMISE: returns this Bird's current altitude

   virtual void fly();
     //PROMISE: altitude() >= 0
};
```
⟶ was "altitude () > 0"

Because the new promise is weaker than the old, the change isn't substitutable, and user code will subtly break. To repair this, the maintenance programmer will have to find all the places that invoke the fly() service and check that they don't rely on the old behavior. The easiest way to ensure that someone actually examines each of these places is to change the name of the service. For example, change it from fly() to flyIfYouCan().

Naturally, the ideal situation would be to avoid making a non-substitutable change. But if you're going to break user code, break it in a way that allows the compiler to help you locate all the (now broken) user code.

What can be done for a wedged design?

Have a "creativity party."

A wedged design is one that has stopped unfolding gracefully, often because the kind-of relationships aren't quite correct. When this happens, developers are often tempted to force-fit whatever is left (for example, they might fall back to the traditional "live code, dead data" metaphor). We have found that the key to unlock a wedged design is almost always to invent new classes. In other words, to get *more* object-oriented rather than less object-oriented. This requires creative, right-brain thinking: a creativity party.

A creativity party is a design meeting where the express purpose is to invent new ideas. No one attending a creativity party is allowed to critique anyone's ideas, including their own, since criticism and creativity are often mutually exclusive human activities. Instead, every creative idea is recorded for later evaluation.

Here are some ideas to seed your creativity parties. If a class has services whose availability or behavior depends on the object's mode, consider putting each such mode into its own class. If a derived class doesn't want all the features of its base class, rethink the inheritance hierarchies or create new hierarchies to absorb the unwanted services. If a class has a large, seemingly unbounded number of services, consider moving each of these services into a class of its own, and relating these new classes using the "action object" design pattern (this design pattern, also called "command hierarchies" or "verb things," is described elsewhere in the literature).

Every class should have a cohesive mission statement. It is cheaper to develop, test, and maintain N classes that each have one basic mission than one class that must coordinate N different missions. Small is beautiful.

This is part of the paradigm shift.

■

Cross reference—

FAQ: 157

How do you prevent the compiler from generating duplicate out-lined copies of inline virtual functions?

If a class has one or more virtual functions (either inherited or first-declared in that class), then the class should have at least one non-inline virtual function.

Many compilers use the location of the first non-inline virtual function to determine the module that will house the class's magical stuff (the virtual table, out-lined copies of inline virtual functions, and so on). These compilers may put a static copy of a class's magical stuff in every module that includes the class's header file if all of the class's virtual functions are defined inline.

Note that this advice is fairly sensitive to the compiler. Some compilers won't proliferate copies of the magical stuff even if all the virtual functions in a class are inline. But even in these compilers, it doesn't cost much to make sure at least one of the class's virtual functions is non-inline.

■

Cross references—
FAQ: 16, 89, 151, 350
See Stroustrup: 6.2, r.10
See Ellis & Stroustrup: 10.2, 10.7c, 10.8c, 10.9c, 11.6

What should you know about a class whose base class has a virtual destructor?

It should have at least one non-inline virtual function.

If the base class has a virtual destructor, the destructor in the derived class will also be virtual, and, unless you say otherwise, will be inline.

The safest bet is to give every derived class at least one non-inline virtual function (assuming the base class has a virtual destructor).

To show how subtle this can be, consider this trivial example.

```
class Base { public: virtual ~Base(); };
class Derived : public Base { };
main() { }
```

Even though no Base or Derived objects are created, the preceding example will fail to link on many systems. The reason is that the only virtual function in class Derived is inline (Derived::~Derived() is a synthesized inline virtual function), so the compiler puts a static copy of Derived::~Derived() into the current module. Since this static copy of Derived::~Derived() invokes Base::~Base(), the linker will need a definition of Base::~Base().

If you add a non-inline virtual function to a derived class (for example, thisDoesNothing()), it will eliminate the linker errors for that derived class, because the compiler will put the (only) copy of the magical stuff into the module that defines the non-inline virtual function.

```
class Derived2 : public Base {
public:
  //...
private:
  virtual void thisDoesNothing();
};

//this goes in exactly one .C file, often called Derived2.C
void Derived2::thisDoesNothing() { }
```

As with the advice from the previous FAQ, this guideline is fairly sensitive to the compiler. Nonetheless it is fairly easy to make sure that a class with virtual functions has at least one non-inline virtual function.

■

Cross references—
FAQ: 16, 89, 97, 98, 150, 170
See Stroustrup: 6.2, r.10
See Ellis & Stroustrup: 10.2, 10.7c, 10.8c, 10.9c, 11.6

What is static typing?

A safety net.

With static typing, the compiler checks the type safety of every operation at compile-time. For example, the compiler checks the parameter types of function arguments; an improper match is flagged as an error at compile-time.

In object-oriented programs, the most common symptom of a type mismatch is the attempt to invoke a member function on an object when that object does not support the service. For example, if class x has member function f() but not g(), and x is an instance of class X, then x.f() is legal and x.g() is illegal.

```
class X {
public:
  void f() { }
};

main()
{
  X x;
  x.f();    //OK
```

```
#ifdef GENERATE_ERROR
  //the following error is caught at compile-time
  //there is no need for run-time checks
  x.g();
#endif
}
```

Fortunately, C++ catches errors like this at compile-time.

■

Cross references—

FAQ: 16, 89, 153, 154
See Stroustrup: 6.2, r.10
See Ellis & Stroustrup: 10.2, 10.7c, 10.8c, 10.9c, 11.6
See Lippman: 10.2

F A Q
153

What is dynamic typing?

When you don't know if a program is type correct until run-time.

With dynamic typing, user code determines whether an object supports a particular service at run-time rather than at compile-time. Dynamic typing is often accompanied by down casts.

Dynamic typing can unnecessarily increase the cost of your C++ software.

■

Cross references—

FAQ: 16, 89, 152, 154, 155, 156, 162
See Stroustrup: 6.2, r.10
See Ellis & Stroustrup: 10.2, 10.7c, 10.8c, 10.9c, 11.6
See Lippman: 10.2

What is the problem with dynamic typing?

It uses code to find code.

With dynamic typing, the user checks the type of the object to see whether it supports a particular set of services (this is the code that is doing the finding). The user may then need to down cast to the appropriate pointer type in order to access those services (this is the code that is being searched for).

By using user code to find server code, the user code becomes more complex and more fragile.

■

Cross references—

FAQ: 16, 152, 153, 155, 156, 162

What are the costs of using code to find code?

Maintenance costs and run-time costs.

Dynamic typing requires the user code to know about the server's inheritance hierarchy; when user code employs dynamic typing, changing the server's inheritance hierarchy often breaks the user code. This is unfortunate, considering that one of the main goals of object-oriented technology is reducing maintenance costs.

Dynamic typing also requires a run-time check to ensure that the object supports the requested service. This is usually implemented using control flow, such as an `if` or `switch` statement. When the design exploits the static typing capabilities of the C++ compiler, these run-time tests become unnecessary.

■

Cross references—

FAQ: 153, 154, 158, 159
See Stroustrup: 6.2, r.10
See Ellis & Stroustrup: 10.2, 10.7c, 10.8c, 10.9c, 11.6
See Lippman: 10.2

FAQ 156

How can you avoid dynamic typing?

Design. Design. Design.

Circumstances sometimes require the use of dynamic typing. Unfortunately, dynamic typing is often used when it is not required.

Often dynamic typing is used because the programmer does not have enough expertise or does not take the time to produce a good object-oriented design.

When you think you need to use dynamic typing, Just Say No, and go back to designing. After you have revised the design, and revised it again, if you still think you need dynamic typing, use it; but be aware of the additional coding, testing, and maintenance costs you will incur.

■

Cross references—

FAQ: 153, 154, 155, 158, 159, 160
See Stroustrup: 6.2, r.10
See Ellis & Stroustrup: 10.2, 10.7c, 10.8c, 10.9c, 11.6
See Lippman: 10.2

FAQ 157

What is a capability query?

A bandage used to patch a bad design.

A capability query is an inspector member function that allows users to determine whether an object is capable of performing a given service. Capability queries invite inflexibility.

The up side of capability queries is that they allow a class designer to avoid thinking about how users will use the objects, because they allow the classes and objects to be manipulated by the user code.

The down side of capability queries is that they allow a class designer to avoid thinking about how users will use the objects, because they allow the classes and objects to be manipulated by the user code.

Capability queries export complexity from the server to the users, from the few to the many. User code often needs explicit control flow to select operations based on the results of a capability query—user code uses code to find code. This impacts existing user code when new derived classes are added.

Capability queries are one more symptom of dynamic typing.

■

Cross reference—
FAQ: 155

What is an alternative to dynamic typing?

Dynamic binding.

One design alternative that often works is replacing dynamic typing and down casts with dynamic binding and virtual functions. When you do that, you must generalize the derived class service and move the declaration of the derived class service up to the base class. By using this approach, the class selection and down cast are performed automatically and safely. Furthermore, this approach produces extensible software because it automatically extends itself whenever a new derived class is created—as if an extra case or if/else magically appeared in the dynamic typing technique. Finally, in this approach the user gives control to the object rather than reasoning about the object.

The following example demonstrates the dynamic typing (or wrong) way to do things. Pretend the various escape sequences toggle italics on the various kinds of printers.

```
#include <iostream.h>

//pretend this is the escape character
const char* const esc = "ESC";

enum Type { EPSON, PROPRINTER, STAR };
```

```cpp
class Printer1 {
public:
  virtual ~Printer1() { }
  virtual Type type() const  = 0;
};              ──► BAD FORM: returns a type field
class EpsonPrinter1 : public Printer1 {
public:
  virtual Type type() const
    { return EPSON; }
  void italicsEpson(const char* s)
    { cout << esc << "i+" << s << esc << "i-"; }
};

class ProprinterPrinter1 : public Printer1 {
public:
  virtual Type type() const
    { return PROPRINTER; }
  void italicsProprinter(const char* s)
    { cout << esc << "[i" << s << esc << "[n"; }
};

class StarPrinter1 : public Printer1 {
public:
  virtual Type type() const
    { return STAR; }
  void italicsStar(const char* s)
    { cout << esc << "x" << s << esc << "y"; }
};

void
printUsingItalics(Printer1& p, const char* s)
{
  switch (p.type()) {
            ──► BAD FORM: uses code to find code
    case EPSON:
      ((EpsonPrinter1&) p).italicsEpson(s);
            ──► BAD FORM: pointer/reference cast
      break;
    case PROPRINTER:
      ((ProprinterPrinter1&) p).italicsProprinter(s);
      break;
    case STAR:
      ((StarPrinter1&) p).italicsStar(s);
      break;
    default:
      cerr << "Call company representative immediately\n";
  }
}          ──► BAD FORM: delays type-checking until run-time
```

The preceding style uses classes and virtual functions, but it is not the best use of OO technology. We call it Pseudo-OO.

Pseudo-OO uses the `type()` service in basically the same way as the old paradigm used tagged unions (that is, tag fields that indicate which piece of the `union` is currently being used). Pseudo-OO is relatively error prone and non-extensible compared to the right way to use classes and virtual functions, shown below.

```cpp
class Printer2 {
public:
  virtual ~Printer2() { }
  virtual void italics(const char* s) = 0;
};


class EpsonPrinter2 : public Printer2 {
public:
  virtual void italics(const char* s)
    { cout << esc << "i+" << s << esc << "i-"; }
};


class ProprinterPrinter2 : public Printer2 {
public:
  virtual void italics(const char* s)
    { cout << esc << "[i" << s << esc << "[n"; }
};


class StarPrinter2 : public Printer2 {
public:
  virtual void italics(const char* s)
    { cout << esc << "x" << s << esc << "y"; }
};


void
printUsingItalics(Printer2& p, const char* s)
{
  p.italics(s);
```

├──► GOOD FORM: known to be type correct at compile-time
├──► GOOD FORM: no "call company representative" message
├──► GOOD FORM: uses data (rather than code) to find code
└──► GOOD FORM: users don't need to know all printer types

```cpp
}
```

■

Cross references—

FAQ: 153, 154, 155, 156, 159, 162
See Stroustrup: 6.2, r.10
See Ellis & Stroustrup: 10.2, 10.7c, 10.8c, 10.9c, 11.6
See Lippman: 9.1

FAQ
159

What is another alternative to dynamic typing?

Templates.

In the past, some people designed container classes (`List`, `Stack`, `Set`, and so on) that inserted or extracted elements as pointers to a base class from which everything else was derived (for example, class `Object`). This approach promotes dynamic typing and should be avoided in C++.

■

Cross references—

FAQ: 153, 154, 155, 156, 158, 275
See Stroustrup: 6.2, 8, r.10
See Ellis & Stroustrup: 10.2, 10.7c, 10.8c, 10.9c, 11.6, 14
See Lippman: 9.3

FAQ
160

Are there cases where dynamic typing is necessary?

Yes; persistent heterogeneous objects.

A program can't have static knowledge about things that existed before the execution of that program. If some other program stores a group of objects from several classes in a database, and your software peels those objects off the disk drive's aluminum platter (or, equivalently, slurps them from a coaxial cable), your software can't know the types of the objects, because your software didn't create them.

In these cases, the objects may need to be queried about their types, especially if the persistent objects are highly heterogeneous. Note that it is possible to avoid the type queries if the objects are known to be of the same class (homogeneous), or at least known to be derived from some common ABC that has a fully functional set of services.

To whatever extent possible, use the maxim, "Ask Once, Then Remember." In other words, try to avoid asking an object its type (or its capabilities) every time you use it. This is especially true if the queries require reasoning about the objects in a non-extensible manner (that is, control flow logic that uses code to find code).

FAQ
161

Given a pointer to an ABC, how can you find out the class of the referent?

Don't try.

The typical reason for trying to find the class of the referent is because you have an algorithm that depends on the object's class. If the algorithm differs depending on the derived class, then the algorithm should be a virtual member function in the class hierarchy. If the algorithm is structurally the same for all derived classes but has little pieces that differ depending on the derived class, then the little pieces should be virtual member functions in the class hierarchy. This technique lets derived classes select the ideal algorithm or algorithm fragments.

For example, finding the minimal distance to a mouse click requires different algorithms for circles, squares, lines, and so forth. One might be tempted to write non-OO code such as the following (pretend `Position`, `Shape`, `Circle`, and so forth, are classes).

```
// int
// dist_BAD_FORM(Shape& s, Position mouse)
// {
//   Circle* cp;
//   Square* sp;
//   Line*   lp;
//
//   if ((cp = dynamic_cast<Circle*>(&s)) != NULL) {
//        └──▶ BAD FORM: uses code to find code
//     //find the distance from mouse to the Circle, *cp
//   } else if ((sp = dynamic_cast<Square*>(&s)) != NULL) {
//     //find the distance from mouse to the Square, *sp
//   } else if ((lp = dynamic_cast<Line*>(&s)) != NULL) {
//     //find the distance from mouse to the Line, *lp
//   }
// }
```

One problem with the above, non-OO technique is that adding a new derived class requires working user code to be modified by adding a new `"else if"` section. Besides the obvious concern that changing working user code may break it, in large systems it is difficult to find all the places that need to be changed, and in very large systems there is typically a scheduling problem to coordinate the changes in diverse teams of developers.

With object-oriented technology, you put the function `dist()` into the Shape rather than putting the Shape into the function `dist()`.

```
class Position { };

class Shape {
public:
  virtual ~Shape() { }
  virtual void draw() const = 0;
  virtual int  dist(Position mouse) const = 0;
};

class Circle : public Shape {
public:
  virtual void draw() const
    { /* draw a Circle */ }
  virtual int dist(Position mouse) const
    { /* find the distance from mouse to this Circle */ }
};
```

```
class Square : public Shape {
public:
  virtual void draw() const
    { /* draw a Square */ }
  virtual int dist(Position mouse) const
    { /* find the distance from mouse to this Square */ }
};
```

Compared to the non-OO solution, the OO solution greatly reduces the amount of existing code that needs to be modified when a new class is added. With a little extra design work, the amount of code that needs to be modified can be reduced to an insignificant level.

■

Cross references—

FAQ: 78, 153, 154, 155
See Stroustrup: 6.2, 6.3, r.10
See Ellis & Stroustrup: 10.2, 10.7c, 10.8c, 10.9c, 11.6
See Lippman: 10.2

What is a down cast?

F A Q
162

Trouble.

A down cast is when a pointer cast is used to convert a `Base*` to a `Derived*`, where class `Derived` is publicly derived from class `Base`. It is used when the developer thinks or hopes that the `Base*` actually points to an object of class `Derived`, or to a class derived from `Derived`. It is normally used when a developer needs to access a service that is provided by `Derived` but not by `Base`.

For example, suppose class `LiquidAsset` is derived from class `Asset`, and `LiquidAsset::liquidValue()` exists but `Asset::liquidValue()` does not. A developer might down cast an `Asset*` to a `LiquidAsset*` in order to access the `liquidValue()` operation.

```
#include <iostream.h>

class Asset {
public:
  virtual ~Asset() { }
  virtual bool isLiquidatable() const   { return false; }
  //
};                        └──► BAD FORM: capability query

class LiquidAsset : public Asset {
public:
  LiquidAsset(int value=100)              : value_(value) { }
  int  getValue() const                   { return value_;  }
  void setValue(int value)                { value_ = value; }
  virtual bool isLiquidatable() const     { return true;    }
  //
                          └──► BAD FORM: capability query
protected:
  int value_;      //value of this asset
};

int
tryToLiquidate(Asset& asset)
{
  int value;
  if (asset.isLiquidatable()) {
    └──► BAD FORM: finds code using code
    value = ((LiquidAsset&)asset).getValue();
                          └──► BAD FORM: down cast
    ((LiquidAsset&)asset).setValue(0);
                    └──► BAD FORM: down cast
    cout << "Liquidated $" << value << '\n';
  } else {
    value = 0;
    cout << "Sorry, couldn't liquidate this asset\n";
  }
  return value;
}

main()
{
  Asset        a;
  LiquidAsset b;

  tryToLiquidate(a);
  tryToLiquidate(b);
}
```

The output of this program follows.

```
Sorry, couldn't liquidate this asset
Liquidated $100
```

■

Cross references—

FAQ: 153, 154, 155, 163, 164, 165
See Stroustrup: 6.2, r.10
See Ellis & Stroustrup: 10.2, 10.7c, 10.8c, 10.9c, 11.6
See Lippman: 10.2

What is an alternative to using down casts?

Move the user code into the object in the form of virtual functions.

An if / down cast pair can often be replaced by a virtual function call. The key insight is to move the *context* of the capability query from the user's code into the virtual function; don't just move the primitive query used in the user's if statements.

To help you find the segments of code that will need to be moved into virtual functions, look for those segments of code whose structure depends on the derived class; these will be the same as the contexts of the capability queries. Segments of code that depend on the derived class should be moved into the hierarchy as virtual functions; segments of code that don't depend on the derived class can remain user code, or can be non-virtual member functions in the base class.

In the previous FAQ, the context of the capability query in the user code included the entire tryToLiquidate operation (this entire operation depended on the derived class). To apply this guideline, move the code for this operation into the class hierarchy as a virtual function.

```cpp
#include <iostream.h>

class Asset {
public:
  virtual ~Asset() { }
  virtual int tryToLiquidate()
    {
      cout << "Sorry, couldn't liquidate this asset\n";
      return 0;
    }
};

class LiquidAsset : public Asset {
public:
  LiquidAsset(int value=100)
    : value_(value) { }
  virtual int tryToLiquidate()
    {
      int value = value_;
      value_ = 0;
      cout << "Liquidated $" << value << '\n';
      return value;
    }

protected:
  int value_;     //value of this asset
};

main()
{
  Asset        a;
  LiquidAsset b;

  a.tryToLiquidate();
  b.tryToLiquidate();
}
```

The output of this program follows.

```
Sorry, couldn't liquidate this asset
Liquidated $100
```

In the previous FAQ, the down cast was explicit, and was therefore subject to human error. In the revised solution, above, the conversion from `Asset*` to `LiquidAsset*` is implicitly part of the virtual function call mechanism: `LiquidAsset::tryToLiquidate()` does not need to down cast the `this` pointer into a `LiquidAsset*`.

Think of a virtual function call as an extensible `if` / down cast pair that never down casts to the wrong type.

■

Cross references—

FAQ: 162, 164, 165, 166
See Stroustrup: 6.2, r.10
See Ellis & Stroustrup: 10.2, 10.7c, 10.8c, 10.9c, 11.6
See Lippman: 9.1

Why are down casts dangerous?

They're like walking a high-wire without a safety net.

Suppose you down cast from base class pointer to derived class pointer for the purpose of accessing an operation provided exclusively by the derived class. If the base class pointer points to an object of that particular derived class, or to an object of a class derived from the target derived class, all is well. Otherwise calling the operation is invalid, and the results are usually disastrous.

■

Cross references—

FAQ: 153, 162, 163, 165
See Stroustrup: 6.2, r.10
See Ellis & Stroustrup: 10.2, 10.7c, 10.8c, 10.9c, 11.6
See Lippman: 10.2

F A Q
164

FAQ 165

Are there any hidden costs for type-safe down casts?

Yes, type-safe down casts have 5 hidden costs.

A type-safe down cast prevents the nightmare scenario described in the previous FAQ by executing a type check before performing the down cast. Users typically code a series of `if`s or a `switch` to determine the object's class. The tests and the down casts are performed by the `dynamic_cast` operator or by some home-brewed variant with similar semantics.

Although type-safe down casts never cast a pointer to an incorrect type, they have 5 hidden costs. They increase coding cost, maintenance cost, testing cost, run-time CPU cost, and extensibility cost.

1. Coding cost: they move mechanical complexity from the servers into the users, from the few to the many.

2. Maintenance cost: moving code from the servers to the users increases the overall software bulk.

3. Testing cost: a test harness must be devised to exercise every if, including the ifs used to test the type safety of the down casts.

4. Run-time CPU cost: additional code must be executed to test the type safety of the down casts.

5. Extensibility cost: the additional control flow code needs to be modified when new derived classes are added.

The underlying cause for these costs lies with the style of programming implied by type-safe down casts, rather than with the down casts themselves. Embracing the more extensible style of programming that does not use down casts is part of the paradigm shift.

■

Cross references—
FAQ: 153, 162, 163, 164
See Stroustrup: 6.2, r.10
See Ellis & Stroustrup: 10.2, 10.7c, 10.8c, 10.9c, 11.6
See Lippman: 10.2

Should the inheritance graph of C++ hierarchies be tall or short?

Short.

When the inheritance graph is too tall, down casts are common. This is because the type of the pointer is often sufficiently different from the type of the object that the desired service is available only by down casting the pointer.

The type-safe philosophy espoused in this book discourages the use of down casting, even if those down casts are checked first.

■

Cross references—

FAQ: 15, 76, 153, 154, 162, 163, 164, 167
See Stroustrup: 6.2, 12.2, 12.3, 12.4, 12.5
See Ellis & Stroustrup: 10.1c, 10.2, 10.7c

Should the inheritance graph of C++ hierarchies be monolithic or a forest?

A forest.

The inheritance hierarchy of well-designed C++ software is normally a forest of little trees rather than a large, monolithic tree. Monolithic trees usually result in excessive use of down casting. The type-safe philosophy espoused in this book discourages the use of down casting.

■

Cross references—

FAQ: 15, 76, 153, 154, 162, 163, 164, 166
See Stroustrup: 6.2, 12.2, 12.3, 12.4, 12.5
See Ellis & Stroustrup: 10.1c, 10.2, 10.7c

What is the purpose of a constructor?

Constructors build objects from dust.

The constructor turns a pile of incoherent, arbitrary bits into a living object. It initializes the object's internal data members, but it may also allocate resources (memory, files, semaphores, sockets, and so on).

The constructors for class x are member functions named x. Here is an example.

```
class Battery {
public:
  Battery(int initialCharge);
  void drain();
protected:
  int charge_;
};

Battery::Battery(int initialCharge)
  : charge_(initialCharge)
{
  //intentionally left blank
}

void
Battery::drain()
{
  charge_ -= 5;
  if (charge_ < 0)
    charge_ = 0;
}
```

```
main()
{
   Battery yourDiscountBattery(20); //a Battery object
   Battery myNameBrandBattery(30);  //another Battery object
}
```

You can define more than one constructor for a class. Each constructor will have the same name so the compiler must be able to distinguish among them by the number and/or types of their parameters.

■

Cross references—

FAQ: 100, 173, 177, 264, 266
See Stroustrup: 5.2, 5.5, 6.2, 6.3
See Ellis & Stroustrup: 12.1, 12.3c, 12.4, 12.7, 12.8
See Lippman: 6.1, 9.2

FAQ
169

What is C++'s constructor discipline?

A constructor is automatically called at the moment an object is created.

Descartes said, "I think, therefore I am." The C++ variation of that is, "I am, therefore I can think." In other words, every object that exists ("I am") has been initialized by one of the class's constructors ("I can think"). Except for pathological cases, by the time an object is accessible, its constructor has already initialized it.

The developers of a class provide a set of constructors that define how objects of that class can be initialized. When users create objects of that class, they must provide arguments that match the signature of one of the class's constructors. Constructors support encapsulation since they allow users to create objects in one of the officially supported ways. Users cannot initialize an object's state directly, since this might place the object in an incoherent or illegal state.

In the example from the previous FAQ, the constructor for class `Battery` is the member function `Battery::Battery(int initialCharge)`. This constructor initializes the `protected:` data member `charge_` to the value passed as the parameter to the constructor. The constructor is called twice in `main()`, once when `yourDiscountBattery` is created, and once when `myNameBrandBattery` is created.

What is the purpose of a destructor?

FAQ
170

To give an object its last rites.

The destructor is the last member function ever called for an object. The destructor's typical purpose is to release resources that the object is holding.

A class can have at most one destructor. For a class named x, the destructor is a member function named ~X().

Just as a constructor turns a pile of incoherent, arbitrary bits into a living object, a destructor turns a living object into a pile of incoherent, arbitrary bits. Destructors blow an object to bits.

∎

Cross references—

FAQ: 89, 97, 98, 100, 103, 178, 179, 196, 267, 268
See Stroustrup: 5.2, 5.5, 6.2, 6.3
See Ellis & Stroustrup: 12.1, 12.3c, 12.4, 12.7, 12.8
See Lippman: 6.1, 9.1

What is C++'s destructor discipline?

FAQ
171

Guaranteed death.

If a class has a destructor, C++ guarantees this destructor will be called whenever an object dies. For an `auto` (local) object, death occurs at the close of the block ({...}) in which the object was created (that is, when it is conceptually popped from the run-time stack). For a temporary object, death occurs at the end of the outermost expression in which the temporary was generated. For an object allocated dynamically (via `new`), death occurs when the object is `deleted`. With a static object, death occurs sometime after `main()` finishes.

Warning: Do not use `longjmp` with C++, because it subverts the guarantee that destructors will be called.

∎

Cross reference—
FAQ: 257

What happens when a destructor is executed?

The object is taken apart piece by piece.

The destructor automatically calls the destructors for all member objects and all immediate non-virtual base classes. First, the destructor's body (`{...}`) is executed, then the destructors for member objects are called in the reverse order that the member objects appear in the class body, then the destructors for immediate base classes are called (in the reverse order they appear in the class declaration). Virtual base classes are special. Their destructors are called immediately after the body of the most derived class's destructor (only).

For example, suppose `lock(int)` and `unlock(int)` provide the primitives to manage mutual exclusion. The C++ interface to these primitives would be a `Lock` class, whose constructor calls `lock(int)`, and whose destructor calls `unlock(int)`.

```cpp
#include <iostream.h>

void lock(int i)
{
  cout << "pretend we acquire lock #" << i << '\n';
  //in reality, this would manipulate semaphore #i
  // (or use some other mutual exclusion primitive).
}

void unlock(int i)
{
  cout << "pretend we release lock #" << i << '\n';
  //in reality, this would manipulate semaphore #i
  // (or use some other mutual exclusion primitive).
}

class Lock {
public:
  Lock(int lockNum) : lockNum_(lockNum) { lock(lockNum_); }
  ~Lock()              { unlock(lockNum_); }
protected:
  int lockNum_;
private:
  //these are never defined (copying a Lock is senseless)
  Lock(const Lock&);
  Lock& operator= (const Lock&);
};
```

```
void
multiThreadedFunction()
{
  cout << "no mutual exclusion here\n";
  {
    Lock lock(42);    //pretend this is critical section #42
    cout << "lock provides mutual exclusion here\n";
  }
```
└──► the lock is automagically released here
```
  cout << "no mutual exclusion here\n";
}
```

If you want to be cute, you can rename class Lock to class Critical, so the user code could declare an object named section: Lock lock(42) would become Critical section(42).

What is the purpose of a copy constructor?

F A Q
173

It initializes an object by copying the state from another object of the same class.

Whenever an object is copied, another object (the copy) is created, so a constructor is called. This constructor is called the copy constructor. If the class of the object being copied is X, the copy constructor's signature is usually X::X(const X&).

In the following example, the copy constructor is String::String(const String&). Notice how it initializes the new String object to be a copy of the source String object.

```
#include <string.h>

class String {
public:

  //constructor to promote a const char* to a String
  String(const char* s)
    : len_(strlen(s)), data_(new char[len_+1])
    { memcpy(data_, s, len_+1); }

  //copy constructor
  String(const String& source)
    : len_(source.len_), data_(new char[source.len_+1])
    { memcpy(data_, source.data_, len_+1); }
```

```
    //destructor
    ~String()
      { delete [] data_; }

    //assignment operator (code not listed here)
    String& operator= (const String& s);

  protected:
    unsigned len_;    //ORDER DEPENDENCY; see FAQ 190
    char*     data_;
};

main()
{
  String a = "xyzzy"; //calls String::String(const char*)
  String b = a;        //calls String::String(const String&)
}
```

└──▶ both strings are destructed here

■

Cross references—

FAQ: 99, 168, 177, 197
See Stroustrup: 5.2, 5.5, 6.2, 6.3
See Ellis & Stroustrup: 12.1, 12.3c, 12.4, 12.7, 12.8
See Lippman: 6.3, 8.8

FAQ
174

What is a ctor?

An abbreviation for constructor.

FAQ
175

What is a dtor?

An abbreviation for destructor.

What does X-X-ref mean?

It's the way a guru says copy constructor.

One way to pronounce X(const X&) is X-X-ref (pretend the const is silent). The first X refers to the name of the member function, and the X-ref refers to the type of the parameter.

Compared to X-X-ref, the term copy constructor has a whopping two extra syllables.

When is a copy constructor invoked?

Pass-by-value, return-by-value, and explicit copy.

An example follows.

```
#include <iostream.h>

class X {
public:
  X()          { cout << "default constructor\n"; }
  X(const X&)  { cout << "copy constructor\n";     }
};

X
userCode(X b)  //pass by value:    copy main()'s a to b
{
  X c = b;     //explicit copy:    copy from b to c
  return c;
}              //return by value: copy from c to main()'s d

main()
{
  X a;
  cout << "calling userCode()\n";
  X d = userCode(a);
  cout << "back in main()\n";
}
```

The (annotated) output of this program is:

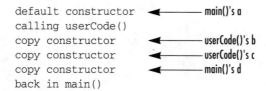

```
default constructor  ◄——————— main()'s a
calling userCode()
copy constructor     ◄——————— userCode()'s b
copy constructor     ◄——————— userCode()'s c
copy constructor     ◄——————— main()'s d
back in main()
```

Note that pass-by-value calls the copy constructor if the caller supplies another object of the same class. Supplying something else may invoke a different constructor. Similar comments apply to return-by-value.

■

Cross references—

FAQ: 168, 173, 197
See Stroustrup: 5.2, 5.5, 6.2, 6.3
See Ellis & Stroustrup: 12.1, 12.3c, 12.4, 12.7, 12.8
See Lippman: 6.3, 8.8

F A Q
178

Does the destructor for a derived class need to explicitly call the destructor of its base class?

No.

The run-time system calls the destructor for the base class after the destructor for the derived class finishes executing.

Never call a destructor explicitly. The only exception to this is the fairly esoteric case of destructing an object that was initialized by the placement new operator.

■

Cross references—

FAQ: 170, 310
See Stroustrup: 5.2, 5.5, 6.2, 6.3
See Ellis & Stroustrup: 12.1, 12.3c, 12.4, 12.7, 12.8
See Lippman: 6.1, 9.1

How do you destruct a local object before the end of its scope?

Use a named member function; do *not* call the destructor explicitly.

If you want an early destruction (for example, to destroy a local object before the object leaves its scope), then the appropriate class should provide a member function that does the same thing the destructor would do. This member function should mark the object so the destructor, which will inevitably be called at the close of the object's scope, will be able to tell if the early destruction member function has been called.

For example, the destructor for a `File` object might close the underlying file. Because users might need to close the file before the end of the block in which an automatic (local) `File` object is created, a named `close()` member function could be defined. This `close()` member function could set the underlying file handle to some invalid state such as -1. This file handle value could be checked in a later operation, such as another call to `close()` or a call to the destructor itself. To avoid duplication of code, the destructor could simply call the `close()` member function.

```
#include <iostream.h>

int
openFile(const char* name)
{
  //normally this code would actually open the named file.
  //for this example, we pretend everything is handle 42.
  int handle = 42;
  cout << "opening " << name << " as #" << handle << '\n';
  return handle;
}

void
closeFile(int handle)
{
  //normally this code would actually close the file.
  cout << "closing file #" << handle << '\n';
}
```

```cpp
class File {
public:
  File(const char* name)
    : handle_( openFile(name) ) { }
  ~File()
    { close(); }
  void close()
    {
      if (handle_ != closed_) closeFile(handle_);
      handle_ = closed_;
    }

protected:
  enum { closed_ = -1 };        //File::CLOSED is a constant
  int handle_;
private:
  //these are never defined; copy semantics are ill defined
  File(const File&);
  File& operator= (const File&);
};

void
userCode(bool throwIt)
{
  File f("sample.txt");
  cout << "after open, before throw-or-close\n";
  if (throwIt) throw "note that the file still gets closed!";
  f.close();
  cout << "after close\n";
}

main()
{
  cout << "====== without throwing an exception ======\n";
  userCode(false);

  cout << "====== with throwing an exception ========\n";
  try {
    userCode(true);
  }
  catch (const char* msg) {
    cout << "exception caught; " << msg << '\n';
  }
}
```

The output of this program follows.

```
====== without throwing an exception ======
opening sample.txt as #42
after open, before throw-or-close
closing file #42
after close
====== with throwing an exception =========
opening sample.txt as #42
after open, before throw-or-close
closing file #42
exception caught; note that the file still gets closed!
```

Don't forget this key observation: Regardless of whether an exception gets thrown, or whether the `f.close()` instruction is reached, `closeFile()` is always called exactly once per open file.

■

Cross references—

FAQ: 170, 196
See Stroustrup: 5.2, 5.5, 6.2, 6.3
See Ellis & Stroustrup: 12.1, 12.3c, 12.4, 12.7, 12.8
See Lippman: 6.1

How can I control the lifetime of class scope static objects, file scope static objects, and file scope global objects?

Replace them with functions which return a reference to a local scope static object that is contained inside the functions.

The lifetimes of class scope static objects, file scope static objects, and file scope global objects are the same. Their constructors are invoked before `main()` begins executing and their destructors are invoked after `main()` finishes. Static local objects, on the other hand, are initialized the first time control flows over their declaration.

The snag with class scope static objects, file scope static objects, and file scope global objects occurs when there is an order dependency between initializations across different compilation units. This can be both dangerous and subtle.

For example, suppose a constructor of class `Fred` uses a static data member of class `Wilma`, and some user creates a global `Fred` object. If the static objects in the user's module get initialized before those in the module containing `Fred`'s static data member, `Fred`'s constructor will access a `Wilma` object before it gets constructed. In the code below, the order of the global `Fred` and the static data member have been arranged to simulate this disaster.

```
#include <iostream.h>

class Wilma {
public:
  Wilma()  { cout << "Wilma ctor\n"; }
  void f() { cout << "Wilma used\n"; }
};

class Fred {
public:
  Fred() { cout << "Fred ctor\n"; wilma_.f(); }
protected:
  static Wilma wilma_;
};

Fred f;
Wilma Fred::wilma_;

main() { }
```

The (annotated) output from this program, below, shows that the `Wilma` object is used before it is initialized. This is a disaster.

```
Fred ctor
Wilma used ◄── the static object gets used
Wilma ctor ◄── the static object gets constructed
```

There are many ways to solve this problem. We've adopted the simplest: change the static data member into a static member function that returns a static local by reference. This provides construct-on-first-use semantics, which is desirable in most situations.

The code below shows how to apply this guideline to the above situation. The static data member `wilma_` has been changed to a static member function that returns a `Wilma&`. All uses of `Fred::wilma_` are therefore changed to `Fred2::wilma_()`. Class `Wilma` remains unchanged.

```
class Fred2 {
public:
  Fred2() { cout << "Fred2 ctor\n"; wilma_().f(); }
```
└──────► new tokens
```
protected:
  static Wilma& wilma_();

};
```
└──┴──► new tokens
```
Fred2 f;
Wilma& Fred2::wilma_() { static Wilma w; return w; }
```

The (annotated) output from this program, below, shows that the Wilma object is initialized before it is used. This is good.

```
Fred2 ctor
Wilma ctor ◄─── the static object gets constructed
Wilma used ◄─── the static object gets used
```

When the constructor of my base class calls a virtual function, why doesn't the override ever get called?

FAQ
181

C++ is helping you by ensuring member objects are initialized before they are used.

Objects of a derived class mature during construction. While the base class's constructor is executing, the object is merely a base class object. Later, during the execution of the derived class's constructor, the object matures into a derived class object. If a virtual function is invoked while the object is still immature, the immature version of the virtual function gets called. It may sound confusing, but it's the only sensible way to do it.

For example, class Derived overrides an inherited virtual function, f(), and Base::Base() calls f(). Since the object is still a Base during the execution of Base::Base(), Base::f() will get invoked. If C++ allowed Base::Base() to call Derived::f(), Derived::f() might invoke services on one of its member objects even though those member objects haven't been constructed yet!

```
#include <iostream.h>

class MemberObject {
public:
  MemberObject()   { cout << "MemberObject ctor\n"; }
  void fred()      { cout << "MemberObject used\n"; }
};

class Base {
public:
  Base()           { cout << "Base ctor\n"; f(); }
  virtual void f() { cout << "Base::f()\n"; }
};

class Derived : public Base {
public:
  Derived()    : Base(), m_() { cout << "Derived ctor\n"; }
  virtual void f() { cout << "Derived::f()\n"; m_.fred(); }
protected:
  MemberObject m_;
};

main()
{
  Derived d;
  cout << "====\n";
  d.f();
}
```

The output of this program follows.

```
Base ctor
Base::f()
MemberObject ctor
Derived ctor
====
Derived::f()
MemberObject used
```

If C++ allowed Base::Base() to call Derived::f(), m_.fred() would get called before m_ was constructed.

Most people think this rule isn't intuitively obvious. That's why it's so necessary.

■

Cross references—

FAQ: 89, 100, 168, 182
See Stroustrup: 5.2, 5.5, 6.2, 6.3
See Ellis & Stroustrup: 12.1, 12.3c, 12.4, 12.7, 12.8
See Lippman: 9.1

When the destructor of my base class calls a virtual function, why doesn't the override ever get called?

C++ is helping you ensure member objects aren't used after they are destructed.

Just as an object of a derived class matures into a derived class object during construction, it reverts back into a base class object during destruction.

Extending the example from the previous FAQ, if `Base::~Base()` called `f()`, `Base::f()` will get invoked, because the object will already have reverted to a mere `Base`.

This is the right thing to do. If `Base::~Base()` could call `Derived::f()`, the `MemberObject` would be used after it was destructed, which would give unpredictable results.

Most people don't think this rule is intuitively obvious, either. That's why it's so necessary.

■

Cross references—

FAQ: 89, 100, 168, 181
See Stroustrup: 5.2, 5.5, 6.2, 6.3
See Ellis & Stroustrup: 12.1, 12.3c, 12.4, 12.7, 12.8
See Lippman: 9.1

How should you initialize member objects?

Use initialization lists.

Initialize all member objects and base classes explicitly in the initialization list of a constructor. Not only does this explicitly express what the compiler is going to do anyway, but it is generally more efficient to initialize a member object properly rather than use default initialization followed by assignment.

The performance benefit gained by initializing member objects via the initialization list can be substantial (as much as three times faster!) compared to using default initialization followed by assignment. There is no performance gain in using initialization lists with member objects of built-in types, but there is no loss either, so initialization lists should be used for symmetry.

Here is an example of using an initialization list in a constructor.

```
class Battery {
public:
  Battery(int initialCharge);
  void drain();
protected:
  int charge_;
};

Battery::Battery(int initialCharge)
  : charge_(initialCharge)
{                        the initialization list
  //intentionally left blank
}
```

```
void
Battery::drain()
{
  charge_ -= 5;
  if (charge_ < 0)
    charge_ = 0;
}

class WristWatch {
public:
  WristWatch();
  void tick();
protected:
  Battery battery_;
};

WristWatch::WristWatch()
  : battery_(100)
{
  //intentionally left blank
}

void
WristWatch::tick()
{
  battery_.drain();
}

main()
{
  WristWatch watch;
  for (int i = 0; i < 10; ++i)
    watch.tick();
}
```

the initialization list

For an exception to this guideline, see FAQ-191.

■

Cross references—
FAQ: 168, 185, 186, 191
See Stroustrup: 8.4
See Ellis & Stroustrup: 5.5, 6.2
See Lippman: 8.3

Is it normal for constructors to have nothing inside their body?

Yes.

The body of a constructor is the {...} part. A constructor should initialize its member objects in the initialization list, often leaving little or nothing to do inside the constructor's body. When the constructor body is empty, you can decorate it with a comment such as:

```
//intentionally left blank.
```

An example follows (Fract is a fraction class).

```
#include <iostream.h>

class Fract {
public:
  Fract(int numerator=0, int denominator=1);
  int numerator() const      { return num_; }
  int denominator() const    { return den_; }
  friend Fract operator+ (const Fract& a, const Fract& b);
  friend Fract operator- (const Fract& a, const Fract& b);
  friend Fract operator* (const Fract& a, const Fract& b);
  friend Fract operator/ (const Fract& a, const Fract& b);
  friend ostream& operator<< (ostream& ostr, const Fract& a)
    { return ostr << a.num_ << '/' << a.den_; }
protected:
  int num_;  //numerator
  int den_;  //denominator
};

Fract::Fract(int numerator, int denominator)
  : num_(numerator),
    den_(denominator)
{
  //intentionally left blank
}

main()
{
  Fract a;                cout << "a = " << a << endl;
  Fract b = 5;            cout << "b = " << b << endl;
  Fract c = Fract(22,7);  cout << "c = " << c << endl;
}
```

The output of this program follows.

```
a = 0/1
b = 5/1
c = 22/7
```

Notice that the initialization list resides in the constructor's definition and not its declaration (in this case, the declaration and the definition are separate).

F A Q
185

How do you initialize a const **data member?**

In the initialization list of each constructor.

Non-static const data members are declared in the class body with a const prefix. Their state is initialized in the constructor's initialization list. The value used to initialize the const data member can be a literal value, a parameter passed to the constructor, or the result of some expression. After initialization, the state of a const data member within a particular object cannot change, however different objects can initialize a const data member to different states.

In the following example, i_ is a non-constant member variable and j_ is a constant member variable.

```
class Fred {
public:

   //initialize constant j_ with a literal value
   Fred(int i) : i_(i), j_(10) { }

   //initialize constant j_ using a constructor parameter
   Fred(int i, int j) : i_(i), j_(j) { }

protected:
   int i_;
   const int j_;
};

main()
{
   Fred a(5);      //a.j_ will always be 10
   Fred b(5,15);   //b.j_ will always be 15
   Fred c(5,20);   //c.j_ will always be 20
}
```

■

Cross references—

FAQ: 168, 183
See Stroustrup: 8.4
See Ellis & Stroustrup: 5.5, 6.2
See Lippman: 6.1

F A Q
186

How do you initialize a reference data member?

In the initialization list of each constructor.

An example follows.

```
class Fred {
public:
  Fred(int& i) : i_(i) { }
protected:
  int& i_;
};

main()
{
  int x;
  Fred a(x);    //a.i_ will always be an alias for x
}
```

Be sure not to bind a reference data member to an object passed to the constructor by value (for example, if i were passed by value), since the reference (i_) would refer to a temporary variable allocated on the stack. Remember, parameters disappear as soon as the function (the constructor in this case) returns; this would create a dangling reference. Depending on the phase of the moon, a dangling reference might crash your program (even scarier than that, the program might *not* crash—until after it ships to your most valuable customer).

■

Cross references—

FAQ: 168, 183, 289
See Stroustrup: 8.4
See Ellis & Stroustrup: 5.5, 6.2
See Lippman: 6.1

Are initializers executed in the same order as they appear in the initialization list?

Not necessarily.

C++ guarantees that base class subobjects and member objects are destructed in the opposite order from which they are constructed. It fulfills this promise by initializing the subobjects of immediate base classes in the order that base classes appear in the class declaration, then initializing member objects in the order that they appear in the class body layout. Destruction is the opposite order: member objects in the reverse order of the class body layout, then subobjects of immediate base classes in the reverse order they appear in the base class list in the class declaration. The order of the initialization list is irrelevant.

The following example demonstrates the fact that initialization order is tied to the order of the class layout rather than to the order of the initialization list.

```
#include <iostream.h>

class Noisy {
public:
  Noisy(const char* msg) : msg_(msg)
    { cout << "construct " << msg_ << "\n"; }
 ~Noisy()
    { cout << "destruct "  << msg_ << "\n"; }
protected:
  const char* msg_;
};

class AB : public Noisy {
public:
  AB()
    : b_("b_"), a_("a_"), Noisy("base") { }
protected:
  Noisy a_;
  Noisy b_;
};

main()
{
  AB ab;
}
```

▶ BAD FORM: see next FAQ

The initialization list order is (b_, a_, base-class), but the class body layout order is (base-class, a_, b_). The output of this program follows.

```
construct base
construct a_
construct b_
destruct b_
destruct a_
destruct base
```

The order of initializers in a constructor's initialization list is irrelevant (but see the next FAQ for a recommendation).

■

Cross references—

FAQ: 168, 183, 188, 189
See Stroustrup: 8.4
See Ellis & Stroustrup: 5.5, 6.2
See Lippman: 8.9

F A Q
188

What should be the order of your constructor initialization lists?

Immediate base classes (left to right), then member objects (top to bottom).

In other words, the order of the initialization list should mimic the order in which initializations will actually take place. This guideline discourages a particularly subtle class of order dependency errors by giving an obvious, visual clue. For example, the following contains a hideous error.

```
#include <iostream.h>

class Y {
public:
  Y()        { cout << "Y ctor\n"; }
  void f()   { cout << "Y used\n"; }
};

class X {
public:
  X(Y& y)    { y.f(); }
};
```

```
class Z {
public:
  Z()           : y_(), x_(y_) { }

protected:
  X x_;
  Y y_;
};

main()
{
  Z z;
}
```

> BAD FORM: y_ is used before it is initialized!

The output of this program follows.

```
Y used
Y ctor
```

Note that `y_` is used (`Y::f()`) before it is initialized (`Y::Y()`). If the guideline espoused by this FAQ was employed, the error would be more obvious: the initialization list of `Z::Z()` would have read `x_(y_)`, `y_()`, visually indicating that `y_` would be used before being initialized.

Not all compilers issue diagnostic messages for these cases.

■

Cross references—

FAQ: 168, 183, 187, 189
See Stroustrup: 8.4
See Ellis & Stroustrup: 5.5, 6.2
See Lippman: 8.9

F A Q

189

How do you initialize one member object using an expression containing another member object?

Just Say No.

In a constructor's initialization list, avoid using one member object from `this` object in the initialization expression of a subsequent initializer for `this` object. This guideline prevents subtle order-dependency errors if someone reorganizes the layout of member objects within the class.

Because of this guideline, the constructor that follows uses `s.len_ + 1` rather than `len_ + 1`, even though they are otherwise equivalent. This avoids an unnecessary order dependency.

```
#include <string.h>

class String {
public:
  String() : len_(0), data_(new char[1]) {data_[0] = '\0';}
 ~String()                               {delete [] data_;}
  String(const String& s);               //copy constructor
  String& operator= (const String& s);   //assignment
protected:
  unsigned len_;
  char*    data_;
};

String::String(const String& s)
  : len_ ( s.len_                ),
    data_( new char[s.len_ + 1] )
{
  memcpy(data_, s.data_, len_ + 1);
}

main()
{
  String a;          //default ctor; zero length String ("")
  String b = a;      //copy constructor
}
```

not "len_"

"len_" OK in a ctor body

An unnecessary order dependency on the class layout of `len_` and `data_` would have been introduced if the constructor's initialization of `data_` had used `len_ + 1` rather than `s.len_ + 1`. However using `len_` within a constructor body (`{...}`) is OK: no order dependency is introduced since the entire initialization list is guaranteed to be finished before the constructor body begins executing.

■

Cross references—

FAQ: 168, 183, 187, 188
See Stroustrup: 8.4
See Ellis & Stroustrup: 5.5, 6.2
See Lippman: 8.9

What if I have to initialize a member object via another member object?

Comment the declaration of the effected data members with //ORDER DEPENDENCY.

If a constructor initializes a member object of this object via another member object of this object, rearranging the data members of the class could break the constructor. This important maintenance constraint should be documented in the class body.

For example, in the constructor that follows, the initializer for data_ uses len_ to avoid a redundant call to strlen(s), thus introducing an order dependency in the class body.

```
#include <string.h>

class String {
public:
  String(const char* s);              //promote const char*
  String(const String& s);            //copy constructor
  String& operator= (const String&);  //assignment
 ~String()                            { delete [] data_; }
protected:
  unsigned len_;     //ORDER DEPENDENCY
  char*    data_;    //ORDER DEPENDENCY
};

String::String(const char* s)
  : len_ ( strlen(s)          ),
    data_( new char[len_ + 1] )
{                      order dependency introduced here
  memcpy(data_, s, len_ + 1);
}

main()
{
  String s = "xyzzy";
}
```

Note that the //ORDER DEPENDENCY comment is attached to the effected data members in the class body, not to the constructor initialization list. This is because the order of member objects in the class body is critical; the order of initializers in the constructor is irrelevant.

Are there exceptions to the rule, "Initialize all member objects in an initialization list?"

Yes, to facilitate argument screening.

Arguments to constructors sometimes need to be checked (or screened) before they can be used to initialize a member object. When it becomes difficult to squeeze the resultant if (...) throw ... logic into the initialization list, it may be more convenient to initialize the member object via its default constructor, then modify its state in the constructor body ({...}) via assignment or some other mutative services.

This situation is usually limited to classes that are built directly on built-in types (int, char*, and so forth), because constructors for user-defined (class) types normally check their own arguments.

For example, in the preceding FAQ, String::String(const char*) passed its parameter to strlen(const char*) without verifying that the pointer was non-NULL. If you want to perform this test, you can use assignment in the constructor.

```
#include <stdlib.h>
#include <string.h>

class NullArgument { };

class String {
public:
  String(const char* s);                //promote const char*
  String(const String& s);              //copy constructor
  String& operator= (const String&);    //assignment
  ~String()                             { delete [] data_; }
protected:
  unsigned len_;
  char*     data_;
};
```

```
String::String(const char* s)
  //no initialization list due to argument screening
{
  if (s == NULL) throw NullArgument();
  len_ = strlen(s);
  data_ = new char[len_ + 1];
  memcpy(data_, s, len_ + 1);
}

main()
{
  String s = "xyzzy";
}
```

Using assignment rather than initialization tends to remove order dependencies. For example, String::String(const char*) no longer introduces an order dependency in the member data of class String. However doing this may introduce performance penalties if the member objects are user-defined (class) types.

■

Cross references—
FAQ: 189, 305

F A Q
192

How should virtual base classes be initialized?

In the constructor initialization list of every concrete class that inherits from a virtual base class, including the concrete classes that inherit indirectly.

Every concrete class that has a virtual base class somewhere in its inheritance hierarchy should mention the virtual base class in the initialization lists of its constructors. The virtual base class should be the very first thing in these initialization lists, before immediate non-virtual base classes and before member objects. The copy constructor may need to be explicit, just so you can initialize the virtual base class appropriately.

If a virtual base class's only constructor cannot accept arguments, this guideline can be softened to allow concrete derived classes to be silent about the virtual base class. However, when the virtual base class's constructor can accept one or more arguments, or when the virtual base class has more than one constructor, explicitly mentioning the virtual base class is usually best.

■

Cross references—

FAQ: 81, 168, 183, 187, 188, 193
See Stroustrup: 8.4
See Ellis & Stroustrup: 5.5, 6.2, 12.6

How should virtual base classes be initialized by ABCs?

The constructor initialization list of an ABC should not mention a virtual base class.

For example, suppose `Vehicle` is an ABC, and that `LandVehicle` and `WaterVehicle` derive from `Vehicle` using `public virtual` inheritance. Suppose further that `AmphibiousVehicle` is an ABC that multiply inherits from `LandVehicle` and `WaterVehicle`. Under these circumstances, none of these classes should mention `Vehicle` in their initialization lists.

The reason for this is that the virtual base class's constructor is called from the constructor of an object's actual class, and an ABC can't be instantiated.

■

Cross references—

FAQ: 78, 168, 183, 187, 188, 192
See Stroustrup: 8.4
See Ellis & Stroustrup: 5.5, 6.2, 12.6
See Lippman: 9.2

How do you initialize an array of objects with specific initializers?

Messy, messy.

Why use arrays in the first place? Why not use container objects? If you *must* use arrays, and if you *must* initialize the elements with specific initializers, the answer you seek is the `{...}` initializer syntax.

```
#include <iostream.h>

class Stack {
public:
  Stack(int maxLen=5)
    { cout << "Stack: maxLen=" << maxLen << '\n'; }
  Stack(const Stack&)
    { cout << "Stack: copy ctor\n"; }
};

main()
{
  //a will be constructed with maxLen=7:
  Stack a(7);

  //all 4 will be constructed without arguments (maxLen=5):
  Stack b[4];

  //c[0] will copy from a, c[1] maxLen=8, c[2] maxLen=7,
  //c[3] will be constructed without arguments (maxLen=5):
  Stack c[4] = { a, Stack(8), 7 };
}
```

The (annotated) output of this program follows.

```
Stack: maxLen=7    ◄──── this is a
Stack: maxLen=5    ◄──── this is b[0]
Stack: maxLen=5    ◄──── this is b[1]
Stack: maxLen=5    ◄──── this is b[2]
Stack: maxLen=5    ◄──── this is b[3]
Stack: copy ctor   ◄──── this is c[0]
Stack: maxLen=8    ◄──── this is c[1]
Stack: maxLen=7    ◄──── this is c[2]
Stack: maxLen=5    ◄──── this is c[3]
```

■

Cross references—

FAQ: 136, 137, 307
See Stroustrup: r.5, r.12
See Ellis & Stroustrup: 5.3, 12.5, 12.6

What are The Big Three?

Destructor, copy constructor, and assignment operator.

These infrastructure routines provide the basic termination and copy semantics for objects of the class.

■

Cross references—

FAQ: 170, 173, 199, 200, 206, 207
See Stroustrup: 5.2, 5.5, 6.2, 6.3
See Ellis & Stroustrup: 12.1, 12.3c, 12.4, 12.7, 12.8, 13.4
See Lippman: 6.1, 6.2, 6.3, 8.8

F A Q 195

What happens if you destroy an object that doesn't have an explicit destructor?

The compiler synthesizes a destructor for that class.

If a class X doesn't provide an explicit destructor, the compiler synthesizes one that destructs all the object's member objects and base class subobjects. This is called memberwise destruction. You can think of built-in types (int, float, and so on) as having a destructor that does nothing.

Thus if class X doesn't have an explicit destructor, and an object of class X contains an object of class Member, then the compiler's synthesized X::~X() invokes Member's destructor.

F A Q 196

```
#include <iostream.h>

class Member {
public:
  ~Member() { cout << "destructing a Member object\n"; }
};

class X {
public:
  //suppose "X" doesn't have an explicit destructor
protected:
  Member member_;
};

main()
{
  {
    X x;
    cout << "before destructing an X\n";
  }      //X::~X() called here
  cout << "after destructing an X\n";
}
```

`X::~X()` calls `Member::~Member()` automatically, so the output of this program is as follows.

```
before destructing an X
destructing a Member object
after destructing an X
```

■

Cross references—

FAQ: 170, 195, 197, 198
See Stroustrup: 5.2, 5.5, 6.2, 6.3
See Ellis & Stroustrup: 12.1, 12.3c, 12.4, 12.7, 12.8, 13.4
See Lippman: 6.1

What happens if you copy an object that doesn't have an explicit copy constructor?

The compiler synthesizes a copy constructor for that class.

If someone copies an object of class X, and X doesn't provide an explicit copy constructor, the compiler synthesizes one that copy constructs all the object's member objects and base class subobjects. This is called member-wise copy construction. You can think of built-in types (int, float, and so on) as having a copy constructor that does a bitwise copy.

Thus if class X doesn't have an explicit copy constructor, and an object of class X contains an object of class Member that has an explicit copy constructor, then the compiler's synthesized X::X(const X&) invokes Member's copy constructor.

```
#include <iostream.h>

class Member {
public:
  Member()
    { cout << "constructing a Member\n"; }
  Member(const Member&)
    { cout << "copying a Member\n"; }
};

class X {
public:
  X() : member_() { }
  //suppose X doesn't have an explicit copy constructor
protected:
  Member member_;
};

main()
{
  X a;
  X b = a;     //X::X(const X&) called here
}
```

X::X(const X&) calls Member::Member(const Member&) automatically, so the output of this program is as follows.

```
constructing a Member
copying a Member
```

■

Cross references—

FAQ: 173, 195, 196, 198, 199
See Stroustrup: 5.2, 5.5, 6.2, 6.3
See Ellis & Stroustrup: 12.1, 12.3c, 12.4, 12.7, 12.8, 13.4
See Lippman: 8.8

F A Q
198

What happens if you assign an object that doesn't have an explicit assignment operator?

The compiler synthesizes an assignment operator for that class.

If someone assigns an object of class X, and X doesn't provide an explicit assignment operator, the compiler synthesizes one that calls the assignment operator on all the object's member objects and base class subobjects. This is called memberwise assignment. You can think of built-in types (int, float, and so on) as having an assignment operator that does a bitwise copy.

Thus if class X doesn't have an explicit assignment operator, and an object of class X contains an object of class Member, then the compiler's synthesized X::operator= (const X&) invokes Member's assignment operator.

```
#include <iostream.h>

class Member {
public:
  Member()
    { cout << "constructing a Member\n"; }
  Member& operator= (const Member&)
    { cout << "assigning a Member\n"; return *this; }
};

class X {
public:
  X() : member_() { }
  //note: X doesn't have an explicit assignment operator
protected:
  Member member_;
};
```

```
main()
{
  X a;
  X b;
  a = b;    //X::operator= (const X&) called here
}
```

`X::operator= (const X&)` calls `Member::operator= (const Member&)` automatically, so the output of this program is as follows.

```
constructing a Member
constructing a Member
assigning a Member
```

■

Cross references—
FAQ: 195, 196, 197, 199
See Stroustrup: 5.2, 5.5, 6.2, 6.3
See Ellis & Stroustrup: 12.1, 12.3c, 12.4, 12.7, 12.8, 13.4
See Lippman: 6.3

What is The Law of The Big Three?

If a class needs a destructor, or a copy constructor, or an assignment operator, it needs them all.

This law was formulated by the author and first appeared in 1991 on the Internet in the comp.lang.c++ FAQ. About 90% to 95% of the time, violations of this law lead to incorrect behavior, and often to disasters.

During code reviews and debugging sessions, we have traced many core dumps back to violations of The Law.

THE BIG THREE
NOT JUST A GOOD IDEA...
IT'S THE LAW!

■

Cross references—

FAQ: 170, 173, 195, 200, 201, 202, 203, 206, 207
See Stroustrup: 5.2, 5.5, 6.2, 6.3
See Ellis & Stroustrup: 12.1, 12.3c, 12.4, 12.7, 12.8, 13.4
See Lippman: 6.1, 6.3, 8.8

Which of The Big Three usually shows up first?

An explicit destructor.

You will typically discover the need to do something special during the constructor, then discover the need to undo that special action during the destructor. In over 90% of the cases, the class also needs a copy constructor so that the special thing will be done during copying. With similar probability, the class needs a nontrivial assignment operator.

The destructor is the signal for applying The Law. Pretend your keyboard's ~ key is painted bright red, and that it's wired up to a siren.

In the following example, the constructor of class String allocates memory, so its destructor deletes that memory. After you type the ~ of ~String(), remember The Law of The Big Three.

```cpp
#include <string.h>

class String {
public:

  String(const char* s)
    : len_(strlen(s)), data_(new char[len_ + 1])
    { memcpy(data_, s, len_ + 1); }

  ~String()
    { delete [] data_; }

  String(const String& s);                //not provided here
  String& operator= (const String& s);    //not provided here

protected:
  unsigned len_;      //ORDER DEPENDENCY; see FAQ 190
  char*    data_;     //ORDER DEPENDENCY; see FAQ 190
};

main()
{
  String s = "xyzzy";
}
```

Classes that own allocated memory (hash tables, linked lists, and so forth) generally need The Big Three.

■

Cross references—

FAQ: 170, 190, 195, 196, 199, 201, 202, 203
See Stroustrup: 5.2, 5.5, 6.2, 6.3
See Ellis & Stroustrup: 12.1, 12.3c, 12.4, 12.7, 12.8, 13.4

What is remote ownership?

When the object that owns a pointer also owns the allocation pointed to by that pointer.

When an object has a pointer and is responsible for whatever "stuff" the pointer refers to, the object is said to have remote ownership. That is, the object owns the referent. When an object has remote ownership, it usually means that the object is responsible for `deleteing` the referent.

Anytime you place a pointer in an object, you should immediately determine whether the object owns the referent (that is, whether the object has remote ownership). When you don't make this determination early enough, you can easily create a schizophrenic implementation, where some of the object's services assume the object owns the referent, others assume someone else owns the referent. The result is generally a mess, and often a disaster.

■

Cross references—

FAQ: 170, 173, 195, 202, 203, 204, 205, 323
See Stroustrup: 5.2, 5.5, 6.2, 6.3
See Ellis & Stroustrup: 12.1, 12.3c, 12.4, 12.7, 12.8, 13.4

FAQ 202

How is remote ownership special?

The copy semantics for an object that owns a referent require the referent to be copied, rather than the pointer. For example, a String class might have a pointer to an array that contains the characters in the string. In this case, the copy semantics of String require that the data in this array be copied, not the pointer to that array.

In contrast, the copy semantics are usually straightforward when an object contains a pointer that doesn't own the referent. Copying such an object involves simply copying the pointer. For example, an iterator object might have a pointer to a node of a linked list. Since the node is owned by the list rather than the iterator, copying an iterator involves copying the pointer; the data in the node is not copied to the new iterator.

When an object has remote ownership, that object needs The Big Three (destructor, copy constructor, and assignment operator). These routines are responsible for destroying the referent, creating a copy of the referent, and assigning the referent, respectively.

■

Cross references—
FAQ: 199, 200, 201, 203, 204, 205
See Stroustrup: 5.2, 5.5, 6.2, 6.3
See Ellis & Stroustrup: 12.1, 12.3c, 12.4, 12.7, 12.8, 13.4

FAQ 203

What if a class owns a referent and doesn't have all of The Big Three?

Mayhem and chaos.

The following EvilString class doesn't have an explicit copy constructor, so the compiler-synthesized copy constructor copies only the pointer rather than copying the pointed-to data.

```
#include <string.h>

class EvilString {
public:
  EvilString(const char* s)
    : len_(strlen(s)), data_(new char[len_ + 1])
    { memcpy(data_, s, len_ + 1); }
```

```
~EvilString()
   { delete [] data_; }
 //since this contains remote ownership, it needs an
 //explicit copy constructor. but pretend the developer
 //failed to provide an explicit copy constructor.
 //similar comments for the assignment operator.
protected:
  unsigned len_;      //ORDER DEPENDENCY; see FAQ-190
  char* data_;        //ORDER DEPENDENCY; see FAQ-190
};
```

If EvilString is copied (passed by value, for example), then the copy points to the same string data as the original. When the copy dies, their shared string data is deleted, leaving the original with a dangling reference. Any use of the original, including the implicit destruction when the original dies, will probably result in a corrupt heap.

```
void
f(EvilString b)
{
  //since EvilString lacks a proper copy constructor,
  //changes to b's string-data will also change a's string
}

void
sampleUserCode()
{
  EvilString a = "xyzzy";
  f(a);
  //any use of a might corrupt the heap
}
```
⌐──➤ a's destructor might corrupt the heap

Note that the problem is not with passing things by value; the problem is that the copy constructor for class EvilString is broken.

■

Cross references—

FAQ: 195, 199, 200, 201, 202, 204, 205, 323, 325, 326
See Stroustrup: 5.2, 5.5, 6.2, 6.3
See Ellis & Stroustrup: 12.1, 12.3c, 12.4, 12.7, 12.8, 13.4
See Lippman: 6.1, 6.3, 8.8

Can you build a C++ class to help manage remote ownership?

Yes.

HeapPtr<T>, shown following, acts like a T* that deletes its referent when it dies. This is used when you need a T* that points to a T object allocated by new and when the owner of the pointer owns the referent. In other words, HeapPtr<T> is useful for managing remote ownership.

```
#include <iostream.h>
#include <stdlib.h>
#include <assert.h>
#include <time.h>

template<class T>
class HeapPtr {
public:

  HeapPtr(T* ptr=NULL)   : ptr_(ptr) { }
 ~HeapPtr()             { deallocate(); }
  T* operator-> ()   { assert(ptr_ != NULL); return ptr_; }
  T& operator* ()    { assert(ptr_ != NULL); return *ptr_; }
  void deallocate() { delete ptr_; ptr_ = NULL; }
  T* relinquishOwnership()
     { T* old = ptr_; ptr_ = NULL; return old; }
  HeapPtr<T>& operator= (T* ptr)
     { deallocate(); ptr_ = ptr; return *this; }

protected:
  T* ptr_;
private:
  //these aren't implemented; their absence prevents copying
  HeapPtr<T>& operator= (const HeapPtr<T>&);
  HeapPtr             (const HeapPtr<T>&);
};
```

HeapPtr<T> acts like a raw pointer, except that it frees users from worrying about ensuring that the delete is executed. More important than the one line of delete code, managed pointers handle exceptions properly: the referent is automagically deleted when an exception causes the HeapPtr object to be destructed. An example follows.

```
bool
heads()      //a coin-toss: true with 50%-50% probability
{
   return (rand() >> 4) % 2 ? true : false;
}

class Fred {
public:
   Fred()                        { cout << "Fred::Fred(); "; }
  ~Fred()                        { cout << "Fred::~Fred(); "; }
   void g()                      { cout << "Fred::g(); ";
                                   if (heads()) throw 5; }
   friend void h(Fred& fred)     { cout << "h(Fred&); ";
                                   if (heads()) throw 7; }
   Fred& operator= (const Fred&);
   Fred               (const Fred&);
};

void
usingRawPointers()
{
   cout << "using a Fred* pointer: ";
   Fred* p = new Fred;

   try {
     p->g();
     h(*p);
   }
   catch (...) {
     delete p;
     throw;
   }

   delete p;      //delete is explicit
   cout << "didn't throw\n";
}
```

```
void
usingManagedPointers()
{
  cout << "using a HeapPtr<Fred>: ";
  HeapPtr<Fred> p(new Fred);
  p->g();
  h(*p);
  cout << "didn't throw\n";
}               //delete is automagic (no need to worry)

main()
{
  srand(time(NULL));    //randomize the random number seed

  for (int i = 0; i < 10; ++i) {
    try {
      usingRawPointers();
      usingManagedPointers();
    } catch (int i) {
      cout << "caught " << i << '\n';
    }
    cout << '\n';
  }
}
```

Note how much simpler the code for usingManagedPointers() is when compared to the functionally similar usingRawPointers(). A significant portion of usingRawPointers() exists just to ensure the referent gets properly deleted; none of this scaffolding is necessary in usingManagedPointers().

In the HeapPtr template, the two assert(ptr_ != NULL) calls test that a NULL pointer doesn't get dereferenced. Defining the preprocessor symbol NDEBUG makes this testing code disappear (many compilers can do this via -DNDEBUG on the command line).

The relinquishOwnership() member function allows a local HeapPtr<T> object to relinquish ownership of its referent. This is useful when the ownership of the managed pointer needs to be transferred to the caller. Having someone else delete what you created can be abused, but experience has shown that this service is convenient in some circumstances.

■

Cross references—

FAQ: 199, 200, 201, 202, 203, 205, 275
See Stroustrup: 5.2, 5.5, 6.2, 6.3
See Ellis & Stroustrup: 12.1, 12.3c, 12.4, 12.7, 12.8, 13.4

F A Q
205

How can a managed pointer object help when an object has remote ownership?

It plugs leaks and enforces The Law of The Big Three.

When a class uses a plain `T*` to implement remote ownership, forgetting any of The Big Three will cause the compiler to silently generate wrong code. The result is almost always a disaster at run-time. By replacing the `T*` with a managed pointer such as `HeapPtr<T>`, the compiler will either synthesize The Big Three correctly, or will cause specific, compile-time errors; it will not cause run-time disasters.

The following example shows a class that implements remote ownership by a managed pointer, `HeapPtr<Fred>`, rather than a plain pointer, `Fred*`. The code for template `HeapPtr` can be found in FAQ-204 and FAQ-460.

```
#include <iostream.h>
#include "FAQ 460/HeapPtr.h"  //see FAQ 460 for this file

class Fred {
public:
  Fred()                      { cout << "Fred::Fred(); "; }
 ~Fred()                      { cout << "Fred::~Fred(); "; }
  Fred& operator= (const Fred&);
  Fred         (const Fred&);
};

class X {
public:
  X() : ptr_(new Fred) { }
  //No destructor needed: The Fred will automagically get
  //deleted. The compiler won't synthesize a copy ctor or
  //assignment operator, since the HeapPtr version of these
  //are private.
protected:
  HeapPtr<Fred> ptr_;          //like 'Fred* ptr_'
};
```

```
main()
{
  X x;  //OK: allocates a new Fred
}       //OK: x is destructed, so its Fred gets deleted
```

Because HeapPtr<Fred>'s destructor deletes the referent, X doesn't need an explicit destructor: the X::~X() synthesized by the compiler will be correct.

Because HeapPtr<Fred>'s copy constructor and assignment operator are private:, the compiler is restrained from synthesizing either the copy constructor or the assignment operator for class X. Therefore someone who (possibly accidentally) copies or assigns an X will get a specific, compile-time error message (if you changed the HeapPtr<Fred> to a Fred*, the compiler would silently synthesize copy or assignment operators that give disastrous results).

For example, when the symbol GENERATE_ERROR symbol is #defined in the following function, the compiler gives an error message rather than silently doing the wrong thing.

```
void
disasterAverted(const X& x)
{
  #ifdef GENERATE_ERROR
    X y = x;  //gives a compile-time error message
      y = x;  //gives a compile-time error message
  #endif
}
```

HeapPtr<T> effectively automates the proper delete, and prevents the compiler from synthesizing improper copy operations. It plugs leaks and enforces The Law of The Big Three.

■

Cross references—

FAQ: 199, 200, 201, 202, 203, 204, 323, 465
See Stroustrup: 5.2, 5.5, 6.2, 6.3
See Ellis & Stroustrup: 12.1, 12.3c, 12.4, 12.7, 12.8, 13.4

Are there any exceptions to The Law of The Big Three?

Yes; `virtual` **destructors,** `protected:` **assignment operators, and recording creation or destruction.**

Virtual Destructors: A base class often has a `virtual` destructor to ensure that the right destructor will be called during `delete basePointer`. If this explicit destructor exists solely to be made `virtual` (for example, if it does what the synthesized destructor would have done, namely `{ }`), the class may not need an explicit copy constructor or assignment operator.

Protected Assignment Operators: An ABC often has a `protected:` assignment operator to prevent users from performing assignment using a reference to an ABC. If this explicit assignment operator exists solely to be made `protected:` (for example, if it does what the synthesized assignment operator would have done, namely memberwise assignment), the class may not need an explicit copy constructor or destructor.

Recording Creation or Destruction: A class sometimes has an explicit destructor and copy constructor solely for the class to record the birth and death of its objects. For example, the class might print a message to a log file or count the number of existing objects. If the explicit destructor or copy constructor exist solely to perform this information recording (for example, if these operations do what the systhesized versions would have done), the class may not need an explicit assignment operator, since assignment doesn't change the number of instances of a class.

Even in cases where all three of The Big Three aren't needed, install them all anyway; that way people don't have to think so intensely during a code review.

■

Cross references—

FAQ: 98, 168, 170, 173, 199
See Stroustrup: 5.2, 5.5, 6.2, 6.3
See Ellis & Stroustrup: 12.1, 12.3c, 12.4, 12.7, 12.8, 13.4
See Lippman: 6.1, 6.3, 8.8

FAQ 207

Are there any other circumstances under which you might explicitly want to have The Big Three?

Yes; if you need them to be non-inline.

When the compiler synthesizes The Big Three, it makes them `inline`. If your classes are exposed to your customers (for example, if your customers `#include` your header files rather than merely using an executable built from your classes), your `inline` code is copied into your customers' executables. If your customers want to maintain binary compatibility between releases of your header files, you must not change any `inline` functions that are visible to the customer, including the versions of The Big Three that are synthesized by the compiler. Because of this, you'll want an explicit, non-`inline` version of The Big Three for all classes that will be used directly by the customer.

■

Cross references—

FAQ: 195, 199
See Stroustrup: 5.2, 5.5, 6.2, 6.3
See Ellis & Stroustrup: 12.1, 12.3c, 12.4, 12.7, 12.8, 13.4
See Lippman: 6.1, 6.3, 8.8

FAQ 208

Why does a program crash when you `memcpy()` an object?

Because bitwise copying is evil.

A class's copy operations (copy constructor and assignment operator) are supposed to copy the logical state of an object. In some cases, the state of an object can be copied using a bitwise copy (e.g., `memcpy()`). However a bitwise copy doesn't make sense for a lot of objects; it may even put the copy in an incoherent state.

If a class `x` has a nontrivial copy constructor or assignment operator, bitwise copying an `x` object often will create wild pointers. One common case where bitwise copy of an object will create wild pointers is when the object owns a referent (i.e., it has remote ownership). The wild pointers are a result of the bitwise copy operation—not due to some failure on the part of the class designer.

For example, consider a class that has remote ownership, such as a String class that allocates an array of char from the heap. If String object a is bitwise copied into String b, then the two objects will both point to the same allocated array. One of these Strings will die first, which will delete the allocated array owned by both of them. BOOM!

```
//see FAQ 459 for the following header file:
#include "FAQ 459/String.h"

main()
{
  String a = "fred";
  String b;

  #if 1
    //good: let the object copy itself:
    b = a;
  #else
    //bad: manipulate the object's bits:
    memcpy(&b, &a, sizeof(String));
  #endif
}
```

Note that a bitwise copy is safe if you know the object's exact class, and you know that the object is (and will always remain!) bitwise copyable. For example, in FAQ-459, class String uses memcpy() to copy its string data because char is, and will always remain, bitwise copyable (the string data is a simple array of char).

■

Cross references—

FAQ: 168, 199, 202, 203, 209, 459
See Stroustrup: 5.2, 5.5, 6.2, 6.3
See Ellis & Stroustrup: 12.1, 12.3c, 12.4, 12.7, 12.8, 13.4
See Lippman: 6.1, 6.3, 8.8

Why does a program crash when you use variable length argument lists?

Because variable length argument lists are evil.

Objects passed into ellipses (. . .) are passed via bitwise copy. The parameter objects get bitwise copied onto the stack, but the va_arg macro uses the copy constructor to copy that pile of bits from the stack. The technical term for this asymmetry is "ouch."

```
#include <stdarg.h>

class Xyz {
public:
  Xyz();
  Xyz(const Xyz& x);
  Xyz& operator= (const Xyz& x);
  ~Xyz();
};

void doSomethingWith(Xyz x);

void f(int count, Xyz first...)
{
  va_list ap;                    └──▶ BAD FORM: variable argument list
  va_start(ap, first);

  doSomethingWith( first );

  for (int i = 1; i < count; ++i) {
    Xyz x = va_arg(ap, Xyz);
                               └──▶ the va_arg macro uses a pointer cast
    doSomethingWith( x );
                          └──▶ x gets used: BOOM!
  }
}  └──▶ x gets destructed: BOOM!

main()
{
  Xyz a, b, c;
  f(3, a, b, c);
          └─┴──▶ a, b, and c get bitwise copied: BOOM!
}
```

"Ladies and gentlemen, this is your pilot speaking; please fasten your seat belts in preparation for the rough air ahead."

main()'s three Xyzs are constructed via Xyz::Xyz(). The call to f(int,Xyz...), passes these Xyzs using bitwise copy. These bitwise copies may not be properly initialized Xyz objects and are not logical copies of a, b, and c. Inside f(int,Xyz...), the va_arg macro uses a pointer cast (shudder) to create an Xyz*, but this Xyz* doesn't point to a valid Xyz object because it points to a bitwise copy of an Xyz object. The va_arg macro then dereferences this (invalid) pointer, and the resultant pile of bits is copied (via Xyz's copy constructor) into the local variable, x.

If Xyz has nontrivial copy semantics, the chance that a bitwise copy is the same as a logical copy is remote at best.

Variable length argument lists are evil.

■

Cross references—

FAQ: 168, 173, 199, 202, 203, 208, 324
See Stroustrup: 5.2, 5.5, 6.2, 6.3
See Ellis & Stroustrup: 12.1, 12.3c, 12.4, 12.7, 12.8, 13.4

Why does a program crash when you use realloc() to reallocate an array of class objects?

Because it is evil to use realloc() on objects of user-defined classes.

When realloc() needs to move the storage that is being reallocated, it uses bitwise copy, rather than invoking the appropriate constructor for the newly allocated objects.

Only use realloc() for objects that guarantee that they will always be bitwise copyable.

■

Cross references—

FAQ: 208, 303
See Stroustrup: 5.2, 5.5, 6.2, 6.3
See Ellis & Stroustrup: 12.1, 12.3c, 12.4, 12.7, 12.8, 13.4

When does the compiler synthesize an assignment operator for a class?

When a class doesn't define its own assignment operator.

The behavior of a compiler-synthesized assignment operator is to copy the state of the source object to the destination object by individually assigning all of the destination object's base class subobjects and member objects.

In general, you should design your classes so that the compiler can synthesize useful assignment operators for you.

∎

Cross references—

FAQ: 212, 217
See Stroustrup: 7.6, r.5, r.12, r.13
See Ellis & Stroustrup: 5.17, 12.3c, 12.6, 12.8, 13.4
See Lippman: 6.3

What can you do to help the compiler synthesize an assignment operator for your class?

Adhere to our assignment operator discipline.

If you follow a few simple rules, then the compiler-synthesized assignment operator will usually do exactly what you want it to do. Without some assignment operator discipline, you will need to provide an explicit assignment operator for an unnecessarily large percentage of your classes, because the compiler-synthesized version will be incorrect an unnecessarily large percentage of the time.

The following FAQs provide guidelines for adhering to an assignment operator discipline that we have found to be effective and practical.

■

Cross references—

FAQ: 211, 217
See Stroustrup: 7.6, r.5, r.12, r.13
See Ellis & Stroustrup: 5.17, 12.3c, 12.6, 12.8, 13.4
See Lippman: 6.3

F A Q

213

What is an effective and practical assignment operator discipline?

Don't fiddle (directly) with your base class's state, and don't fiddle (indirectly) with your derived class's state.

An assignment operator in a derived class should call the assignment operator in its direct base classes (to change its base class subobjects), then call the assignment operator of its member objects (to change its member objects). These assignments should be in the same order as the declaration order of the class's base classes and member objects.

The following is an example of this.

```
class Base {
public:
  Base& operator= (const Base& b)
    { i_ = b.i_; return *this; }
protected:
  int i_;
};

class Derived : public Base {
public:
  Derived& operator= (const Derived& d);
protected:
  int j_;
};
```

```
Derived&
Derived::operator= (const Derived& d)
{
  Base::operator= (d);
  j_ = d.j_;
  return *this;
}
```

Typically, a `Derived::operator=` shouldn't fiddle with member objects defined in a base class; instead it should call its base class's assignment operator. Nor should a `Base::operator=` normally fiddle with member objects defined in a derived class (that is, it usually shouldn't call a virtual `copyState()` routine that a derived class will use to copy the derived class's state).

If a `Base::operator=` tried to copy a derived class's state via a virtual function, the compiler-synthesized assignment operators in derived classes would be invalidated. This will require you to define an explicit assignment operator in an unnecessarily large percentage of your derived classes. This added work often negates any common code that is shared in the base class's assignment operator.

For example, suppose `Base` defines `Base::operator= (const Base& b)`, and this assignment operator calls virtual function `copyFrom(const Base&)`. If the derived class `Derived` overrides `copyFrom(const Base&)` to change the entire abstract state of the `Derived` object, then the compiler-synthesized implementation of `Derived::operator= (const Derived&)` is likely to be unacceptable. The compiler-synthesized `Derived::operator= (const Derived&)` calls `Base::operator= (const Base&)` which calls back to `Derived::copyFrom(const Base&)`; after returning, the `Derived` state is assigned a second time by `Derived::operator= (const Derived&)`.

At best, this will be a waste of CPU cycles because it will reassign the `Derived` member objects. At worst, this will be semantically incorrect, because special changes made during `Derived::copyFrom(const Base&)` may get wiped out when the `Derived` member objects are subsequently assigned by `Derived::operator= (const Derived&)`.

■

Cross references—

FAQ: 211, 212, 217
See Stroustrup: 7.6, r.5, r.12, r.13
See Ellis & Stroustrup: 5.17, 12.3c, 12.6, 12.8, 13.4
See Lippman: 6.3, 8.11

What should be returned by assignment operators?

A reference to this object.

Assignment operators should generally return *this by reference. This means they adhere to the same convention used by the built-in types by allowing assignment to be used as an expression rather than simply a statement. It also allows assignment to be cascaded into larger expressions. An example follows.

```
#include <iostream.h>

class X {
public:
  X(int i=3)
    : i_(i) { }
  X& operator= (const X& x)
    { i_ = x.i_; return *this; }
  friend int operator== (const X& a, const X& b)
    { return a.i_ == b.i_; }
protected:
  int i_;
};

main()
{
  X x, y, z;
  x = y = 5;
  if ((z = x) == y)
    cout << "z (which was assigned from x) is equal to y\n";
}
```

■

Cross references—

FAQ: 215
See Stroustrup: 7.6, r.5, r.12, r.13
See Ellis & Stroustrup: 5.17, 12.3c, 12.6, 12.8, 13.4
See Lippman: 6.3

What should be returned by private and protected assignment operators?

Either return a reference to this object, or make the return type void.

Assignment operators that are private or protected needn't return *this. The reason is that private and protected assignment operators have very few users, so the advantage of returning *this is limited.

Assignment operators are often declared as private to prevent users from assigning objects of the class; they are often left undefined, just in case they are accidentally called by a member function or a friend function. Assignment operators are often declared as protected in abstract base classes to ensure assignment doesn't occur when the destination is a reference to an abstract class (for example, assigning a circle to a square).

■

Cross references—

FAQ: 82, 214, 216
See Stroustrup: 7.6, r.5, r.12, r.13
See Ellis & Stroustrup: 5.17, 12.3c, 12.6, 12.8, 13.4
See Lippman: 6.3

How should the assignment operator be declared in an ABC?

The assignment operator of an ABC should generally be protected.

By default, assignment operators for all classes are public, including those for ABCs. For ABCs, this default should usually be changed so attempts to assign incompatible objects are trapped as compile-time errors. An example follows.

```
class Shape { };
class Square : public Shape { };
class Circle : public Shape { };
```

```
main()
{
  Square s;    Shape& ss = s;
  Circle c;    Shape& cc = c;
  ss = cc;                      //nonsensical, but legal
}
```

Instead, the assignment operator for an ABC should be `protected`, as the following shows.

```
class Shape {
protected:
  void operator= (const Shape& s)    { p_ = s.p_; }
  Position p_;
};
```

Note that the `protected` assignment operator assigns the internal state of one `Shape` to another `Shape`. If it didn't assign the `Shape`'s `p_` member object, all derived classes would have to override their assignment operators in order to do what the base class's assignment operator should have done in the first place.

■

Cross references—

FAQ: 76, 78, 214, 215, 218
See Stroustrup: 7.6, r.5, r.12, r.13
See Ellis & Stroustrup: 5.17, 12.3c, 12.6, 12.8, 13.4
See Lippman: 6.3

When should you define an assignment operator that mimics the compiler-synthesized assignment operator?

When a `protected` assignment operator is needed.

When a `protected` assignment operator contains the same code as the compiler would have synthesized automatically, its only purpose is to prevent users from assigning an object of the class. This is common with abstract base classes.

An example follows.

```
class Position { };

class Shape {
public:
  virtual void draw() const = 0;
  virtual ~Shape() { }
protected:
  Position pos_;
  void operator= (const Shape& s)
    { pos_ = s.pos_; }
};                 ┗━━▶ assign all members from s into this
```

Note that such an assignment operator does not automatically trigger The Law of The Big Three.

■

Cross references—

FAQ: 206, 211, 212
See Stroustrup: 7.6, r.5, r.12, r.13
See Ellis & Stroustrup: 5.17, 12.3c, 12.6, 12.8, 13.4
See Lippman: 6.3

Can an ABC's assignment operator be `virtual`?

F A Q
218

Sometimes.

An ABC's assignment operator can be virtual only if all derived classes of the ABC will be assignment compatible with all other derived classes and if you're willing to put up with a bit of extra work.

Classes derived from a base class are assignment compatible if and only if there's an isomorphism between the abstract states of the classes. For example, the abstract class `Stack` has concrete derived classes `StackBasedOnList` and `StackBasedOnArray`. These concrete derived classes have the same abstract state space, as well as the same set of services and the same semantics. Thus, any `Stack` object can be assigned to any other `Stack` object whether or not they are instances of the same concrete class.

If all derived classes from an ABC are assignment compatible with all other derived classes from that ABC, the ABC's assignment operator may be `protected`, or it may be a `virtual` that is overridden by most (if not all) derived classes.

It is easiest on the class implementor if the base class's assignment operator is `protected`, but this approach restricts users from assigning arbitrary pairs of objects of derived classes.

Making the base class's assignment operator `public` and `virtual` allows any arbitrary `Stack&` to be assigned to any other `Stack&`, even if they are `Stack` objects of different derived classes. The overridden assignment operators in the derived classes should copy the entire abstract state of the other `Stack`.

```
class Stack {
public:
  virtual ~Stack()                        { }
  virtual void    push(int elem)        = 0;
  virtual int     pop()                 = 0;
  virtual int     getElem(int n) const = 0;
  virtual Stack& operator= (const Stack& s)
    { n_ = s.n_; return *this; }
protected:
  int n_;
};

void
userCode(Stack& s, Stack& s2)
{
  s = s2;
}
```

The overridden assignment operator and the overloaded assignment operator in a derived class, such as the `StackArray` class that follows, are often different.

```
class StackArray : public Stack {
public:
  StackArray()                          : Stack() { }
  virtual void push(int x)              { data_[n_++] = x; }
  virtual int  pop()                    { return data_[--n_]; }
  virtual int  getElem(int n) const     { return data_[n]; }
  virtual StackArray& operator= (const Stack& s); //override
  StackArray& operator= (const StackArray& s);     //overload
protected:
  int data_[10];
};
```

```
StackArray&
StackArray::operator= (const Stack& s)              //override
{
  Stack::operator= (s);
  for (int i = 0; i < n_; ++i)
    data_[i] = s.getElem(i);
  return *this;
}

StackArray&
StackArray::operator= (const StackArray& s)          //overload
{
  Stack::operator= (s);
  for (int i = 0; i < n_; ++i)
    data_[i] = s.data_[i];
  return *this;
}

main()
{
  StackArray s, s2;
  userCode(s, s2);
}
```

Note that the override (`StackArray::operator=(const Stack&)`) returns a `StackArray&` rather than a mere `Stack&`. This is called a contravariant return type.

■

Cross references—
FAQ: 89, 214, 215, 216
See Stroustrup: 7.6, r.5, r.12, r.13
See Ellis & Stroustrup: 5.17, 12.3c, 12.6, 12.8, 13.4
See Lippman: 6.3, 8.11

What should you do if a base class's assignment operator is virtual?

F A Q
219

You should probably override the base class's assignment operator and provide your own overloaded assignment operator.

For example, when base class B declares `B::operator= (const B&)` to be virtual, a publicly derived class D should provide both the override (`D::operator= (const B&)`) and the overload (`D::operator= (const D&)`).

```
#include <iostream.h>

class B {
public:
  virtual ~B() { }
  virtual B& operator= (const B& b)
    { cout << "B::operator=(const B&)\n"; return *this; }
};

class D : public B {
public:
  virtual D& operator= (const B& b)              //override
    { cout << "D::operator=(const B&)\n"; return *this; }
  D& operator= (const D& d)                      //overload
    { cout << "D::operator=(const D&)\n"; return *this; }
};

void
userCode(D& d, B& b, D& d2, B& b2)
{
  cout << "d = d2:  ";  d = d2;
  cout << "d = b2:  ";  d = b2;
  cout << "b = b2:  ";  b = b2;
  cout << "b = d2:  ";  b = d2;
}

main()
{
  D d, b, d2, b2;
  userCode(d, b, d2, b2);
}
```

Because b and b2 in userCode() are actually of class D, the output of this program is as follows.

```
d = d2:  D::operator=(const D&)
d = b2:  D::operator=(const B&)
b = b2:  D::operator=(const B&)
b = d2:  D::operator=(const B&)
```

The dynamically bound calls (the last two) resolve to the override (D::operator= (const B&)) because the actual class of b in userCode() is D. If b had actually been a B, the last two calls would have resolved to B::operator= (const B&). Naturally, these calls could also resolve to some other override if the object's actual class had been some other derived class that provided an override.

Note that D::operator= (const B& b) cannot assume its parameter, b, is also of class D, therefore it cannot assume that b contains data members that are defined by class D.

■

Cross references—
FAQ: 89, 214, 215
See Stroustrup: 7.6, r.5, r.12, r.13
See Ellis & Stroustrup: 5.17, 12.3c, 12.6, 12.8, 13.4
See Lippman: 6.3, 8.11

F A Q
220

What should happen when an object is assigned to itself?

Nothing; but unless you're careful, a disaster may occur.

Users never intentionally assign an object to itself (a = a). However, since two different pointers or references could refer to the same object (aliasing), it is possible that statements like a = b will assign an object to itself.

If you don't handle self-assignment in your explicit assignment operators, a disaster might occur. Especially when you have remote ownership. An example follows.

```
#include <iostream.h>

class String {
public:
  String();
  String(const char* s);
  String(const String& s);
 ~String();
  String& operator= (const String& s);
protected:
  unsigned len_;
  char*    data_;
};
```

```
String&
String::operator= (const String& s)
{
  //fail to check for self-assignment: BAD FORM!

  //delete the old before allocate the new: BAD FORM!
  delete [] data_;

  data_ = new char[len_ + 1];
  memcpy(data_, s.data_, s.len_ + 1);
  len_ = s.len_;
  return *this;
}

void
f(String& a, String& b)
{
  a = b;
}

main()
{
  String a = "xyzpqr";
  f(a, a);
}
```

There are two problems with the String assignment operator: we delete our old state before we allocate our new state (this leaves the this object in an incoherent state when new throws an exception), and we fail to test for self-assignment (during self-assignment, deleteing our old state also deletes the state of the other String). These problems are repaired in the following.

```
String&
String::operator= (const String& s)
{
  //ensure that self-assignment is harmless: GOOD FORM!
  if (this == &s)
    return *this;

  //allocate the new before deleting the old: GOOD FORM!
  char* newData = new char[s.len_ + 1];
  delete [] data_;
  data_ = newData;
  memcpy(data_, s.data_, s.len_ + 1);
  len_ = s.len_;
  return *this;
}
```

Self-assignment can also be rendered harmless by performance-driven tests. For example, there is no need to replace the allocated memory if the old allocation is big enough to handle the new state.

```
String&
String::operator= (const String& s)
{
  if (s.len_ > len_) {
    //the above test makes self-assignment harmless
    char* newData = new char[s.len_ + 1];
    delete [] data_;
    data_ = newData;
  }
  memcpy(data_, s.data_, s.len_ + 1);
  len_ = s.len_;
  return *this;
}
```

Since self-assignment is rare, you should not optimize in favor of self-assignment. For example, during self-assignment, the above assignment operator calls memcpy() unnecessarily; this call can be removed by a special if test, but puts more overhead on the normal path in an attempt to optimize the pathological case. The goal is to make self-assignment harmless, not to make it fast.

■

Cross references—

FAQ: 89, 211, 212, 217
See Stroustrup: 7.6, r.5, r.12, r.13
See Ellis & Stroustrup: 5.17, 12.3c, 12.6, 12.8, 13.4
See Lippman: 6.3, 8.11

F A Q
221

When is a class correct?

When it abides by its own internal constraints, and when it meets or exceeds its external agreements.

A class's internal constraints define the allowed states of data structures associated with objects of the class. Every object of the class must abide by these restrictions at all times.

A class's external agreements include requirements imposed on users of the class and promises made to those users. This behavior is observable in the sense that it is expressed in terms of the class's public services.

■

Cross references—
FAQ: 222, 226
See Stroustrup: 12.2

F A Q
222

What is a class invariant?

Stuff that's true whenever anyone else is looking.

The class invariant is the collection of all the invariant fragments for the class. An invariant fragment is a boolean expression that is always true for objects of the class. An invariant fragment is always true whenever a user has the thread of control. An invariant fragment might temporarily lapse within a member or friend function, but the member or friend function must restore the invariant fragment before returning to the user.

Here are a few of the invariant fragments for a Date class.

```
#include <assert.h>

class Date {
public:
  //public interface for Date would go here...
protected:
  int day_;
  int month_;
  int year_;

  void testInvariant() const
  {
    assert(day_   >=  1);
    assert(day_   <= 31);
    assert(month_ >=  1);
    assert(month_ <= 12);
  }
};
```

The statement assert(expression) evaluates expression as a boolean. If expression is false, then the assertion fails, and the program is killed with an appropriate error message. Compiling this compilation unit with the symbol NDEBUG defined (for example, via the -DNDEBUG option on many command-line driven compilers) causes the assert(expression) code to vanish (assert(expression) is a macro).

■

Cross references—
FAQ: 223, 224, 226
See Stroustrup: 12.2

F A Q
223

How can you ensure an object remains in a self-consistent state?

Empower the object to test itself at the end of every mutative service.

The class invariant should be recorded, if for no other reason than as documentation for future maintainers. Since this documentation is expressed in the unambiguous form of source code, it is better than documentation written in a natural language which is relatively imprecise.

Encode the class invariant in a member function called `testInvariant()` const, and use `assert()` macros (or equivalent) to express the various invariant fragments.

■

Cross references—

FAQ: 221, 222, 224
See Stroustrup: 12.2

F A Q
224

What are the two rules that guide invariant testing?

Establish and maintain—get it started and keep it going.

Rule #1: Every Public Constructor Must Establish The Invariant. Every public constructor must initialize its object so it passes the invariant test. Thus every public constructor should call `testInvariant()` as the last thing it does (this call should be in an `#ifdef` so it can be easily removed or reinstalled as desired).

Rule #2: Every Public Service Must Maintain The Invariant. Every public service may assume its object passes the invariant test at the beginning, and must restore its object's invariant by the time it returns. Thus every public service that mutates the object should call `testInvariant()` as the last thing it does (this call should also be in an `#ifdef`).

■

Cross references—

FAQ: 221, 222, 223, 337
See Stroustrup: 12.2

F A Q
225

How can you ensure an object doesn't get blown away by a wild pointer?

Empower the object to test its invariant at the beginning of every service.

Wild pointers can corrupt a sleeping object. Wild pointers are the SCUD missiles of the software world—they are undirected, terrorist instruments that wreak havoc in chaotic ways.

Once a wild pointer has scribbled on an object, that object also exhibits chaotic behavior, often developing wild pointers of its own. The chain reaction spreads like a virus—each wild pointer infects a few more objects. Eventually one of these wild pointers attempts to scribble on something protected by the hardware; then the system crashes.

Looking for the root of the problem is mostly based on intuition and blind luck. We call this Voodoo debugging, since it is about as effective as a fortune teller reading chicken entrails—indeed, the technology of reading entrails is surprisingly similar to that of reading a core dump after corruption by wild pointers.

An object can help detect wild pointers by beginning all its services with a call to testInvariant(). This will ensure that the object is still in a consistent state. This call to testInvariant() should also be in an #ifdef so it can easily be removed or reinstalled if desired.

```
#include <assert.h>

class Date {
public:
  Date();
 ~Date();
  Date            (const Date& date);  //copy constructor
  Date& operator= (const Date& date);  //assignment operator
  Date& operator++ ();
protected:
  int month_;
  int day_;
  int year_;

  void testInvariant() const
  {
    assert(day_ >=  1);
    assert(day_ <= 31);
    assert(month_ >=  1);
    assert(month_ <= 12);
  }
};
```

```
Date::Date()
   : month_(8),
     day_   (1),
     year_  (1994)
{
  testInvariant();
}

Date::~Date()
{
  testInvariant();
}

Date&
Date::operator++ ()
{
  testInvariant();
  //put code to increment the date here
  testInvariant();
  return *this;
}
```

Since the testInvariant() const service is inline, calls to it will vanish when its body goes away. The body of testInvariant() const will go away when all the assert() macros expand to nothing, which happens when the symbol NDEBUG is defined.

■

Cross references—

FAQ: 221, 222, 323, 327
See Stroustrup: 5.2, 7.10, 12.2

What is behavioral self-testing?

When an object checks its work before letting others see what happened.

The promises made by a service can be encoded as a test that is executed at the end of the service. For example, if the List::removeFirst() service promises that List::numElems() will return one less than it did before, an explicit test to this effect can be made at the end of the List::removeFirst() member function. The code associated with behavioral self-tests can be wrapped in an #ifdef so it can be easily removed or reinstalled as desired.

```cpp
#include <assert.h>
#include <stdlib.h>

class List;

class Node {
private:
  friend List;
  int    elem_;
  Node* next_;
  Node(int elem, Node* next) : elem_(elem), next_(next) { }
};

class Empty { };

class List {
public:
  List           (const List& list);  //copy constructor
  List& operator= (const List& list);  //assignment operator
  List()                  : first_(NULL) { }
  ~List()                 { while (first_) removeFirst(); }
  bool empty() const      { return first_ != NULL;        }
  int  numElems() const;  //count number of nodes...
  int  peekAtFirst() const { return first_->elem_;        }
  void prepend(int x)     { first_ = new Node(x, first_); }
  int  removeFirst() throw(Empty);
    //REQUIRE:
    //  !empty()
    //PROMISE:
    //  RESULT == INITIAL(peekAtFirst())
    //  numElems() == INITIAL(numElems()) - 1
protected:
  Node* first_;
};
```

```
int
List::removeFirst() throw(Empty)
{
  if (empty()) throw Empty();

  #ifndef NDEBUG
    int INITIAL_peekAtFirst = peekAtFirst();
    int INITIAL_numElems = numElems();
  #endif

  //remove first element from the List
  int result = first_->elem_;
  Node* oldFirstNode = first_;
  first_ = first_->next_;
  delete oldFirstNode;
  --numElems_;

  #ifndef NDEBUG
    assert(result == INITIAL_peekAtFirst);
    assert(numElems() == INITIAL_numElems - 1);
  #endif
  return result;
}

main()
{
  List a;
  a.prepend(42);
  a.prepend(24);
  int elem = a.removeFirst();
}
```

Naturally the assert(expression) statements can be replaced by other assertion-checking techniques, if desired. The key is that the object checks its own results, so test harnesses can be simpler. Indeed, every user of the class becomes an impromptu test harness.

■

Cross references—

FAQ: 221, 223, 224
See Stroustrup: 12.2

FAQ

227

What are the advantages of objects that test themselves?

Testing starts earlier, continues longer, requires nearly no human intervention, and focuses on the most commonly used paths.

There is very little human effort required for objects that test themselves, other than writing the behavioral self-tests and the `testInvariant()` member function. The run-time system works a lot harder because it must continually re-verify the object's state and its transitions there is very little human (payroll intensive) intervention.

By integrating an object's test harnesses with the object, the self-testing strategy reduces reliance on big-bang testing. In practice, self-testing detects defects earlier than they otherwise would be with traditional, big-bang testing. This reduces the cost of finding and repairing defects, and improves the business efficiency during system integration.

The self-testing technique is similar to the quality mandate in manufacturing. The whole will be correct because every part is correct, and because every combination of parts is tested.

■

Cross references—

FAQ: 221, 222, 223, 224, 225, 226
See Stroustrup: 11.3, 12.2

What is a friend?

An entity to which a class grants access authority.

Friends can be functions, other classes, or individual member functions of other classes. Friend classes are used when two or more classes are designed to work together and need access to each other's implementation in ways that the rest of the world shouldn't be allowed to have. In other words, they help keep private things private. For instance, it may be desirable for class DatabaseCursor to have more privilege to the internals of class Database than main() has.

Friend classes normally imply that one abstraction (a database with multiple cursors, for example) is implemented using several distinct classes (Database and DatabaseCursor). This is especially useful when the various classes have different lifetimes or different cardinalities. For example, it is likely that there is an arbitrary number of DatabaseCursor objects for any given Database object.

```
#include "FAQ 459/String.h"    //see FAQ 459 for this file

class BTree { /*...*/ };
class Cache { /*...*/ };
class DatabaseCursor;

class Database {
public:
  unsigned numRecords() const;
protected:
  friend DatabaseCursor;    //grant access to DatabaseCursor
  BTree btree_;
  Cache cache_;
};
```

```
class DatabaseCursor {
public:
  String getCurrentRecord() const;
  void   insertRecord(String record);
  void   goToNextRecord();
protected:
  Database* db_;    //the Database to which we are attached
};
```

In general, it is a bad idea to force class `Database` and class `DatabaseCursor` together into one class by moving the services of `DatabaseCursor` into class `Database` (for example, `Database::getCurrentRecord()`, and so on). Not only would this impose a one-cursor-per-database policy, it would make `Database` schizophrenic—`Database` would need to manage both the data and a current position within that data.

■

Cross references—
FAQ: 24, 229, 230, 231, 232, 459
See Stroustrup: 5.4, 7.12, 7.2
See Ellis & Stroustrup: 9.1, 11.4, 12.3c
See Lippman: 5.5, 8.4

FAQ 229

What's a good mental model for friend classes?

A "Hogan's Heros" tunnel.

Users (Shultz and Colonel Klink) don't see the information being exchanged through the tunnels that connect the various objects (POW barracks). The special friendship relationship (the tunnels) lets the classes keep private things private.

The alternative to granting special access privileges between the classes would be for the classes to expose services that allow anyone to manipulate a class's private members (in the `DatabaseCursor` example, class `Database` would need to provide public services to manipulate its cache, B-tree, file system, and so on). Although the implementation bits would be encapsulated, the implementation technique would be exposed. Subsequently changing the implementation technique would break users.

In the traditional software realm, friendship is called tight cohesion, and is, within limits, considered good.

■

Cross references—

FAQ: 228, 230, 231
See Stroustrup: 5.4, 7.12, 7.2
See Ellis & Stroustrup: 9.1, 11.4, 12.3c
See Lippman: 5.5, 8.4

What are some advantages of using friend classes?

Objects as interfaces.

Friend classes are useful when a class wants to hide features that are needed by another, tightly cohesive class.

Friend classes arise when a member function on a class needs to maintain state between calls, and when multiple copies of this state must exist. Under these circumstances, the member function becomes a friend class, and the multiple copies of the state become multiple objects of that friend class.

■

Cross references—

FAQ: 228, 229, 231
See Stroustrup: 5.4, 7.2, 7.12
See Ellis & Stroustrup: 9.1, 11.4, 12.3c
See Lippman: 5.5, 8.4

Do friends violate the encapsulation barrier?

Not necessarily.

If you define the encapsulation barrier as the suite of member functions on a class, then friends violate the encapsulation barrier. However, this is a naive view of encapsulation, and applying it consistently actually degrades the overall encapsulation of a system. For example, if another entity needs to be part of the same abstraction, this naive approach suggests that the first class should expose its implementation technique via an unnecessarily large suite of get/set member functions.

The enlightened view is that the encapsulation barrier encapsulates an abstraction, not just a class. For example, the previous example illustrates an abstraction (database with multiple cursors) that is too rich to be implemented by a single class. In cases like this, friend classes are a valuable way of hiding the (possibly complex) interrelationships between the various pieces of the abstraction.

Friends don't violate the encapsulation barrier; they are the encapsulation barrier (more precisely, they are part of the encapsulation barrier).

■

Cross references—

FAQ: 24, 72, 228, 229, 230
See Stroustrup: 5.4, 7.12, 7.2
See Ellis & Stroustrup: 9.1, 11.4, 12.3c
See Lippman: 5.5, 8.4

FAQ 232 What is a friend function?

A way of improving an interface without breaking encapsulation.

A friend function is a non-member function that has been granted access to a class's non-public members.

For example, the syntax most objects use for printing is cout << x, where x is the object being printed, and cout is the output stream (ostream) on which the object is being printed. This printing service is provided by operator<<, which needs to be a friend function of the class of x rather than a member function of the class of x, because you want the ostream on the left side of the << operator and the object being printed on the right side. In general, operators can be member functions only if the member function is attached to the leftmost argument of the operator.

```
#include <iostream.h>
#include <string.h>
#include <stdlib.h>

class String {
public:
```

```
  String(const char* s)              : s_(strdup(s)) { }
  ~String()                          { free(s_); }

  String(const String& s);
  String& operator= (const String& s);

  friend ostream& operator<< (ostream& o, const String& s)
    { return o << s.s_; }
protected:
  char* s_;
};

void userCode()
{
  String s = "fred";
  cout << s << "\n";
}
```

■

Cross references—

FAQ: 228, 233, 234, 239
See Stroustrup: 5.4, 7.12, 7.2
See Ellis & Stroustrup: 9.1, 11.4, 12.3c
See Lippman: 8.4

What are some advantages of using friend functions?

Readability of user code.

Friend functions allow the class designer to choose the syntax for the user code interface that is the most intuitive while still maintaining the class's encapsulation barrier. This lets developers make an abstraction easier to use, which reduces education costs and improves the quality of the user code— intuitive interfaces are abused less often.

■

Cross references—

FAQ: 228, 232, 234, 239
See Stroustrup: 5.4, 7.2, 7.12
See Ellis & Stroustrup: 9.1, 11.4, 12.3c
See Lippman: 5.5, 8.4

FAQ
234

What are some guidelines when using friend functions?

Friend functions should be part of the class's public interface, and their code should be owned by the class's owner.

Guideline #1: Friend functions should be used only for operations that are part of the public interface of a class. They should not be used every time someone wants to do something tricky with the class. If users ask you to let their functions be friends of your class, this is a sign that your interface is inadequate; fix the problem (the interface) rather than patching the symptoms. Don't grant friendship to everyone.

Guideline #2: A friend function or class should be under the political and technical authority of the same team that owns the class itself. Granting friendship status to a function or class under the political authority of a team other than the one implementing the class results in a scheduling nightmare—changes involve coordinating multiple participants who may not always be in a position to handle your requested modifications in a timely manner.

■

Cross references—

FAQ: 232, 233, 239, 240
See Stroustrup: 5.4, 7.12, 7.2
See Ellis & Stroustrup: 9.1, 11.4, 12.3c
See Lippman: 5.5, 8.4

FAQ
235

What does it mean that friendship isn't transitive?

A friend of a friend isn't (necessarily) a friend.

Friendship is personal; it is explicitly granted to a particular, named individual. All friends of a class are declared explicitly in the body of the class. This clearly identifies the entities that need to be updated when the private part of a class is changed.

In the following code, operator<< is a friend of BinaryTree, and BinaryTree is a friend of BinaryTreeNode, but this does not make operator<< a friend of BinaryTreeNode.

```
#include <iostream.h>

class BinaryTreeNode;

class BinaryTree {
public:
  friend ostream& operator<< (ostream&, const BinaryTree&);
protected:
  BinaryTreeNode* root_;
};

class BinaryTreeNode {
public:
  //public interface for BinaryTreeNode goes here...
protected:
  friend BinaryTree;
  BinaryTreeNode* left_;
  BinaryTreeNode* right_;
};

ostream& operator<< (ostream& ostr, const BinaryTree& bt)
{
  //bt.root_ can be accessed (we're a friend of BinaryTree),
  //but bt.root_->left_ cannot be accessed.
  return ostr;
}
```

If operator<< needs to access BinaryTreeNode::left_ or BinaryTreeNode::right_, it must be made a friend of BinaryTreeNode as well.

■

Cross references—

FAQ: 228, 232, 236, 237
See Stroustrup: 5.4, 7.12, 7.2
See Ellis & Stroustrup: 9.1, 11.4, 12.3c
See Lippman: 5.5, 8.4

What does it mean that friendship isn't inherited?

I may trust you, but I don't (necessarily) trust your children.

Suppose class X grants friendship privileges to another class Base and someone derives class Derived from class Base. Derived is not a friend of X just because its base class is a friend of X. This rule improves encapsulation.

```
class Base;

class X {
  friend Base;
};

class Base {
  //member functions of Base are friends of X
};

class Derived : public Base {
  //member functions of Derived are not friends of X
};
```

In the following example, an EggCarton is not supposed to have more than a dozen eggs (numEggs_ <= 12). Class EggCartonFiller is trusted not to break the semantics of an EggCarton, so EggCarton makes EggCartonFiller a friend. This friendship allows EggCartonFiller::addAnEgg() to access EggCarton::numEggs_.

```
class EggCartonFiller;

class EggCarton {
public:
  EggCarton() : numEggs_(0) { }        //an empty carton
private:
  friend EggCartonFiller;
  int numEggs_;                        //can't exceed a dozen
};

class EggCartonFiller {
public:
  void addAnEgg(EggCarton& carton)
    {
      if (carton.numEggs_ < 12)
        ++ carton.numEggs_;
    }
};
```

If friendship were inherited, anyone could create a class derived from EggCartonFiller and possibly break the semantics of an EggCarton.

```
class SubversiveFiller : public EggCartonFiller {
public:
  void violateEncapsulation(EggCarton& carton)
    {
      #ifdef GENERATE_ERROR
        carton.numEggs_ = 13;  //compile-time error:
      #endif                   //access to carton is denied
    }
};
```

■

Cross references—
FAQ: 15, 24, 228, 232, 235, 237
See Stroustrup: 5.4, 7.12, 7.2
See Ellis & Stroustrup: 9.1, 11.4, 12.3c
See Lippman: 9.1

What does it mean that friends aren't virtual?

F A Q
237

Friend functions don't bind dynamically.

If you need the functionality of a virtual function and the syntax of a friend function, use the virtual friend function idiom.

■

Cross references—
FAQ: 238
See Stroustrup: 5.4, 7.12, 7.2
See Ellis & Stroustrup: 9.1, 11.4, 12.3c

What is the virtual friend function idiom?

An idiom that provides the effect of friend functions that bind dynamically.

If you need the syntax of a friend function, yet the operation must be dynamically bound, use an `inline` friend function that calls a `protected:` virtual member function.

Suppose class Shape is an abstract base class (ABC), and a Shape is printed via cout << aShape, where aShape is a Shape& which refers to an object of a derived class such as Circle. To use the virtual friend function idiom, operator<< would be a friend of Shape and would call a `protected:` pure virtual member function such as print(ostream&) const.

```
#include <iostream.h>

class Shape {
public:
  virtual ~Shape() { }
  friend ostream& operator<< (ostream& ostr, const Shape& s)
    { s.print(ostr); return ostr; }
protected:
  virtual void print(ostream& ostr) const = 0;
};

class Circle : public Shape {
public:
  Circle() : radius_(42) { }
protected:
  virtual void print(ostream& ostr) const
    { ostr << "Circle of radius " << radius_; }
  float radius_;
};

void
userCode(Shape& s)
{
  cout << s << '\n';
}

main()
{
  Circle c;
  userCode(c);
}
```

The output of this program follows.

```
Circle of radius 42
```

Because `print()` is virtual, the right implementation will always be invoked. Because `print()` is pure virtual, concrete derived classes are required to provide a definition—`Shape` doesn't have enough knowledge about itself to print itself. Because `print()` is `protected:`, users must use the official syntax provided by `operator<<` (this avoids cluttering the interface with two ways of doing the same thing).

Note that there is only one `operator<<` for the entire `Shape` hierarchy. Derived classes provide a definition for `print(ostream&) const`, but they do not declare or define `operator<<`.

■

Cross references—

FAQ: 235, 237, 241
See Stroustrup: 5.4, 7.12, 7.2
See Ellis & Stroustrup: 9.1, 11.4, 12.3c
See Lippman: 5.5, 8.4, 9.1

Which is better, a member function or a friend function?

Use a member function when you can and a friend function when you have to.

As in real life, family members have benefits that friends don't have. For example, making friends that bind dynamically requires an extra line of code.

See the answer to the next FAQ for details on when a friend function is superior to a member function.

■

Cross references—

FAQ: 232, 233, 234, 240
See Stroustrup: 5.4, 7.127.2
See Ellis & Stroustrup: 9.1, 11.4, 12.3c
See Lippman: 5.5, 8.4

When do I need to use a friend function rather than a member function?

The three P's of friendship: Position, Promotion, or Perception.

Position: Use a friend function when the object being operated on can't appear as the leftmost argument. For example, the syntax to print an object n is usually cout << n, where cout can be replaced by any ostream. Notice that n is not the leftmost argument and therefore operator<< cannot be a member of n's class. If operator<< needs access to n's internal state, it must be a friend of n's class.

```
#include <iostream.h>

class Fraction {
public:
  Fraction(int num=0, int denom=1)
    : num_(num), denom_(denom) { }
  friend ostream& operator<< (ostream& o, const Fraction& f)
    { return o << f.num_ << '/' << f.denom_; }
protected:
  int num_, denom_;
};

main()
{
  Fraction n = Fraction(3,8);     // "3/8"
  cout << "n is " << n << '\n';
}
```

Promotion: Use a friend function when you want to allow promotion of the leftmost argument. For example, the Fraction class might want to support 5*n, where n is a Fraction object. This may require promoting the leftmost argument from an int to a Fraction where this is implemented by passing a single int parameter to Fraction's constructor—Fraction(5). The operator* needs to be a friend because C++ never automatically promotes the this object in a member function invocation.

```
#include <iostream.h>

class Fraction {
public:
  Fraction(int num=0, int denom=1)
    : num_(num), denom_(denom) { }
  friend ostream& operator<< (ostream& o, const Fraction& f)
    { return o << f.num_ << '/' << f.denom_; }
  friend Fraction operator*(const Fraction&,const Fraction&)
    { return Fraction(a.num_*b.num_, a.denom_*b.denom_); }
protected:
  int num_, denom_;
};

main()
{
  Fraction n = Fraction(3,8);        // "3/8"
  cout << "If n is " << n << ", 5*n is " << 5*n << '\n';
}
```

Perception: Use a friend function when it leads to a user syntax that is more intuitive. For example, two possible syntaxes for computing the square of a fraction n are n.square() and square(n) (for example, 1/2 squared is 1/4). If the operation is constructive (if n is unchanged), square(n) may be preferred because n.square() might be incorrectly perceived as squaring n itself.

```
#include <iostream.h>

class Fraction {
public:
  Fraction(int num=0, int denom=1)
    : num_(num), denom_(denom) { }
  friend ostream& operator<< (ostream& o, const Fraction& f)
    { return ostr << f.num_ << '/' << f.denom_; }
  friend Fraction square(const Fraction& n)
    { return Fraction(n.num_*n.num_, n.denom_*n.denom_); }
protected:
  int num_, denom_;
};

main()
{
  Fraction n = Fraction(3,8);        // "3/8"
  cout << "If n=" << n << ", n*n is " << square(n) << "\n";
}
```

Of the three P's for choosing between friend functions and member functions, perception is the most subjective. In many cases involving perception, a static member function (for example, `Fraction::square(n)`) is better than a friend function.

■

Cross references—

FAQ: 232, 233, 234, 239
See Stroustrup: 5.4, 7.12, 7.2
See Ellis & Stroustrup: 9.1, 11.4, 12.3c
See Lippman: 5.5, 8.4

F A Q
241

Should friend functions be declared in the `private`, `protected`, **or** `public` section of a class?

For documentation purposes, `public`.

The compiler ignores the access level (`private`, `protected`, or `public`) where friend functions are declared. However, for documentation purposes, they should be declared in the `public` part of the class, since friend functions are inherently `public` (most friend functions are top-level functions, and are therefore conceptually at file scope).

■

Cross references—

FAQ: 82, 232, 239, 240, 242
See Stroustrup: 5.4, 7.12, 7.2
See Ellis & Stroustrup: 9.1, 11.4, 12.3c
See Lippman: 5.5, 8.4

F A Q
242

Should friend classes be declared in the `private`, `protected`, **or** `public` section of a class?

For documentation purposes, `private`.

The compiler ignores the access level (`private`, `protected`, or `public`) where friend classes are declared. However, for documentation purposes, they should be declared in the `private` part of the class, since friend classes are part of a class's implementation.

Friend classes allow two or more classes to work together in a secret manner. Therefore, a friend class is interested in the implementation of its friend but doesn't become part of its friend's interface.

∎

Cross references—

FAQ: 82, 228, 229, 230, 241
See Stroustrup: 5.4, 7.12, 7.2
See Ellis & Stroustrup: 9.1, 11.4, 12.3c
See Lippman: 5.5, 8.4

What is a private class?

A class created only for implementation purposes.

A private class is a class that is completely hidden from users. Typically all its constructors (and often everything else) are `private`, and it declares another class as its `friend`. Because the private class lacks public constructors or services, only the designated `friends` and other instances of the private class can create or use instances of the private class.

For example, the `Node` class associated with a linked list class might be so specialized that no other class would benefit from reusing it. In this case the `Node` class can be a private class, and can declare the linked list class a friend.

```
#include <stdlib.h>

class List;

//Node is a private class; it is only usable by class List
class Node {
private:
  friend List;
  Node(int e, Node* next=NULL) : next_(next), elem_(e) { }
  Node* next_;
  int   elem_;
};
```

```
class List {
public:
  List()                          : first_(NULL) { }
  List(const List& a)             : first_(NULL) { *this = a; }
  ~List()                         { clear(); }
  List& operator= (const List& a);
  void prepend(int e)             { first_ = new Node(e, first_); }
  bool empty() const              { return first_ == NULL; }
  void clear();
protected:
  Node* first_;
};

main()
{
  List a;
  a.prepend(4);
  a.prepend(3);
  a.prepend(2);
  List b;
  b = a;
}
```

Many private classes are nested inside their friend class. For example, class Node could have been nested inside class List in the preceding example, thereby reducing global name space pollution (nesting Node inside List removes the name Node from the global name space).

■

Cross references—

FAQ: 54
See Ellis & Stroustrup: 12.2c
See Lippman: 3.12, 6.1, 8.5

What's the best way to handle catastrophic errors?

Throw an exception.

Avoid "soft" error-handling mechanisms such as using error codes.

A class whose error handling is too soft allows disastrous errors to remain uncorrected. For example, if a hash table can't allocate memory for its hash buckets, it might return an error code hoping the caller will do the right thing. This allows (but doesn't require) the hash table's users to deal with the problem, and leaves us with a partially initialized, incoherent hash table.

■

Cross references—
FAQ: 53, 245, 246, 247
See Stroustrup: 9, 9.8
See Ellis & Stroustrup: 15
See Lippman: Appendix B

What error-propagation strategy should you use instead of error codes?

try / catch / throw.

In C++, a server that detects something unusual can throw an exception object. The caller that has enough context to handle the unusual event can catch the thrown exception object. Callers can specify the types of exception objects they are willing to handle; exception objects that don't match the specified types are automatically propagated to the caller's caller. Thus

```
void g(bool throwIt) throw(int)
{
  cout << "F, ";
  try {
    h(throwIt);
  }
  catch (float f) {
    cout << "G, ";
  }
  cout << "H, ";
}

void h(bool throwIt) throw(int)
{
  cout << "I, ";
  if (throwIt) {
    cout << "throw, ";
    throw 42;
  } else {
    cout << "no-throw, ";
  }
  cout << "J, ";
}
```

The output of this program follows.

```
throwIt == false: A, B, F, I, no-throw, J, H, C, E, done
throwIt == true: A, B, F, I, throw, D, E, done
```

The catch clause in g() is bypassed in both cases, because h() throws an int (which g() is not willing to catch), rather than a float (which g() is willing to catch).

■

Cross references—

FAQ: 53, 244, 246, 247, 248, 261
See Stroustrup: 9, 9.8
See Ellis & Stroustrup: 15
See Lippman: Appendix B

intermediate callers (between the thrower and the catcher) can simply ignore the exception; only the original thrower and the ultimate catcher need to know about the unusual event.

This separates policy from mechanism; objects at low levels have the mechanism to detect and throw exceptions, objects at higher levels specify the policy of how exceptions are to be handled.

In the example that follows, function f() calls g(), g() calls h(), and h() throws an int. During the stack unwinding process, g() never wakes up—control immediately passes to the catch clause inside f().

```cpp
#include <iostream.h>

void f(bool throwIt) throw();
void g(bool throwIt) throw(int);
void h(bool throwIt) throw(int);

main()
{
  cout << "throwIt == false: ";
  f(false);
  cout << "done\n";

  cout << "throwIt == true: ";
  f(true);
  cout << "done\n";
}

void f(bool throwIt) throw()
{
  cout << "A, ";
  try {
    cout << "B, ";
    g(throwIt);
    cout << "C, ";
  }
  catch (int i) {
    cout << "D, ";
  }
  cout << "E, ";
}
```

FAQ 246

What is the purpose of the C++ exception-handling mechanism?

Error handling.

The purpose of the C++ exception-handling mechanism is to handle errors in software composed of independently developed components operating under synchronous control. It is not intended for handling asynchronous events such as interrupts.

There are other situations in which exceptions can legitimately be used, but they are rare and extreme caution should be used so that exception handling is not abused.

Note that the error-handling strategy for your system must be designed as carefully as the rest of the system (often more carefully). Without such a careful design, exception handling will be applied inconsistently and will create more problems than it solves.

■

Cross references—

FAQ: 53, 244, 245, 247, 248
See Stroustrup: 9, 9.1
See Ellis & Stroustrup: 15
See Lippman: Appendix B

FAQ 247

What is an error?

Anything that prevents a function from fulfilling its promises.

Obviously a function must have a clear definition of its promises before you can ascertain whether or not there is an error. For example, assume that one of the services provided by class `Gardener` is mowing the lawn.

```
class Gardener {
public:
  void mowTheLawn();
};

main()
{
  Gardener mac;
  mac.mowTheLawn();
}
```

Is it an error if you ask mac to mow the lawn and the lawn mower runs out of gas? Or if the lawn mower breaks and cannot be fixed until a new part arrives? Or if mac is home sick today? Or if mac is too busy? Or if mac gets hit by lightning (a truly exceptional event)?

Ten different people will give ten different answers as to which, if any, of these are errors. The only way to be sure is to refer to the agreement you have with mac the Gardener.

If the agreement says that someone (not necessarily mac) will mow the lawn sometime after a request is submitted, then none of the previously mentioned situations is an error, because mac, or one of his heirs, can eventually fulfill the agreement.

If the agreement says the lawn will be mowed on the same day that the request is submitted, then running out of gas might not be an error, but mac's illness and a breakdown requiring overnight repairs are errors.

■

Cross references—
FAQ: 244, 245, 246, 248
See Stroustrup: 9, 9.5
See Ellis & Stroustrup: 15
See Lippman: Appendix B

When should a function throw an exception?

When it can't fulfill its promises.

When a function detects a problem that prevents it from fulfilling its promises, the function should throw an exception. If the function can recover from the problem so that it can still provide its user with the services it promised, then it has handled the problem and should not throw an exception.

In the following example, the gardener throws an exception if he cannot mow the lawn on the same day that the user requests that the lawn be mowed. This occurs when the gardener's lawn mower runs out of gas after 5 p.m. (when the gas stations close).

```
#include <iostream.h>
#include <stdlib.h>

class NoGas { };
```

```
class LawnMower {
public:
  LawnMower()                    : gasLeft_(10) { }
  void mowOneRow()              { if (!empty()) --gasLeft_; }
  void fillErUp()               { gasLeft_ = 10;            }
  bool empty() const            { return gasLeft_ == 0;     }
protected:
  unsigned gasLeft_;
};

class Gardener {
public:
  Gardener()                    : mower_(), rowsInLawn_(25) { }
  void mowTheLawn() throw(NoGas);
protected:
  LawnMower mower_;
  int       rowsInLawn_;
};

//pretend this returns the current hour (0 .. 23):
int currentHourHand()                 { return rand() % 24; }

void
Gardener::mowTheLawn() throw(NoGas)
{
  for (int row = 0; row < rowsInLawn_; ++row) {
    if (mower_.empty()) {
      if (currentHourHand() >= 17) throw NoGas();
      cout << "filling up tank\n";
      mower_.fillErUp();
    }
    cout << "mow one row\n";
    mower_.mowOneRow();
  }
}

main()
{
  Gardener mac;
  try {
    cout << "Mac is trying to mow the lawn\n";
    mac.mowTheLawn();
    cout << "Mac succeeded at mowing the lawn!\n";
  }
  catch (NoGas) {
    cout << "sorry, Mac ran out of gas\n";
  }
}
```

■

Cross references—

FAQ: 53, 247, 250, 252, 253, 254
See Stroustrup: 9, 9.1
See Ellis & Stroustrup: 15, 15.2c
See Lippman: Appendix B

What is an exception specification?

F A Q
249

A specification indicating which exception objects a function expects to `throw`.

For example, in FAQ-248, the service `Gardener::mowTheLawn()` was decorated with the specification `throw(NoGas)`. This specification indicates that `Gardener::mowTheLawn()` expects to throw `NoGas` (or some object derived from `NoGas`), but nothing else. The presence of `throw()` indicates that the function doesn't expect to throw any exceptions.

If a function throws an exception other than those listed in the exception specification, the `unexpected()` function is called, which (by default) calls `terminate()`, which (by default) calls `abort()`.

In general, exception specifications should be used. One place where they are contraindicated, however, is where bug-fixes for very large systems are shipped to customers in small pieces. This is because exception specifications unnecessarily increase the number of modules that must be shipped with such a bug-fix. In other cases where bug-fixes are shipped as the entire executable, exception specifications should be used.

■

Cross references—

FAQ: 248, 271
See Stroustrup: 9
See Ellis & Stroustrup: 15
See Lippman: Appendix B

FAQ

250

How often should exceptions be thrown relative to calls that return by the normal return path?

A throw should be the exception rather than the rule.

Ideally, exceptions will be rare in practice (less than 1% of the time). If you have an event that happens more often than this, perhaps it is not an error, and perhaps you should avoid using the exception-handling mechanism to signal this event.

Because most compilers optimize for the normal (non-throw) case, this guideline produces optimal performance, especially if there are a number of stack frames between the thrower and the ultimate catcher.

■

Cross references—

FAQ: 53, 247, 248, 252, 253, 254
See Stroustrup: 9, 9.1, 9.8
See Ellis & Stroustrup: 15, 15.2c
See Lippman: Appendix B

FAQ

251

Should a function catch all exceptions generated by the functions it calls?

Not usually.

If every function had an explicit try and catch for all functions it calls, two of the benefits of C++ exceptions (reduced coding and testing costs) would be lost. Errors are commonly handled several (often many) stack frames above where they are detected. Intermediate stack frames normally ignore exceptions that they can't handle.

■

Cross references—

FAQ: 53, 247, 259, 260
See Stroustrup: 9, 9.1, 9.2
See Ellis & Stroustrup: 15, 15.4c
See Lippman: Appendix B

How can `throw` (versus error codes) make the system cheaper to write?

Fewer tests to write.

Error codes are a nice-guy approach; they allow (but don't require) the caller to do something when an error occurs. This spreads the error handling code into every caller of every function, rather than focusing it on the relatively few routines that can actually correct the problem. Error codes therefore create a complex telephone chain that is hard to test and maintain—everyone percolates the error information backwards until finally someone is capable of handling it.

■

Cross references—
FAQ: 53, 247, 248, 253, 255
See Stroustrup: 9, 9.1, 9.8
See Ellis & Stroustrup: 15
See Lippman: Appendix B

How can `throw` (versus error codes) make the system faster?

It avoids passing space for exceptions that aren't needed.

The C++ exception-handling mechanism allows an arbitrarily large amount of information to be transferred from the `throw` point to the `catch` clause. The size of the thrown objects are independent of, and often much larger than, the the size of a function's normal return type. For example, a function might normally return an `int`, but in the case of an error might need to return a large exception object.

Using error codes requires a function to return (or, equivalently, be passed a pointer to) the large exception object (even when it is not used), plus the `int`, plus another flag that tells callers whether they got a normal return code or an exceptional return code. The `throw` strategy is based on the pay-for-it-only-when-you-use-it philosophy.

Furthermore, testing for error codes requires a conditional branch in the normal execution path, and therefore run-time testing is done for situations that almost never occur. When functions were hundreds of lines long, checking for error codes was a small percentage of the executable code. But with OO, where member functions are often less than ten lines of code, error codes impose an unnecessary performance penalty.

■

Cross references—

FAQ: 53, 247, 248, 252, 254, 256
See Stroustrup: 9, 9.1, 9.8
See Ellis & Stroustrup: 15
See Lippman: Appendix B

F A Q
254

How can `throw` (versus error codes) make the system easier to understand?

Exception-handling separates the normal logic from the exception handling logic.

When a function call uses error codes to signal exceptions, the caller must check the error code with control flow logic (`if`). This mingles the normal logic with the exception handling logic, increasing the complexity of both paths. The biggest advantage of using C++'s exception handling is its clear separation of the normal code from the error-handling code.

■

Cross references—

FAQ: 53, 247, 248, 252, 253, 255
See Stroustrup: 9, 9.1, 9.8
See Ellis & Stroustrup: 15
See Lippman: Appendix B

Why is it helpful to separate the normal logic from the exception handling logic?

So the normal logic doesn't get lost in the error-handling code.

Suppose you want to read in two matrices, add them, subtract them, multiply them, and divide them, assuming a suitable definition for matrix division. The calling code wants to catch any Overflow errors because it can recover from them, but it wants any other errors to be propagated to the calling function. In this case you can use a try block as follows.

```cpp
#include <iostream.h>

class BadIndex { };

class Overflow {
public:
  Overflow(const char* errorMsg)   : errorMsg_(errorMsg) { }
  const char* errorMsg() const     { return errorMsg_; }
protected:
  const char* errorMsg_;
};

class Matrix {
public:
  Matrix();

  float& operator() (unsigned row, unsigned col)
    throw(BadIndex);
  float  operator() (unsigned row, unsigned col) const
    throw(BadIndex);

  friend Matrix operator+ (const Matrix& a, const Matrix& b)
    throw(Overflow);
  friend Matrix operator- (const Matrix& a, const Matrix& b)
    throw(Overflow);
  friend Matrix operator* (const Matrix& a, const Matrix& b)
    throw(Overflow);
  friend Matrix operator/ (const Matrix& a, const Matrix& b)
    throw(Overflow);

  friend ostream& operator<< (ostream& o, const Matrix& a);
  friend istream& operator>> (istream& i,       Matrix& a);
};
```

```
void
usingExceptions()
{
  Matrix m1, m2, m3, m4, m5, m6;
  try {
    cin >> m1;
    cin >> m2;
    m3 = m1 + m2;
    m4 = m1 - m2;
    m5 = m1 * m2;
    m6 = m1 / m2;
  }
  catch (Overflow e) {
    cout << "overflow: " << e.errorMsg() << endl;
  }
}
```

Now consider what you have to do to handle this situation using error codes.

```
enum ErrorCode {
  OK,
  OVERFLOW_ERROR
};

ErrorCode add(Matrix& r, const Matrix& a, const Matrix& b);
ErrorCode sub(Matrix& r, const Matrix& a, const Matrix& b);
ErrorCode mul(Matrix& r, const Matrix& a, const Matrix& b);
ErrorCode div(Matrix& r, const Matrix& a, const Matrix& b);
```

```
ErrorCode
usingErrorCodes()
{
  Matrix m1, m2, m3, m4, m5, m6;
  cin >> m1;
  cin >> m2;

  ErrorCode errorCode = add(m3, m1, m2);
  if (errorCode == OVERFLOW_ERROR) {
    cout << "overflow error: Matrix + Matrix\n";
    return errorCode;
  }

  errorCode = sub(m4, m1, m2);
  if (errorCode == OVERFLOW_ERROR) {
    cout << "overflow error: Matrix - Matrix\n";
    return errorCode;
  }

  errorCode = mul(m5, m1, m2);
  if (errorCode == OVERFLOW_ERROR) {
    cout << "overflow error: Matrix * Matrix\n";
    return errorCode;
  }

  errorCode = div(m6, m1, m2);
  if (errorCode == OVERFLOW_ERROR) {
    cout << "overflow error: Matrix / Matrix\n";
    return errorCode;
  }

  return OK;
}
```

In this case, the normal algorithm gets lost in the code for error detection and error recovery.

■

Cross references—

FAQ: 246, 247, 252, 254
See Stroustrup: 9, 9.1, 9.8
See Ellis & Stroustrup: 15
See Lippman: Appendix B

FAQ
256

What happens to objects in stack frames that get unwound during the `throw` / `catch` **process?**

They are properly destructed.

Local objects that reside on the stack between the `throw` and the `catch` are properly destructed in stack order; last constructed, first destructed. The result is an extension of the C++ destructor discipline; allocated resources can be safely kept in an object whose destructor releases the resource. This resource is often memory, but it could also be files that need to be closed, semaphores that need to be unlocked, and so on.

■

Cross references—

FAQ: 53, 170
See Stroustrup: 9, 9.1, 9.2
See Ellis & Stroustrup: 15, 15.4c
See Lippman: Appendix B

FAQ
257

Where should you want to see `setjmp` **and** `longjmp` **in C++?**

In your competitor's code.

Never use `setjmp()` and `longjmp()` in C++. Use `try` / `catch` / `throw` instead. The major problem with `longjmp()` is that it doesn't destroy local (`auto`) objects properly.

■

Cross references—

FAQ: 53, 170
See Stroustrup: 9
See Ellis & Stroustrup: 15
See Lippman: Appendix B

What should be placed in a `try` block?

Code that may `throw` an exception from which this function might be able to recover.

If the code called from a `try` block cannot `throw` an exception, then there is no need for the `try` block. Similarly, if the code called from a `try` block can `throw` exceptions but this function cannot recover from these exceptions, then there is no point in catching the exception and no point in putting the code in a `try` block.

■

Cross references—
FAQ: 53, 259
See Stroustrup: 9
See Ellis & Stroustrup: 15
See Lippman: Appendix B

What should be placed in a `catch` block?

Full recovery, then continued processing; or partial recovery, then rethrow.

If you can completely recover from the error, then you can either continue with normal processing or you can restart the `try` block again (put the `try` block in a loop, for example).

If you can effect a partial recovery from the error, your `catch` clause can propagate the exception to the calling function by either throwing the same exception object (`throw;`) or by throwing a different exception object.

```
#include <iostream.h>
#include "FAQ 459/String.h"    //see FAQ 459 for this file

class AccessViolation { };
class BadFileName    { };
```

```cpp
class File {
public:
  File(const String& filename)
    throw(AccessViolation, BadFileName)
    {
      cout << "Open " << filename << "\n";
      if (filename == "badAccess.txt")
        throw AccessViolation();
      if (filename == "badName.txt")
        throw BadFileName();
    }
};

class UserClass {
public:
  void f(const String& filename) throw(BadFileName);
};

void
UserClass::f(const String& filename) throw(BadFileName)
{
  try {
    File f(filename);
  }
  catch (const AccessViolation& e) {
    cout << "  FULLY recover from access-violation\n";
  }
  catch (const BadFileName& e) {
    cout << "  PARTIALLY recover from bad-file-name\n";
    throw;
  }
}

void
tryIt(const String& filename)
{
  try {
    UserClass u;
    u.f(filename);
    cout << "  OK\n";
  }
  catch (const BadFileName& e) {
    cout << "  Finish recovering from bad-file-name\n";
  }
}
```

```
main()
{
  tryIt("goodFile.txt");
  tryIt("badAccess.txt");
  tryIt("badName.txt");
}
```

The output of this program is as follows.

```
Open goodFile.txt
  OK
Open badAccess.txt
  FULLY recover from access-violation
  OK
Open badName.txt
  PARTIALLY recover from bad-file-name
  Finish recovering from bad-file-name
```

■

Cross references—

FAQ: 53, 251, 258, 260, 459
See Stroustrup: 9, 9.1, 9.2, 9.7
See Ellis & Stroustrup: 15, 15.4c
See Lippman: Appendix B

What should not be placed in a catch block?

F A Q
260

Catching exceptions you can't do anything about, or killing the process.

Catching exceptions that you can't do anything about is confusing to those who will have to maintain your code.

Killing the process (for example, calling abort()) puts too much policy in the lower layers of the system. You normally don't know whether the calling function might be able to recover from the error; the only way to find out is to throw something at them and let them make their own decisions.

■

Cross references—

FAQ: 53, 251, 258, 259
See Stroustrup: 9, 9.1, 9.2, 9.7
See Ellis & Stroustrup: 15, 15.4c
See Lippman: Appendix B

What sorts of objects should be thrown when an exception is detected?

Design a monolithic hierarchy of exception classes for this purpose.

Within the limited realm of exception classes, a singly rooted inheritance tree is superior to a forest of trees. This is an exception (pun intended) to the usual guideline that C++ class hierarchies should be a forest of trees.

One advantage of a monolithic hierarchy for exception classes is in catch-all situations. For example, main() often uses a try block that catches all possible exceptions. This catch-all block logs the uncaught exception, and possibly restarts main(). This can be done via ellipses (catch (...)), but a monolithic hierarchy of exception classes allows main()'s catch clause to extract information from the exception object by means of services provided by the root class of the exception hierarchy. This allows a more detailed description of the unknown exception to be logged.

For example, suppose all exceptions are derived from class xmsg.

```
#include <iostream.h>

class xmsg {
public:
  friend ostream& operator<< (ostream& ostr, const xmsg& e)
    { e.print(ostr); return ostr; }
protected:
  virtual void print(ostream& ostr) const
    { ostr << "xmsg\n"; }
};
```

```
int
theActualMain(int argc, char** argv)
{
  //the code that would normally go into main() goes here
  return 0;
}

main(int argc, char** argv)
{
  for (;;) {
    try {
      return theActualMain(argc, argv);
    }
    catch (const xmsg& e) {
      //Oh No! somehow an exception leaked.
      cerr << "uncaught exception: " << e << '\n';
    }
    catch (...) {
      cerr << "an exception didn't inherit from xmsg!\n"
           << "contact the company at 1-800-BAD-BUGS\n";
    }
  }
  //UNREACHED
  return 1;
}
```

The for loop is an infinite loop; it is designed to restart the program after an uncaught exception. Restarting may be more involved than it appears in the preceding example, such as resetting global objects to some initial state. This initialization code can appear at the top of theActualMain(). Resetting static objects to their pristine state can also appear just before the end of the for loop.

■

Cross references—

FAQ: 15, 53, 76, 77, 167, 248, 254
See Stroustrup: 9, 9.3
See Ellis & Stroustrup: 15, 15.1c, 15.2c
See Lippman: Appendix B

How should exception classes be named?

F A Q
262

Name the error, not the thrower.

The server should throw an exception whose class name describes the error that occurred, rather than describing the code that detected the exception. In other words, the type of the exception object should embody the meaning of what went wrong.

For example, if a List class is asked to remove an element and the List is empty, the List should throw an exception such as EmptyContainer, rather than an exception such as ListError.

The purpose of this advice is to enhance information hiding. For example, suppose class List is used to build class Queue; the EmptyContainer exception might be meaningful to users of Queue. Eventually someone may have to catch the exception, repackage it, and throw the repackaged exception, but the goal is to make the exception useful for as many callers and callers' callers as possible.

■

Cross references—

FAQ: 250, 251, 261
See Stroustrup: 9, 9.3
See Ellis & Stroustrup: 15
See Lippman: Appendix B

Under what circumstances can an overridden virtual member function throw exceptions other than those mentioned by the specification of the member function in the base class?

F A Q
263

Only when doing this won't surprise users of the base class.

Specifically, it is safe for an override to throw an object of a class that is publicly derived from a class mentioned in the list of possible exceptions given in the specification of the base class's member function.

Suppose class Base has service f() that promises to throw only objects of class X. If class Derived overrides f() and throws an object of unrelated class Y, user code will break, because users will get an exception they aren't expecting. Derived::f() *can* throw an X2 if X2 is derived from X, due to the kind-of relationship between X2 and X.

```
#include <stdlib.h>
#include <iostream.h>

class X { };
class Y { };
class X2 : public X { };

class Base {
public:
  virtual void f() throw(X);
    //PROMISE: may throw 'X', but never throws anything else
  virtual ~Base() { }
};

void
userCode(Base& base)
{
  try {
    base.f();
    cout << "OK: base.f() didn't throw anything\n";
  }
  catch (X& x) {
    cout << "OK: base.f() threw an X\n";
  }
  catch (...) {
    cout << "huh? base.f() threw something other than X!\n";
  }
}

class Derived : public Base {
public:
  virtual void f() throw(X,X2,Y);
    //PROMISE:
    //   may throw X    ◄──── OK: users will be expecting this
    //   may throw X2   ◄──── OK: X2 is derived from X
    //   may throw Y    ◄──── BAD FORM! VIOLATES PROMISE OF BASE
};
```

```
void
Base::f() throw(X)
{
  if (rand() % 2 == 0) throw X();
}

void
Derived::f() throw(X, X2, Y)
{
  int r = rand() % 4;
  if (r == 0) throw X();    //OK: users are expecting X
  if (r == 1) throw X2();   //OK: Base users are expecting X
  if (r == 2) throw Y();    //BAD! Base users don't expect Y
}

main()
{
  Base    base;
  Derived derived;
  cout << "using 'Base'\n";
  for (int i = 0; i < 10; ++i)
    userCode(base);
  cout << "using 'Derived'\n";
  for (int j = 0; j < 10; ++j)
    userCode(derived);
}
```

The overridden service in the derived class has a weaker promise than that made by the base class: Base promised not to throw a Y, and Derived broke this promise.

Weakened promises break user code.

■

Cross references—

FAQ: 120
See Lippman: Appendix B

How do you handle failures detected inside a constructor?

Throw an exception.

Constructors cannot return an error code, so attempting to use error codes is inappropriate. Besides, a failed constructor usually indicates that the object did not achieve a self-consistent state (for example, it may not have been able to allocate sufficient memory, the appropriate file may not have existed, and so on). This is an error.

If your compiler doesn't support the C++ exception-handling mechanism, and you can't switch compiler vendors, the third-best strategy is to mark the object as a zombie.

■

Cross references—
FAQ: 53, 168, 247, 265
See Stroustrup: 9, r.15
See Ellis & Stroustrup: 15, 15.3c
See Lippman: Appendix B

What is a zombie object?

C++'s version of the living dead—object's that aren't quite alive but aren't quite dead either.

When an environment doesn't support throw, an object that can't finish its constructor can set an internal status flag to indicate that the object is unusable. When this technique is used, a query (inspector) service should be provided so users can see whether the object is usable or a zombie.

The zombie-object technique has the unfortunate side effect of allowing objects to survive even though their constructor failed. This means that all member functions must first check to make sure the object isn't a zombie before they use the data inside the object.

In general, the zombie technique is inferior to throwing an exception. You can think of throwing an exception as immediately burying a zombie object.

■

Cross references—

FAQ: 264, 266
See Stroustrup: 9, r.15
See Ellis & Stroustrup: 15, 15.3c
See Lippman: Appendix B

F A Q

266

What do you do if a member object's constructor might throw an exception?

Every member object must manage its own destruction.

The easiest way to make things work correctly is to ensure that the destructor for a composite doesn't need to do anything important to its member objects.

When the constructor of a member object throws an exception, member objects that have already been initialized will be destructed. For example, if a composite contains member objects x_ and y_, and if x_'s constructor succeeds (doesn't `throw`) and y_'s constructor throws, then x_'s destructor will be invoked, but the composite's destructor will not be. Thus the composite's destructor must not do anything important to x_. This is illustrated in the following example.

```
#include <iostream.h>

class X {
public:
  X()            { cout << "X ctor\n"; }
  ~X()           { cout << "X dtor\n"; }
};

class Y {
public:
  Y() throw(int) { cout << "Y ctor throwing\n"; throw 42; }
};
```

```
class A {
public:
  A() throw(int)   : x(), y() { cout << "A ctor\n"; }
  ~A()                        { cout << "A dtor\n"; }
protected:
  X x_;
  Y y_;
};

main()
{
  try {
    A a;
    cout << "never gets here\n";
  }
  catch (int i) {
    cout << "main caught " << i << endl;
  }
}
```

The output of this program follows.

```
X ctor
Y ctor throwing
X dtor
main caught 42
```

Because A::~A() was never invoked, it had better not do something important to x_, because those important things won't happen if y_'s constructor throws an exception.

Rule of thumb: Every member object must manage its own destruction.

■

Cross references—

FAQ: 53, 168, 264
See Stroustrup: 9, r.15
See Ellis & Stroustrup: 15, 15.3c
See Lippman: Appendix B

Should destructors throw exceptions when they fail?

FAQ 267

No.

If a destructor gets invoked due to the stack-unwinding process initiated by the throwing of another exception, and that destructor throws an exception, `terminate()` is invoked, which (by default) calls `abort()`.

■

Cross references—

FAQ: 53, 170, 268, 269
See Stroustrup: 9, r.15
See Ellis & Stroustrup: 15, 15.3c
See Lippman: Appendix B

Should destructors call routines that may throw exceptions?

FAQ 268

Only if the destructor catches whatever the routines might throw.

If a destructor is called while unwinding the stack caused by another exception, and that destructor calls a routine `f()` that throws an exception, the destructor must catch the second (nested) exception, otherwise the exception-handling mechanism calls the `terminate()` function. In plain English: If you call something from a destructor that might `throw` an exception, `catch` that exception in the destructor.

```
#include <iostream.h>

void fred() throw(const char*)
  { cout << "fred() throwing\n"; throw "barney"; }

class X {
public:
  ~X() throw();
};
```

```
X::~X() throw()
{
  try {
    fred();
  }
  catch (const char* msg) {
    cout << "handling fred()'s exception: " << msg << '\n';
  }
}

main()
{
  try {
    X x;
    cout << "main() throwing\n";
    throw "main";
  }
  catch (const char* msg) {
    cout << "handling main()'s exception: " << msg << '\n';
  }
}
```

`X::~X()` is called as a result of the exception thrown by `main()`. But `X::~X()` calls `fred()`, which also throws an exception. Fortunately `X::~X()` catches the exception thrown by `fred()`, otherwise `terminate()` would be called at the end of `X::~X()`.

The output of this program follows.

```
main() throwing
fred() throwing
handling fred()'s exception: barney
handling main()'s exception: main
```

■

Cross references—

FAQ: 53, 170, 267, 269
See Stroustrup: 9, r.15
See Ellis & Stroustrup: 15, 15.3c
See Lippman: Appendix B

Should resource deallocation primitives signal failure by throwing an exception?

No.

Resource deallocation primitives are things like overloads of `operator delete`, closing files, unlocking semaphores, and so on.

Because these are commonly called from destructors, they should signal failure by some means other than throwing an exception. This reduces the circumstances in which `terminate()` will inadvertently be called.

■

Cross references—

FAQ: 53, 170, 267, 268
See Stroustrup: 9, r.15
See Ellis & Stroustrup: 15, 15.3c
See Lippman: Appendix B

What should the `terminate()` function do?

Log the error, release all known system-wide resources, and call `abort()`.

The terminate function is called when the exception-handling system encounters an error from which it can't recover. This happens when `main()` fails to catch an exception and when a destructor called by the exception handler throws an exception. It is also the default behavior of the unexpected function. You can change the behavior of `terminate()` by using the `set_terminate()` function.

The terminate function must not return, nor may it `throw` an exception. The best thing to do is log the catastrophe (but be sure to flush the file after logging the error, because `abort()` doesn't close open files), release any known system-wide resources (things that other applications depend on), and call `abort()`.

Good night, Nurse.

■

Cross references—
FAQ: 271
See Lippman: Appendix B

What should the unexpected() function do?

Log the error and rethrow the current exception.

When a function has an exception specifier, and that function throws an exception that doesn't match anything in its exception specifier list (Murphy's Law), the exception-handling mechanism calls unexpected(). By default, the unexpected() function calls the terminate() function, which is terminal. You can, and probably should, change the behavior of unexpected() by using the set_unexpected() function.

A better implementation of the unexpected function is to log the error, then rethrow the current exception. An example follows.

```
#include <stdlib.h>
#include <iostream.h>

class Fred    { };
class Wilma   { };

void
userCode()
throw(Fred)
{
  if (rand() % 3)
    { cout << "throwing a Fred; ";  throw Fred();  }
  if (rand() % 2)
    { cout << "throwing a Wilma; "; throw Wilma(); }
  cout << "returning normally; ";
}
```

Note that the preceding user code expected to throw a Fred, but never expected to throw a Wilma (see the exception specification below userCode()). Such user functions normally throw extra things by accident (for example, it calls a function that calls a function that calls a function that throws a Wilma). In any event, the function is erroneous; either it must catch the Wilma, or it must broaden its exception specification list to tell its users that it may throw a Wilma.

```
#include <unexpected.h>

void
myUnexpected()
{
  cout << "unexpected exception!" << endl;
  throw;      //rethrow the (unexpected) exception
}
```

```
main()
{
  //without this, the program would silently crash:
  set_unexpected(myUnexpected);

  for (int i = 0; i < 10; ++i) {
    try {
      cout << "trying: ";
      userCode();
      cout << "no exception thrown\n";
    }
    catch (Fred) {
      cout << "caught a Fred\n";
    }
    catch (Wilma) {
      cout << "caught a Wilma\n";
    }
    catch (...) {
      cout << "this should never happen\n";
    }
  }
}
```

If you use a global variable to record the exception object to be thrown just before throwing it, the error message in myUnexpected() can be more intelligent, especially if all exceptions inherit from a common base class that provides some identification services. Obviously, you must be careful when using such global variables in multi-threaded environments.

If your program is crashing silently before main() begins, you may be getting an unexpected exception during static initialization. In this case, you will need to set the unexpected function (set_unexpected (myUnexpected);) inside a constructor of a file-scope static object.

∎

Cross references—

FAQ: 249, 270
See Stroustrup: 9
See Ellis & Stroustrup: 15
See Lippman: Appendix B

FAQ
272

Does a function decorated with `throw()` guarantee not to throw an exception?

No!

The unexpected function (the one most recently passed to `set_unexpected()`) can—and often does—throw an exception.

If a function has an exception specifier, and that function throws an exception that doesn't match any exception specifier on its list, then the exception-handling mechanism calls the function `unexpected()`, which invokes the function that was most recently passed to `set_unexpected()`. By default, `unexpected()` ends up calling `abort()`. This behavior can be changed, however. In particular, the function called by `unexpected()` can throw an exception!

■

Cross references—
FAQ: 271
See Lippman: Appendix B

FAQ
273

Should you assume that every function will throw an exception?

Yes, unless the function explicitly guarantees not to throw an exception.

For example, `strcpy()` doesn't throw exceptions. However any user-defined functions (including those provided by a library), must be assumed to throw an exception.

Software gets changed, and dependencies don't always get checked. Unless a function *explicitly* guarantees *never* to throw an exception, you must assume that it either does or it will.

How might the exception-handling mechanism cause your program to silently crash?

Out of the 4 zillion reasons a program might silently crash, we'll point out two that are related to the C++ exception-handling mechanism.

Possibility #87642: If someone threw an exception that no one caught, terminate() will get called, which calls abort() by default. The solution is to wrap main() in a try block that has a catch (...) clause. If that doesn't work, look for a constructor of a file-scope static object that might throw an exception. Another way to attack this problem is to replace the terminate function with one that prints an appropriate message before it calls abort().

Possibility #253375: If someone threw an exception that didn't match anything on their exception specifications list, unexpected() will get called, which calls terminate() by default, which calls abort() by default. The solution is to replace the behavior of unexpected() with a function that prints an appropriate message.

■

Cross references—

FAQ: 271, 272

What's the idea behind templates?

Templates share source code among structurally similar families of classes or functions.

Many data structures and algorithms can be defined independently of the type of data they manipulate. A template allows you to separate the type-dependent part from the type-independent part. The result is a significant amount of code sharing.

You can think of a template as a cookie cutter: all the cookies it creates have the same basic shape, though they might be made from different kinds of dough. A class template describes how to build classes that implement the same data structure and algorithm, and a function template describes how to build functions that implement the same algorithm.

■

Cross references—
FAQ: 52, 276, 278
See Stroustrup: 8, 8.1
See Ellis & Stroustrup: 14, 14.1c, 14.2c, 14.4c
See Lippman: 7.0

What are the syntax and semantics for a class template?

Like a class, but prefixed with the keyword `template` along with some parameters.

Consider a container class that acts like an array of integers. When you discover the need for an `Array` of `float`, of `long`, of `String`, of `Set`, and of `FileSystem`, you'll quickly tire of writing classes that look almost identical except for the type stored in the array. Mindless repetition is an ideal job for a computer, hence a class template.

```
#include "FAQ 459/String.h"                 //see FAQ 459

template<class T>
class Array {
public:
  Array(unsigned len=10)  : len_(len), arr_(new T[len]) { }
  Array(const Array<T>&);                   //copy constructor
  Array<T>& operator= (const Array<T>&);    //assignment
  ~Array()                                  { delete [] arr_; }
  unsigned len() const                      { return len_;    }
  const T& operator[] (unsigned i) const { return arr_[i]; }
  T&       operator[] (unsigned i)       { return arr_[i]; }

protected:
  unsigned  len_;
  T*        arr_;
};

main()
{
  Array<int>    ai;    ai[5] = 42;
  Array<float>  af;    af[5] = 42.0;
  Array<char>   ac;    ac[5] = char(42);
  Array<String> as;    as[5] = "42";
}
```

The `<class T>` following the `template` keywords indicates that occurrences of `T` in the class template definition represents a yet unspecified type. Note that the keyword `class` doesn't imply that `T` must be a user-defined type; it might be a built-in type such as `int` or `float`.

Note that template classes (instantiations of class templates) need to be explicit about the parameters over which they are being instantiated. This is different from template functions, which don't normally need any special syntax at the caller indicating which template parameters to use.

■

Cross references—
FAQ: 275, 278, 459
See Stroustrup: 8, 8.1, 8.2
See Ellis & Stroustrup: 14, 14.2c, 14.5c
See Lippman: 7.0, 7.1

What's the difference between a class template and a template class?

F A Q
277

A class template is a cookie cutter used to stamp out various template classes.

A class template is the `class` definition when preceded by the `template` keyword; the compiler creates template classes from a class template when it sees a novel sequence of parameters to that class template.
An example follows.

```
template<class T>
class Array {
public:
  Array(unsigned len=10)  : len_(len), arr_(new T[len]) { }
  Array(const Array<T>&);                 //copy constructor
  Array<T>& operator= (const Array<T>&); //assignment
 ~Array()                       { delete [] arr_; }
  unsigned len() const          { return len_;    }
  const T& operator[] (unsigned i) const { return arr_[i]; }
  T&       operator[] (unsigned i)       { return arr_[i]; }

protected:
  unsigned  len_;
  T*        arr_;
};
```

When a class template is supplied with a particular sequence of template arguments (in this case, the only template argument is a type that replaces template argument T), the compiler produces a template class. In the following example, Array<int> is a template class that was produced from the class template Array.

```
main()
{
  Array<int> ai;
  ai[5] = 42;
}
```

To simplify the terminology, just use the terms *template* and *instantiation of a template*.

■

Cross references—
FAQ: 276, 279
See Stroustrup: 8, 8.4
See Ellis & Stroustrup: 14, 14.4c
See Lippman: 7.1

FAQ 278

What are the syntax and semantics for a function template?

Like a function, but prefixed with the keyword template along with some parameters.

Consider a function that swaps its two integer arguments. Just as with Array in the preceding example, repeating the code for swap() for swapping float, char, String, and so on, will become tedious. Hence we create a single function template.

```
template<class T>
void
swap(T& x, T& y)
{
  T tmp = x;
  x = y;
  y = tmp;
}
```

Every time we use swap() with a given pair of arguments, the compiler creates yet another template function based on the function template. An example follows.

```
#include "FAQ 459/String.h"        //see FAQ 459

main()
{
  int    i, j;  /*...*/  swap(i,j);  //swap(int&,    int&)
  char   a, b;  /*...*/  swap(a,b);  //swap(char&,   char&)
  float  c, d;  /*...*/  swap(c,d);  //swap(float&, float&)
  String s, t;  /*...*/  swap(s,t);  //swap(String&,String&)
}
```

■

Cross references—
FAQ: 275, 276, 459
See Stroustrup: 8, 8.4
See Ellis & Stroustrup: 14, 14.4c
See Lippman: 4.2

What's the difference between a function template and a template function?

A function template is a cookie cutter used to stamp out various template functions.

An example follows.

```
template <class T>          //the function template
inline
T
min(const T& a, const T& b)
{
  return a < b ? a : b;
}

main()
{
  int i = min(42, 24);        //creates a template function
  float f = min(42.0, 24.0);  //another template function
}
```

To simplify the terminology, just use the terms *template* and *instantiation of a template.*

■

Cross references—

FAQ: 277, 278
See Stroustrup: 8, 8.4
See Ellis & Stroustrup: 14, 14.4c
See Lippman: 4.2

F A Q

280

What is a container?

A container is an object whose job is to hold other objects.

A container is a collection of elements (objects). The container normally provides services to access these elements in some random or sequential order. Typically, every element has an index, every index has a successor, and the successor of the last index is some special value such as NO_ELEMENT.
Containers are often implemented as class templates.

■

Cross references—

FAQ: 275, 276
See Stroustrup: 13

F A Q

281

What's the difference between a homogeneous and a heterogeneous container?

The elements of a homogeneous container are all of the same type; the elements of a heterogeneous container are of different types.

Containers come in many shades of gray. Generally speaking, the more homogeneous the element types are, the more type-safe the container is. For example, the ultimate heterogeneous container is a container of void*, in which the various elements could point to objects of any type. Even though this seems to optimize flexibility, in practice such containers are nearly worthless. In particular, it's easy to put things into such a container (any object of any type can be inserted), but the user of the container knows nothing of the element's type when it is removed.

A more useful form of heterogeneous container is one that requires its elements to point to objects derived from some specific base class (often an ABC). This base class typically has all, or nearly all, the services provided by the actual objects referenced by the container. For example, one might have a list of Shape*, where the actual referents might be objects of class Square, Circle, Hexagon, and so on.

Should a template use memcpy() on objects of its template argument?

No.

The only time you should bitwise copy an object is if you know that the class of the object will forever be amenable to bitwise copy. But you can't know the class of a template argument. Here is an example.

```cpp
template<class T>
class Array {
public:
  Array(unsigned len=10)  : len_(len), arr_(new T[len]) { }
  Array(const Array<T>&);                 //copy constructor
  Array<T>& operator= (const Array<T>&); //assignment
  ~Array()                               { delete [] arr_; }
  unsigned len() const                   { return len_;    }
  const T& operator[] (unsigned i) const { return arr_[i]; }
  T&       operator[] (unsigned i)       { return arr_[i]; }

protected:
  unsigned  len_;
  T*        arr_;
};
```

```
template<class T>
Array<T>::Array(const Array<T>& a)
  : len_(a.len_),
    arr_(new T[a.len_])
{
  #if 1
    //GOOD FORM: lets the T objects copy themselves:
    for (unsigned i = 0; i < len_; ++i)
      arr_[i] = a.arr_[i];
  #else
    //BAD FORM: manipulates (i.e., "manipulates") the bits of
    //the T objects:
    memcpy(arr_, a.arr_, len_ * sizeof(T));
  #endif
}


template<class T>
Array<T>&
Array<T>::operator= (const Array<T>& a)
{
  if (len_ != a.len_) {    //renders self-assignment harmless
    T* newArr = new T[a.len_];
    delete [] arr_;
    arr_ = newArr;
    len_ = a.len_;
  }

  #if 1s
    //GOOD FORM: lets the T objects copy themselves:
    for (unsigned i = 0; i < len_; ++i)
      arr_[i] = a.arr_[i];
  #else
    //BAD FORM: manipulates the bits of the T objects:
    memcpy(arr_, a.arr_, len_ * sizeof(T));
  #endif

  return *this;
}
```

If a template has been designed to work only with types that can be bit-wise copied (for example, if you use memcpy() to copy some T objects), the template must have a big, fat, juicy comment warning potential users that a class with nontrivial copy semantics might destroy the world (and who wants to be responsible for unleashing such a monster).

■

Cross references—

FAQ: 275
See Stroustrup: 8
See Ellis & Stroustrup: 14

Why does the compiler complain about >> when you use a template inside another template?

Maximal munch.

The compiler's tokenizer (something the compiler does to figure out what your program means) has a rule called the maximal munch rule: Read characters out of the source file until adding one more character causes the current token to stop making sense. For example, the keyword int is one token, rather than three separate tokens, i, n, and t. Therefore, if you put two > symbols together with no whitespace between them, the maximal munch combines them into one token: >>.

In the following example, an array of array-of int might look like the following (go all the way down to main() to see this in action):

```
template<class T>
class Array {
public:
  Array(unsigned len=10)  : len_(len), arr_(new T[len]) { }
  Array(const Array<T>&);                 //copy constructor
  Array<T>& operator= (const Array<T>&); //assignment
  ~Array()                          { delete [] arr_; }
  unsigned len() const              { return len_;    }
  const T& operator[] (unsigned i) const { return arr_[i]; }
  T&       operator[] (unsigned i)       { return arr_[i]; }

protected:
  unsigned  len_;
  T*        arr_;
};
```

```
main()
{
  #if 1
    Array< Array<int> >  a;
  #else                      ──► This works as expected
    Array< Array<int>>  a;
  #endif
}                          ──► Error: looks like a ">>" token
```

■

Cross references—

FAQ: 275, 276, 278
See Stroustrup: 8
See Ellis & Stroustrup: 14

FAQ 284

Can you have file-scope static data with the same name in distinct .c files?

Yes, but don't.

Avoid using file-scope static data with the same name in distinct .c files, especially within .c files that define templates. Note that this is defensive advice to avoid getting stung by less-than-perfect compilation tools.

Depending on the template expansion strategy used by the compiler, several .c files may get #included into the same compilation unit (for example, if several .c files define function templates). If the name of file-scope static entities is the same in two distinct modules, such as a file-scope static int called x in one .c file, and a file-scope static char called x in another .c file, spurious compilation errors can result.

```
//module A.C
static int x;

//module B.C
static char x;    //can cause a "redefined static data" error
```

■

Cross reference—

FAQ: 285

How should you handle copyright notices in .c files that contain templates?

Protect them with "do once" logic using #ifndef **and** #define.

Company copyright notices (copyleft notices, too) in .c files should be protected by a do once, #ifndef/#define pair (similar to what appears in .h files). This is because copyright notices are typically static data, and static data can collide with first-generation template schemes that combine .c files via #include.

For example, the following logic should appear in every .c file.

```
#ifndef COPYRIGHT_NOTICE
#define COPYRIGHT_NOTICE
static const char copyright[] = "Copyright (C) blah blah";
static const char rcs_info[]  = "RCS info goes here ....";
#endif
```

Note that the symbol COPYRIGHT_NOTICE is the same in all .c files (this is different from the way the #ifndef/#define logic is used in .h files), because we are trying to protect against the symbol copyright from being defined more than once when *different* .c files are concatenated.

■

Cross reference—
FAQ: 284

How should you organize code that includes both templates and non-templates?

Don't mix them.

Avoid putting both templates and non-templates into the same .c file. This is because some template expansion strategies require only template functions to be #included together, with non-templates precompiled into the usual object files and object libraries.

FAQ
287

What are parameterized types?

Class templates.

Parameterized types are types (such as `Array`) that are parameterized over another value or type (such as `int`). For example, `List<int>` is a type that is parameterized over another type, `int`.

The C++ rendition of parameterized types is provided by class templates.

■

Cross references—

FAQ: 275, 276
See Stroustrup: 8
See Ellis & Stroustrup: 14

FAQ
288

What is genericity?

Class templates.

Genericity is another word for parameterized types, which is provided in C++ by class templates. Genericity should not to be confused with generality, which just means avoiding solutions that are overly specific.

Cross references—

FAQ: 275, 276
See Stroustrup: 8
See Ellis & Stroustrup: 14
See Lippman: 7.1

What is a reference?

An alias for an object.

A reference is an alternate name for an object, frequently used for passing parameters by reference (pass-by-reference). For example, in the following function swap(), the actual parameters i and j are passed by reference so their values may be changed.

```
#include <iostream.h>

void
swap(int& x, int& y) throw()
{
  int tmp = x;
  x = y;
  y = tmp;
}

main()
{
  int i = 5;
  int j = 7;
  cout << "before: i=" << i << ", j=" << j << '\n';
  swap(i, j);
  cout << "after:  i=" << i << ", j=" << j << '\n';
}
```

Here x and y become aliases for main()'s i and j, respectively. The effect is similar to the C-style pass-by-pointer, but without the caller having to take the address of the parameters and without the callee having to dereference pointers. That is, there is no need to use & in main(), and no need to use * in swap().

■

Cross references—

FAQ: 290, 292, 298
See Stroustrup: 2.3, 4.6, r.8
See Ellis & Stroustrup: 8.2, 8.3, 8.4
See Lippman: 1.5

F A Q
290

When can you attach a reference to its referent?

A reference is attached to its referent when it is created (only).

The following example initializes j to be an alias for i, but the initialization of k is illegal because k is not attached to an object.

```
main()
{
  int  i;
  int& j = i;

#ifdef GENERATE_ERROR
  int& k;    //ERROR: references must be initialized
#endif
}
```

When a function receives parameters by reference, the references are attached (bound) to the actual arguments provided by the caller.

■

Cross references—

FAQ: 289, 292
See Stroustrup: 2.3, 4.6, r.8
See Ellis & Stroustrup: 8.2, 8.3, 8.4
See Lippman: 1.5

What does referent mean?

The object to which a reference refers.

Referent is a synonym for the object to which the reference refers. In the following example code, j is the reference and i is the referent.

```
main()
{
  int  i;
  int& j = i;
}
```

What happens when you assign to a reference?

The referent is changed, not the reference itself.

Because a reference is an alias for its referent, anything done to the reference is actually done to the referent. In particular, a reference is an lvalue (an expression that can appear on the left side of an assignment operator) for the referent. Therefore, assigning to a reference changes the referent.

Said another way, a reference *is* its referent—not a copy of the referent, nor a pointer to the referent, but the referent itself.

For example, in the following function f(), the first statement changes main()'s i, because the formal parameter x is an alias for i. The second statement also changes i (as well as x), because the address of i is stored in y. The third statement does not change i, because z is a copy of the original value of i.

```
void
f(int& x, int* y, int z) throw()
{
  x = 5;   //main's i changed to 5
  *y = 6;  //main's i changed to 6
  z = 7;   //no change to main's i
}
```

```
main()
{
  int i = 4;
  f(i, &i, i);
}
```

■

Cross references—

FAQ: 289, 290, 296, 298
See Stroustrup: 2.3, 4.6, r.8
See Ellis & Stroustrup: 8.2, 8.3, 8.4
See Lippman: 1.5

F A Q
293

What is a local reference?

A local (auto) reference variable that isn't a parameter.

The following example illustrates how local references provide a temporary alias relationship. Integer reference j is an alias for integer i, so changing i to 5 changes j, and changing j changes i.

```
main()
{
  int  i;
  int& j = i; //establish the alias relation between j and i
  i = 5;      //assigning 5 to i, changes both i and j
  j = 6;      //assigning 6 to j, changes both i and j
}
```

Local references are uncommon. They are normally used to avoid recalculating the same location several times; they allow a function to attach a handle to an object that would otherwise require nontrivial address computation to access.

■

Cross references—

FAQ: 291
See Stroustrup: 2.3, 4.6, r.8
See Ellis & Stroustrup: 8.2, 8.3, 8.4
See Lippman: 1.5

What does it mean to return a reference?

The function call expression is the referent.

When a function returns a reference, the function call becomes an lvalue for the referent. This is normally used to allow operator expressions to be used as lvalues—the subscript operator, the dereference operator, and so on. The following example shows how returning a reference allows a subscript operator to be an lvalue.

```cpp
#include <iostream.h>
class BadIndex { };

class Array {
public:
   float& operator[] (unsigned i) throw(BadIndex);
protected:
   float data_[100];
};

inline
float&
Array::operator[] (unsigned i) throw(BadIndex)
{
   if (i >= 100u) throw BadIndex();
   return data_[i];
}

main()
{
   Array a;
   for (unsigned i = 0; i < 100; ++i)
     a[i] = 3.14 * i;
   for (unsigned j = 0; j < 100; ++j)
     cout << a[j] << '\n';
}
```

Returning a reference to `data_[i]` doesn't return a copy of `data_[i]`; it returns `data_[i]` itself. Therefore, anything done to the expression in the caller (`a[i]`) is actually done to `data_[i]`.

■

Cross references—

FAQ: 289, 298
See Stroustrup: 2.3, 4.6, r.8
See Ellis & Stroustrup: 8.2, 8.3, 8.4
See Lippman: 1.8, 3.8

F A Q

295

What happens when you take the address of a reference?

You get the address of the referent.

Remember, the reference is the referent. Anything done to the reference—including taking its address—is actually done to the referent. For example, the following code will print `yes`.

```
#include <iostream.h>

main()
{
    int  i = 5;
    int& j = i;
    if (&j == &i)
        cout << "yes\n";
    else
        cout << "no\n";
}
```

■

Cross references—

FAQ: 289, 298
See Stroustrup: 2.3, 4.6, r.8
See Ellis & Stroustrup: 8.2, 8.3, 8.4
See Lippman: 1.5

How can you make a reference refer to a different referent?

You can't.

Unlike a pointer, once a reference is bound to an object, it cannot be made to refer to a different object. You can't separate the alias from the referent.

For example, the last line of the following example changes i to 6; it does not make the reference k refer to j. Throughout its short life, k will always refer to i.

```
main()
{
  int  i = 5;
  int  j = 6;
  int& k = i;    //bind k so it is an alias for i
        k = j;   //change i to 6 -- does NOT bind k to j
}
```

■

Cross references—
FAQ: *289, 290, 292, 298*
See Stroustrup: *2.3, 4.6, r.8*
See Ellis & Stroustrup: *5.3, 8.2, 8.3, 8.4*
See Lippman: *1.5*

Why would you use references when pointers can do everything references can do?

References are sometimes the right tool for the right job.

Using a pointer when all you need is a reference is like using a chain saw to trim your fingernails—it will do the job, but you'd better be extremely careful.

In C, pointers are used for a variety of purposes because there is no other tool available for doing the tasks they do. Programmers learn to live with the dangers of pointers in C because there is no alternative. It's as if C gives you a chain saw and expects you to use it for building houses, shredding paper, trimming fingernails, and cutting hair.

When all you need is an alias for an object, you're only using some of the capabilities of a pointer—you don't need all of the power and responsibility of a pointer. This is an ideal situation for a reference.

Pointers are a powerful and valuable part of any programmer's toolbox. However, you should use this heavy machinery only when necessary. Don't give a chain saw to a user who just wants a manicure.

Use references when you can, use pointers only when you have to.

■

Cross references—

FAQ: 298
See Stroustrup: 2.3, 4.6, r.8
See Ellis & Stroustrup: 8.2, 8.3, 8.4

FAQ
298

How do you know whether to use references or pointers?

Use references in function signatures, and pointers for local variables and member variables.

References are usually preferred over pointers unless you need to change the binding to a different referent, or to refer to a non-object (a NULL pointer). By implication, references are most useful in parameter lists and return values. Pointers are usually preferred over references for local variables and member objects. An example of this can be seen in the class Array that follows.

```
class Array {
public:
  //references in signatures can make interfaces intuitive
  int& operator[] (int i);
protected:
  //pointers as member data allows reallocation
  int* data_;
};
```

When a function needs a sentinel reference as a parameter or return value, the function can accept or return a pointer and use the NULL pointer as the sentinel value. This is an exception to the guideline provided by this FAQ.

■

Cross references—

FAQ: 201, 289, 296
See Stroustrup: 2.3, 4.6, r.8
See Ellis & Stroustrup: 8.2, 8.3, 8.4
See Lippman: 1.5

Why do I feel like I hate references?

Breathe deeply and relax; you'll get over it.

It often takes C programmers some time to get used to references. In the beginning, C programmers typically complain that pass-by-reference doesn't require explicit syntax in the caller's source code (for example, no & in the caller code). After using C++ for a while, however, developers realize that this is information hiding, which is an asset rather than a liability.

Migrating the level of abstraction from the language of the machine into the language of the problem domain is an important step toward reuse in OO technology. The information hiding provided by a reference is a small step in this migration.

In C, the maxim is, "No hidden mechanism." Since this maxim is inconsistent with the C++ goal of programming in the language of the problem domain rather than the language of the machine, C++ intentionally discards the C maxim. The new maxim is, "Pay for it only if you use it."

Write your C++ code in the language of the problem domain, not the language of the machine.

■

Cross references—

FAQ: 289, 296, 298
See Stroustrup: 2.3, 4.6, r.8
See Ellis & Stroustrup: 8.2, 8.3, 8.4
See Lippman: 1.5

Does int& const x = y; **make sense?**

No.

Because a reference is always bound to the same referent, the const is superfluous and may confuse people. The following examples assume that Fred is some type.

```
//BAD:                        //GOOD:
Fred& const a = b;            Fred& a = b;
const Fred& const c = d;      const Fred& c = d;
void f(Fred& const e);        void f(Fred& e);
void g(const Fred& const e);  void g(const Fred& e);
```

Does new **do more than allocate memory?**

Yes, it also initializes the new object.

Assuming Fred is a known type, the expression new Fred is a two-phase operation; first it allocates memory (using a primitive that is conceptually similar to malloc(sizeof(Fred))), then it calls the appropriate constructor of the class (Fred::Fred(), in this case). Similarly, delete p first calls the destructor on the object *p, then releases the memory pointed to by p using a primitive that is conceptually similar to free(p).

Why should you use new **instead of trustworthy** malloc()**?**

It does more.

Object construction: In C++, new and delete create and destroy objects. In contrast, malloc() and free() merely allocate and deallocate memory.

Safety: The function malloc() isn't type safe. It returns a void* rather than a pointer of the correct type. Note that the ANSI-C rule that allows a void* to be converted to any other pointer is a dangerous hole in the typing system that has been removed in C++.

Flexibility: The new operator can be overridden by a class. For example, new Fred can use a different memory allocation primitive than is used by new Wilma. In contrast, malloc() cannot be overloaded on a class-by-class basis.

■

Cross references—

FAQ: 168, 303
See Stroustrup: 3.2, r.5, r.12, r.18
See Ellis & Stroustrup: 5.3, 12.2c, 12.5, 12.6, 12.7
See Lippman: 3.11

F A Q
303

Does C++ have something like realloc() **that goes along with** new **and** delete**?**

No; and don't use realloc() **directly, since bitwise copying an object of a user-defined class is evil.**

When realloc() needs to move data during the reallocation, it uses a bitwise copy, which is disastrous for many user-defined classes. C++ objects know how to copy themselves using their own copy constructors and assignment operators.

Never use realloc() on objects of user-defined classes. Let the objects copy themselves.

■

Cross references—

FAQ: 210, 302
See Stroustrup: 3.2, r.5, r.12, r.18
See Ellis & Stroustrup: 5.3, 12.2c, 12.5, 12.6, 12.7
See Lippman: 3.11

Does `delete p` delete the pointer `p`, or the referent `*p`?

The referent.

If verbosity were a virtue, the keyword would be changed from `delete` to `deleteTheThingPointedToBy`. One could argue that the keyword is misleading, but the same abuse of English occurs with `free()`: `free(p)` frees the memory pointed to by `p` rather than freeing `p` itself.

```
free(p);   /* why not freeTheStuffPointedToBy(p) ? */
```

■

Cross references—

FAQ: 305, 306
See Stroustrup: 3.2, r.5, r.12, r.18
See Ellis & Stroustrup: 5.3, 12.2c, 12.5, 12.6, 12.7
See Lippman: 3.11

What happens if you pass a NULL pointer to `delete`?

Nothing.

Passing a NULL pointer to `delete` is safe and is guaranteed to do nothing. This simplifies code that uses `delete` by allowing such code to `delete` a pointer that may be NULL without a special `if`.

■

Cross references—

FAQ: 304, 306
See Stroustrup: 3.2, r.5, r.12, r.18
See Ellis & Stroustrup: 5.3, 12.2c, 12.5, 12.6, 12.7
See Lippman: 3.11

What happens when a pointer is deleted twice?

Catastrophe.

Suppose you have a pointer variable p. The first time you delete p, the object *p is safely destructed, and the memory pointed to by p is safely returned to the heap. The second time you pass the same pointer to delete without a subsequent new that returned that pointer, the remains of what used to be an object at *p is passed to the destructor (which could be disastrous), and the memory pointed to by p is handed back to the heap a second time. This will likely corrupt the heap and its list of free memory.

The following example illustrates this situation.

```
class Fred { };

main()
{
  Fred* p1 = new Fred;
  Fred* p2 = p1;
  delete p1;
  delete p2;    //delete the same pointer twice: DISASTER!
}
```

■

Cross references—
FAQ: 304, 305
See Stroustrup: 3.2, r.5, r.12, r.18
See Ellis & Stroustrup: 5.3, 12.2c, 12.5, 12.6, 12.7
See Lippman: 3.11

How do you allocate or deallocate an array of things?

Use new[] and delete[].

Any time you allocate an array of things (that is, any time you use the [...] in the new expression) you *must* use the [] in the delete statement, and vice versa. Here is an example.

```
class Thing { };

main()
{
  Thing* p = new Thing[100];
  delete [] p;
}
```

There is no syntactic difference between the type of a pointer to a thing and a pointer to the first element of an array of things, a feature that C++ inherited from C. The purpose of the syntactic difference between delete and delete[] is to distinguish deleting a thing from an array of things.

■

Cross references—
FAQ: 136, 137, 194, 308
See Stroustrup: r.5, r.12
See Ellis & Stroustrup: 5.3, 12.5, 12.6
See Lippman: 6.3

What if you forget the [] **when you use** delete **to delete an array allocated via** new X[n]**?**

F A Q
308

Catastrophe.

It is the programmer's responsibility—not the compiler's—to make sure the connection between new[] and delete[] is correct. If you get it wrong, don't expect either a compiler error message or a clean run-time exception.

Depending on the implementation, the results may be harmless in some circumstances, but changing the compiler vendor, or even changing the compiler version, could make it fail. The only safe way to write code is to make it correct according to the *language* rather than to some particular implementation of the language.

Some implementations will immediately corrupt the heap if you forget the [] when deleting an array of objects; other implementations will fail to destruct all but the first object in the array. The latter would cause memory leaks if the destructors release memory; cause deadlock if the destructors unlock semaphores; compromise system integrity in other ways; or trigger some combination of any or all of these.

In other words, the best you can hope for is a disaster.

Class libraries can provide simple abstractions that eliminate mismatches between new[] and delete.

■

Cross references—

FAQ: 304, 305, 306
See Stroustrup: 3.2, r.5, r.12, r.18
See Ellis & Stroustrup: 5.3, 12.2c, 12.5, 12.6, 12.7
See Lippman: 6.3

FAQ 309

How do you construct an object at a predetermined position in memory?

Use the placement syntax of the new operator.

Objects are normally created on the stack, on the heap, or in static memory. These correspond to automatic allocation, dynamic allocation, and static allocation, respectively. None of these situations allow the programmer to specify the address where the object will live.

Occasionally an object's desired location is known before the object is created, such as when the hardware uses a piece of storage as a way of communicating with the software. Under these circumstances, use the placement syntax of the new operator.

For example, to place an object of class Fred at the hexadecimal address 0xDEADBEEF, and to pass in values (42, 42) as arguments to the Fred constructor, you would use the following.

```
void* place = (void*) 0xDEADBEEF;
Fred* p = new(place) Fred(42, 42);
```

The storage pointed to by place must be large enough to hold sizeof(Fred) bytes, and must be properly aligned to hold a Fred. The returned pointer p will be numerically the same as place, but p will be a Fred* rather than a void*.

■

Cross references—

FAQ: 168, 302, 310
See Stroustrup: 3.2, r.5, r.12, r.18
See Ellis & Stroustrup: 5.3, 12.2c, 12.5, 12.6, 12.7
See Lippman: 3.11

How do objects created by placement new get destroyed?

**FAQ
310**

Placement destruction.

Use of placement destruction is normally restricted to objects created by placement new. For example, if p is a Fred* that was returned from placement new, *p can be destructed as shown in the following example.

```
p -> ~Fred();
```

Caution: Do not use placement destruction on an object that will later be automatically destroyed, such as an object on the stack, an object on the heap that will be deleted, or a static object. Use placement destruction only when you are in *total control* of the storage allocation and lifetime of the object. In other words, only with objects initialized by the placement new syntax.

■

Cross references—
FAQ: 309
See Stroustrup: 3.2, r.5, r.12, r.18
See Ellis & Stroustrup: 5.3, 12.2c, 12.5, 12.6, 12.7
See Lippman: 3.11

How can you ensure that objects of type Fred are created only with new and not on the stack?

**FAQ
311**

Hide the constructors and provide special creation functions.

Make sure all constructors are non-public (including the copy constructor, whether or not you need to provide an explicit copy constructor); and define static (or friend) functions that return a pointer to objects created via new.

Here's an example.

```
class Fred {
public:
  static Fred* create()          { return new Fred();  }
  static Fred* create(int i)      { return new Fred(i); }
  static Fred* create(const Fred& x) { return new Fred(x); }
protected:
  Fred(int i=10)                 : i_(i)     { }
  Fred(const Fred& x)            : i_(x.i_) { }
  int i_;
};

void
sampleUserCode()
{
  Fred* p = Fred::create(5);
  delete p;
}
```

Note that derived classes can't be instantiated since all of the constructors are private. Derived classes could only be instantiated if some of the constructors were protected.

■

Cross references—

FAQ: 168, 302
See Stroustrup: 3.2, r.5, r.12, r.18
See Ellis & Stroustrup: 5.3, 12.2c, 12.5, 12.6, 12.7
See Lippman: 3.11

How should you manage pointers to allocated objects?

Very carefully.

In languages with explicit memory management such as C and C++, programmers are responsible to ensure there are no memory leaks. A memory leak occurs when an object is allocated but is not subsequently deallocated.

■

Cross references—
FAQ: 313
See Stroustrup: 2.3, r.5, r.8
See Ellis & Stroustrup: 5.17, 8.2, 8.4

What is the cleanest way to avoid memory leaks?

Place pointers inside objects.

The pointer returned from new should always be stored in a member variable of an object. That object's destructor should delete the heap allocation.

In the following example, class Array acts like an array of int. Note that the allocation is remembered by the Array object, whose destructor performs the appropriate delete.

```
#include <stdlib.h>

class BadIndex { };

class Array {
public:
  Array(unsigned len=10) : len_(len), arr_(new int[len]) { }
  Array(const Array& a);            //copy constructor
  Array& operator= (const Array& a);//assignment operator
 ~Array()                           { delete [] arr_; }
  unsigned len() const              { return len_; }
  int  operator[] (unsigned i) const{ return arr_[chk(i)]; }
  int& operator[] (unsigned i)      { return arr_[chk(i)]; }

protected:
  unsigned chk(unsigned i)          //checks index i
    { if (i >= len_) throw BadIndex();
      return i; }
  unsigned  len_;
  T*        arr_;
};

main(int, char** argv)
{
  unsigned len = 100;
  if (argv[0] != NULL)
    len = strtol(argv[0], NULL, 10);
  Array a(len);
  for (unsigned i = 0; i < a.len(); ++i)
    a[i] = 2*i - 47;
}
```
 ───▶ the array of ints is automagically deleted here

■

Cross references—

FAQ: 170, 312, 318
See Stroustrup: 2.3, r.5, r.8
See Ellis & Stroustrup: 5.17, 8.2, 8.4

Why should every allocation be remembered by some object?

To exploit a powerful "hook" in the C++ language: destructors.

Ensuring that every allocation is remembered by some object is the keystone to the C++ resource management discipline. We have found this discipline to be practical in systems and applications ranging in size from very small to huge.

■

Cross references—
FAQ: 313, 315
See Stroustrup: 2.3, r.5, r.8
See Ellis & Stroustrup: 5.17, 8.2, 8.4

What is a practical discipline for resource management?

Ownership, responsibility, focus.

Ownership: Every allocated resource is owned by exactly one resource manager object, which must be a local (`auto`) variable in some scope.
Responsibility: The resource manager object is charged with the responsibility to release the allocated resource. This is the only place that the resource is released.
Focus: The resource manager object does nothing other than manage this individual resource.
A leak is simply a `new` that lacks a corresponding `delete`. Either the `delete` isn't physically in the source code, or it is in the source code but is bypassed due to run-time control flow. Both of these situations are handled by the resource management discipline described above, since the destructor for a local object will always run when control leaves the scope where the local object was created. In other words, the resource management discipline relies on the guarantees provided by the language rather than the good intentions of programmer self-discipline.

The resource management discipline can be applied to the management of all kinds of resources. Memory is being used here by way of example, not limitation.

■

Cross references—
FAQ: 171, 316, 317
See Stroustrup: 2.3, r.5, r.8
See Ellis & Stroustrup: 5.17, 8.2, 8.4

F A Q
316

Is it OK for an object to manage a resource and also perform operations that may throw exceptions?

No.

In the following example, class Fred both manages a resource (an X allocation), and performs some operations that may throw exceptions (it calls mayThrow()). In other words, Fred violates this guideline. When Fred's constructor throws an exception (as a result of calling mayThrow()), there is a resource leak.

```
#include <iostream.h>

class X { };
void mayThrow() throw(int) { throw 42; }

class Fred {
public:
  Fred()
    : p_(new X())
    { mayThrow(); }

  ~Fred()          ──▶ BAD FORM: resource managers must not throw
    { cout << "Not reached #1\n"; delete p_; }
private:
  X* p_;
      ──▶ BAD FORM: throwers must not be resource managers
};
```

```
main()
{
  try {
    Fred f;
    cout << "Not reached #2\n";
  }
  catch (int e) {
    cout << "Exception caught: " << e << "\n";
  }
}
```

Because this guideline was violated, the X object leaked: the delete p_ instruction in Fred::~Fred() is never executed. Either Fred should focus on being a resource manager—and nothing but a resource manager—or Fred should delegate the resource management aspect to some other class. In other words, either get rid of the code that mayThrow() from Fred, or change the X* to a HeapPtr<X>.

■

Cross references—
FAQ: 171, 315, 317, 460
See Stroustrup: 2.3, r.5, r.8
See Ellis & Stroustrup: 5.17, 8.2, 8.4

Is it OK for an object to manage two or more resources?

F A Q
317

No.

An object that manages a resource should manage exactly one resource. Use composition to combine multiple "pure" resource manager objects (for example, multiple HeapPtr objects, File objects, and so forth). This guideline is a (very common) special case of the guideline presented in the previous FAQ.

If your object manages two or more resources, the first resource may leak if the second allocation throws an exception. In particular, when an exception occurs during the execution of a constructor, the object's destructor is not executed, so the destructor won't release the resource that was successfully allocated.

In the following example, class `Fred` manages two resources: an `X` allocation and a `Y` allocation. In other words, `Fred` violates this guideline. When `Fred`'s constructor throws an exception (as a result of allocating a `Y`), the `X` resource leaks.

```
#include <iostream.h>

class X { };

class Y {
public:
  Y() throw(int) { throw 42; }
};

class Fred {
public:
  Fred() throw(int)
    : x_(new X()), y_(new Y()) { }
  ~Fred() throw()
    { cout << "Not reached #1\n"; delete y_; delete x_; }
protected:
  X* x_;
  Y* y_;
};

main()
{
  try {
    Fred f;
    cout << "Not reached #2\n";
  }
  catch (int e) {
    cout << "Exception caught: " << e << "\n";
  }
}
```

In the code above, an arrow points from the `X* x_;` line labeled **BAD FORM**.

Because this guideline was violated, the `X` object leaked: the `delete x_` instruction is never executed. Either `Fred` should focus on being a manager of a resource—not two or more resources—or `Fred` should delegate the resource management aspects to some other class. In other words, either get rid of the `Y` resource from `Fred`, or change the `X*` to a `HeapPtr<X>`.

■

Cross references—

FAQ: 168, 170, 171, 183, 312, 313, 315, 316, 460
See Stroustrup: 2.3, r.5, r.8
See Ellis & Stroustrup: 5.17, 8.2, 8.4

FAQ 318

What if an object has a pointer to an allocation, and one of the object's member functions deletes the allocation?

That member function must immediately restore the integrity of the object holding the pointer.

If some member function (other than the destructor) `deletes` an allocation, then the member function must either replace the allocation with a new allocation, or set a flag that tells the destructor to skip the `delete`. Setting the pointer to NULL is such a flag.

For example, the assignment operator must often `delete` an old allocation as well as allocate a new one. In such cases, the new allocation should be performed before the old is deleted in case the allocation fails. The goal is for the assignment operator to be atomic: it should either succeed completely (no exceptions, and all states successfully copied from the source object), or it should fail (throw an exception) but not change the state of `this`. It is not always possible to meet this atomicity goal, but the assignment operator must never leave `this` object in an incoherent state.

Another guideline is to use a local `HeapPtr` to point to the new allocation. This will ensure the new allocation gets deleted if an exception is thrown by some subsequent operation in the assignment operator code. If you use the `HeapPtr` from FAQ 460, the `relinquishOwnership()` service can be used to transfer the allocation's ownership from the local `HeapPtr` to the `HeapPtr` that is a member of `this` object.

■

Cross references—

FAQ: 170, 313, 320, 460
See Stroustrup: 2.3, r.5, r.8
See Ellis & Stroustrup: 5.17, 8.2, 8.4

How should a pointer variable be handled after being passed to `delete`?

Immediately put the pointer variable into a safe state.

After calling `delete p`, unless the pointer `p` is just about to go out of scope, immediately set `p = NULL` or `p = anotherHeapPtr`. The goal is to prevent a subsequent operation from either following the pointer `p` (which now points at garbage) or calling `delete p` a second time.

Note that setting `p = new Fred` is not acceptable, since the `Fred` allocation may throw an exception before `p` gets changed to a safe state.

We recommend setting `p = NULL` immediately, in case an exception subverts the normal flow of control.

■

Cross references—
FAQ: 312, 313, 320
See Stroustrup: 2.3, r.5, r.8
See Ellis & Stroustrup: 5.17, 8.2, 8.4

How should you handle a pointer to an object that is allocated and deallocated in the same scope?

Place the pointer in a local managed pointer object.

The goal is to make it unnecessary for you to remember to `delete` the temporary object, and to make your code immune to modifications in the control flow logic. Using a managed pointer (for example, a `HeapPtr`) meets this goal since the managed pointer's destructor can `delete` the temporary object.

Here's an example.

```
#include <iostream.h>
#include "FAQ 460/HeapPtr.h"    //see FAQ 460 for this file

class Fred {
public:
  ~Fred() throw() { cout << "Fred dtor\n"; }
};
```

```
main()
{
  HeapPtr<Fred> ptr( new Fred() );
              └──────► a managed pointer, not a Fred*
  if (rand() % 2) {
    cout << "randomly returning from main\n";
    return 0;
  }
  //we do NOT say delete ptr, since ptr is a managed pointer
}
```

■

Cross references—

FAQ: 170, 312, 313, 460
See Stroustrup: 2.3, r.5, r.8
See Ellis & Stroustrup: 5.17, 8.2, 8.4

What does the compiler mean by the warning, "Returning a reference to a local object"?

Bad hair day!

Never return a reference or a pointer to a local (auto) object. As soon as the function returns, the local object is destructed, and the reference or pointer refers to garbage.

Note that returning a copy of a local object (returning "by value") is fine.

■

Cross references—

FAQ: 289, 322, 325
See Stroustrup: 2.3, r.5, r.8
See Ellis & Stroustrup: 5.17, 8.2, 8.4
See Lippman: 3.10

How can you manage pointers across block boundaries?

Avoid storing the address of an object from an inner scope into a pointer in an outer scope.

Here's an example.

```
class A { };

void f()
{
  A* p;
  {
    A a;
    p = &a;      //suspect!
  }
}
```

When control flow leaves the inner block, a will be destroyed and p will be pointing at garbage. Because control can leave the inner scope a number of different ways (including an uncaught exception), setting the outer scope's pointer to point to an inner scope's object can lead to subtle errors and should be avoided on principle.

If you must store the address of an inner scope's object into an outer scope's pointer, then the outer scope's pointer should be changed to NULL (or some other safe value) before leaving the inner scope. To avoid control flow errors, you should guarantee this occurs by creating a local object whose destructor automagically changes the pointer to NULL.

Note that the problem addressed by this FAQ can only occur with a pointer, not with a reference. This is because a reference is permanently bound to its referent at the moment it is initialized. This is another reason to prefer references over pointers.

■

Cross references—

FAQ: 289, 321, 325
See Stroustrup: 2.3, r.5, r.8
See Ellis & Stroustrup: 5.17, 8.2, 8.4
See Lippman: 3.10

What is a wild pointer?

A pointer that refers to garbage.

There are three ways to get a wild pointer.

1. An uninitialized pointer that contains garbage bits.

2. A pointer that gets inadvertently scribbled on.

3. A pointer that refers to something that is no longer there (a dangling reference).

No matter how they happen, wild pointers are bad news. Bad enough that we've devoted this entire chapter to the subject.

■

Cross references—
FAQ: 325, 326
See Stroustrup: 2.3, r.5, r.8
See Ellis & Stroustrup: 5.17, 8.2, 8.4

When should you use pointer casts?

Rarely.

Pointer casts are the `goto` of OO programming. A `goto` complicates the control flow, making it difficult to statically reason about the flow of control. To determine the code's behavior, you must simulate the dynamic flow of control. A pointer cast complicates the type flow, making it difficult to statically reason about the type of an object. To determine the code's behavior, you must simulate the dynamic flow of types.

Pointer casts are also error prone. The basic problem is that the compiler believes you when you do a pointer cast. This can result in a wild pointer. Shudder.

Developers with a background in untyped languages tend to produce designs whose implementations employ an excessive number of pointer casts. These old habits must be terminated without prejudice. The lowest levels of memory management are among the few places where pointer casts are necessary.

Reference casts are just like pointer casts, and are equally dangerous.

Use a pointer cast as often as you would use a `goto`.

■

Cross references—
FAQ: 323, 326

What is a dangling reference?

A reference or pointer to an object that has been destructed.

In C, the classic example of a dangling reference occurs when a function returns a pointer to a local variable, or when someone uses a pointer that has already been passed to `free`. Both situations can occur in C++, too.

■

Cross references—

FAQ: 323, 326
See Stroustrup: 2.3, r.5, r.8
See Ellis & Stroustrup: 5.17, 8.2, 8.4

What happens to a program that has even one wild pointer?

Misery, destruction, and death.

A wild pointer is to software what a car bomb is to a busy street: both are undirected purveyors of pain and suffering.

After a program spawns its first wild pointer, an awesome chain reaction begins. The first wild pointer scribbles on a random memory location, which will likely corrupt the object at that location, creating other wild pointers. Eventually—almost mercifully—one of these wild pointers attempts to scribble on something protected by the hardware, and the program crashes.

By the time that happens, finding the root cause of the error with a debugger is nearly hopeless; what was once a cohesive system of objects is now only a pile of rubble. The system has literally been blown to bits.

■

Cross references—

FAQ: 323, 325, 327
See Stroustrup: 2.3, r.5, r.8
See Ellis & Stroustrup: 5.17, 8.2, 8.4

What is Voodoo debugging?

When developers feel their way through the rubble left behind by wild pointers.

F A Q
327

Wild pointers create true chaos. Arbitrarily small changes, such as inserting an extra semicolon, running the program on a different day of the week, or changing the way you smile as you press the enter key, can cause arbitrarily large effects. Sometimes the program deletes user files, sometimes it just gives the wrong answer, sometimes it actually works! But deep inside, you know the system is very, very sick.

■

Cross references—

FAQ: 323, 325, 326
See Stroustrup: 2.3, r.5, r.8
See Ellis & Stroustrup: 5.17, 8.2, 8.4

Is it safe to bind a reference variable to a temporary object?

F A Q
328

Yes, as long as you don't copy that reference into another reference or pointer.

In the following example, an unnamed temporary String object is created at line A. A (const) reference is bound to this temporary (main()'s x). The language guarantees the unnamed temporary will live until the reference x dies, which in this case is at the end of main(). Therefore, line B is safe: the compiler isn't allowed to destruct the unnamed temporary String object until after line B.

```
#include "FAQ 459/String.h"        //see FAQ 459

String createTemp()               { return "fred"; }

main()
{
  const String& x = createTemp();  //line A
  cout << "x = " << x << "\n";     //line B: this is safe
}
```

There is a caveat—don't copy reference x into a pointer variable that's out of the scope in which the temporary was created. For a subtle example of this, see the next FAQ.

■

Cross references—

FAQ: 289, 290, 325, 329, 459
See Stroustrup: 2.3, r.5, r.8
See Ellis & Stroustrup: 5.17, 8.2, 8.4

**FAQ
329**

Should a parameter passed by const **reference be returned by** const **reference?**

No; it might create a dangling reference, which might destroy the world.

Returning an object by reference is not dangerous in and of itself, provided you ensure that the lifetime of the referent exceeds the lifetime of the returned reference. You can't make this assurance when a const reference parameter is returned by const reference, because the original argument might have been an unnamed temporary.

In the following example, an unnamed temporary String object is created at line A. A (const) reference is bound to this temporary (unsafe()'s x parameter). Even though x is copied into another reference (main()'s y), x itself dies immediately, so the unnamed temporary will live until control flows over the ; on line A. Therefore, line B is unsafe—the compiler is required to destruct the unnamed temporary String object at the end of line A, so line B is working with a dangling reference.

```
#include "FAQ 459/String.h"        //see FAQ 459

String createTemp()               { return "fred"; }
```

```
const String&
unsafe(const String& x)              { return x; }

main()
{
  const String& y = unsafe( createTemp() ); //line A
  cout << "y = " << y << "\n";              //line B: BOOM!
}
```

Note if a function accepts a parameter by non-const reference (for example, `f(String& s)`), returning a copy of this reference parameter is safe, because a temporary cannot be passed by non-const reference.

■

Cross references—
FAQ: 289, 325, 328, 459
See Stroustrup: 2.3, r.5, r.8
See Ellis & Stroustrup: 5.17, 8.2, 8.4

Should template functions for `min(x,y)` **or** `abs(x)` **return a** const **reference?**

F A Q
330

No!

When the following example is compiled and the symbol UNSAFE is defined, `min(x,y)` avoids an extra copy operation by returning a const reference parameter by const reference. As discussed in the previous FAQ, this can create a dangling reference, which can destroy the world.

```
template<class T>
  #ifdef UNSAFE
    const T&
  #else
    T
  #endif
min(const T& x, const T& y)
{
  return x < y ? x : y;
}
```

Returning a const reference parameter by const reference is normally done as an optimization to avoid an extra copy operation. If you're willing to sacrifice correctness, you can make your software very fast!

■

Cross references—

FAQ: 278, 289, 325, 329
See Stroustrup: 2.3, r.5, r.8
See Ellis & Stroustrup: 5.17, 8.2, 8.4
See Lippman: 4.2

F A Q
331

Are the bits of a NULL pointer guaranteed to be all zeros?

No.

Depending on the hardware, the operating system, or the compiler, a pointer whose bits are all zeros may not be the same as the NULL pointer. For example, using memset() to set all the bits of a pointer to zero may not make that pointer equal to NULL. Alternatively, setting a pointer to NULL may set some of the bits of that pointer to 1.

All conforming C++ compilers will print "p1 is NULL" in the program that follows, but some may print "p2 is not NULL".

```
#include <iostream.h>

main()
{
  char* p1 = 0;                    //OK: the NULL pointer
  cout << "p1 is " << (p1==NULL ? "" : " not") << " NULL\n";

  char* p2;
  memset(&p2, '\0', sizeof(p2));  //BAD: undefined pointer!
  cout << "p2 is " << (p2==NULL ? "" : " not") << " NULL\n";
}
```

■

Cross references—

FAQ: 323, 326, 430
See Stroustrup: 2.3, r.5, r.8
See Ellis & Stroustrup: 5.17, 8.2, 8.4

What is const **correctness?**

A program is const **correct if it never changes a constant object.**

C++ achieves const correctness by using the keyword const. For example, a const String could safely be passed to any of the following functions.

```
#include "FAQ 459/String.h"    //see FAQ 459 for this file

void f(       String  s);      //pass by value
void g(const  String& s);      //by reference-to-const
void h(const  String* s);      //by pointer-to-const
```

Function f() cannot change the caller's String due to pass-by-value. By their placement of the const keyword, functions g() and h() promise not to change the caller's String. If g() or h() attempts to modify the String, the compiler generates a compile-time error.

Continuing with the additional declarations that follow, neither g() nor h() can pass their String to i() or j(), because i() and j() don't promise to leave the String unchanged.

```
void i(String& s);             //by reference-to-nonconst
void j(String* s);             //by pointer-to-nonconst
```

Although g() and h() aren't allowed to pass their String's to i() or j(), the opposite is legal; i() can pass its String to g(), and j() can pass its

String to h(), because g() and h() make promises that are at least as strong as (and in this case, stronger than) the promises made by i() and j().

∎

Cross references—

FAQ: 334, 335, 336, 459
See Stroustrup: 2.5, r.7
See Ellis & Stroustrup: 7.1, 9.3
See Lippman: 1.4, 3.7

FAQ 333

Does const **imply run-time overhead?**

No.

All tests for constness are done at compile-time. Neither run-time space nor speed are degraded.

∎

Cross references—

FAQ: 332
See Stroustrup: 2.5, r.7
See Ellis & Stroustrup: 7.1, 9.3
See Lippman: 1.4, 3.7

FAQ 334

Is const **correctness worthwhile?**

Yes.

Declaring the constness of a parameter or variable is just another form of type safety; therefore, const correctness can be considered an extension of C++'s type system. Type safety provides some degree of semantic integrity by promising that, for instance, something declared as a String cannot be used as an int. However, const correctness guarantees even tighter semantic correctness by making sure that data that is not intended to be changed cannot be changed. With const correctness, it is easier to reason about the correctness of your software and aids during software inspection.

It is almost as if const String and String are of different, but related, types. Because type safety helps produce correct software (especially large systems and applications), you should take advantage of const correctness.

■

Cross references—

FAQ: 332, 335, 336
See Stroustrup: 2.5, r.7
See Ellis & Stroustrup: 7.1, 9.3
See Lippman: 1.4, 3.7

Is const **correctness tedious?**

No more tedious than declaring the type of a variable.

In C++, const correctness is simply another form of type information. In theory, expressing any type information is unnecessary, given enough programmer discipline and testing. In practice, developers often leave a lot of interesting information about their code in their heads where it cannot be exploited or verified by the compiler. For instance, when programmers write a function such as the following print() function, they know implicitly that they are passing by reference merely to avoid the overhead of passing by value; there is no intention of changing the String during the print() operation.

```
class String { };
void print(String& s);
```

If this information is documented only by comments in the code or in a separate manual, it is easy for these comments to become inconsistent with the code; the compiler can't read comments or manuals. The most cost-effective way to document this information is with the five-letter word const.

```
void print(const String& s);
```

This form of documentation is succinct, in one place, and can be verified and exploited by the compiler.

■

Cross references—

FAQ: 332, 334, 336
See Stroustrup: 2.5, r.7
See Ellis & Stroustrup: 7.1, 9.3
See Lippman: 1.4, 3.7

FAQ
336

Should you try to get things const **correct sooner or later?**

Sooner; retrofitting const **correctness is expensive.**

Adding constraints later can be difficult and expensive. If a function was not designed to handle a const object from the beginning, trying later to change it to handle a const object can cause a ripple through the system. For instance, suppose f() calls g(), and g() calls h().

```
#include "FAQ 459/String.h"    //see FAQ 459 for this file

void f(String& s);
void g(String& s);
void h(String& s);

void f(String& s)
{
  g(s);
}

void g(String& s)
{
  h(s);
}

void h(String& s)
{
  cout << s << '\n';
}

main()
{
  String s;
  f(s);
}
```

Changing f(String& s) to f(const String& s) will cause error messages until g(String&) is changed to g(const String&). But this change will cause error messages until h(String&) is changed to h(const String&), and so on. The ripple effect is magnificent—unless you have to pay for it.

The moral is: const correctness should be installed from the very beginning.

■

Cross references—
FAQ: 332, 334, 335, 459
See Stroustrup: 2.5, r.7
See Ellis & Stroustrup: 7.1, 9.3
See Lippman: 1.4, 3.7

What's the difference between an inspector and a mutator?

F A Q
337

Inspectors inspect, mutators mutate.

An inspector is a member function that returns information about an object's state without changing the object's abstract state. A mutator changes the state of an object in a way that is visible to outsiders: it changes the object's abstract state.

Here is an example.

```
class Stack {
public:
  int pop();              //mutator
  int numElems() const;   //inspector
};
```

The pop() service is a mutator because it changes the Stack by removing the top element. The numElems() service is an inspector because it simply counts the number of elements in the Stack without changing the Stack in a visible way. The const decoration after numElems() indicates that numElems() promises not to change this Stack.

Only inspectors may be applied to const objects.

```
void
sampleUserCode(const Stack& s)
{
  s.numElems();  //OK: You can inspect a const Stack

  #ifdef GENERATE_ERROR
    s.pop();      //Error: You cannot mutate a const Stack
  #endif
}
```

■   .

Cross references—

FAQ: 332, 336, 338, 339
See Stroustrup: 2.5, r.7
See Ellis & Stroustrup: 7.1, 9.3
See Lippman: 1.4, 3.7

F A Q 338

What is a const member function?

A member function that guarantees not to change this object's abstract state.

A const member function guarantees to leave this object unchanged. The compiler won't allow a const member function to change *this or to invoke a non-const member function for this object.

```
class Stack {
public:
  Stack();
  void push(int elem);
  int  pop();
  int  numElems() const;
protected:
  int numElems_;
  int data_[10];
};

int
Stack::numElems() const
{
  #ifdef GENERATE_ERROR
    ++numElems_;    //ERROR: can't modify *this
    pop();          //ERROR: pop() isn't an inspector
  #endif
  return numElems_;
}
```

■

Cross references—

FAQ: 332, 336, 337, 339
See Stroustrup: 2.5, r.7
See Ellis & Stroustrup: 7.1, 9.3
See Lippman: 5.3

F A Q

339

Does const **refer to the object's bitwise state or abstract state?**

Abstract state.

The const modifier is a part of the class's public interface; therefore, it means what the public interface designer wants it to mean. From the user's perspective, the most important thing is that the compiler allows a const member function to be invoked on a const object.

As an interface designer, the most useful strategy is to tie const to the object's abstract state rather than to its bitwise state. There are situations when an object will change its bitwise state but not its abstract state, and vice versa.

For example, the following String class stores its string data on the heap, pointed to by the member datum data_.

```
class String {
public:
  String(const char* s);
 ~String();
  String(const String& s);
  String& operator= (const string& s);
  unsigned len() const;
  char& operator[] (unsigned index);
  char  operator[] (unsigned index) const;
  void toUpper();  //capitalizes (*this)[i] for valid i
protected:
  unsigned len_;
  char* data_;
};
```

The abstract state of an object s of class String is represented by values returned from s[i], where i ranges from 0 to s.len() - 1 inclusive. The bitwise state of a String is represented by the bits of s itself (that is, by s.len_ and s.data_).

Even though s.toUpper() doesn't change s.len_ or s.data_, String::toUpper() is a non-const service because it changes the abstract state (the state from the user's perspective).

■

Cross references—

FAQ: 332, 337, 338
See Stroustrup: 2.5, r.7
See Ellis & Stroustrup: 7.1, 9.3
See Lippman: 1.4

F A Q
340

When should you avoid using const in declaring formal parameters?

When const doesn't make sense.

Do not use const for formal parameter types that are passed by value. This is because passing parameters by value already implies that the caller's object isn't changed. That is, when const is used with pass by value, it uses the function's interface to export implementation details that are superfluous to users. In practice, this can be confusing. For example, replace f(const Fred x) with either f(const Fred& x) or f(Fred x).

Additionally, do not use Fred* const in a formal parameter list. The rationale is the same as described above. For example, replace f(Fred* const p) with f(Fred* p), and replace g(const Fred* const p) with g(const Fred* p).

Finally, do not use Fred& const in any context, because a reference can never be rebound to a different object.

■

Cross references—
FAQ: 300, 341
See Lippman: 3.7

When should you avoid using const in declaring a function return type?

When const **doesn't make sense.**

In a function that returns its result by value, avoid const in the return type. For example, replace const Fred f() with either Fred f() or const Fred& f(). Using const Fred f() can be confusing to users, especially in the idiomatic case of copying the return result into a local.

The exception to this rule is when users apply a member function of Fred directly to the temporary returned from the function, and when the user wants to get const overloading on that member function. An example follows.

```
#include <iostream.h>

class Fred {
public:
  void wilma()            { cout << "Fred::wilma()\n"; }
  void wilma() const      { cout << "Fred::wilma() const\n"; }
};

      Fred f()            { return Fred(); }
const Fred g()            { return Fred(); }

main()
{
  f().wilma();
  g().wilma();
}
```

Because f() returns a Fred, f().wilma() invokes the non-const version of Fred::wilma(); in contrast, g().wilma() invokes the const version of Fred::wilma(). Thus, the output of this program is as follows.

```
Fred::wilma()
Fred::wilma() const
```

■

Cross references—
FAQ: 300, 340

What is operator overloading?

Syntactic sugar for normal functions.

Operator overloading allows existing C++ operators to be redefined so that they work on objects of user-defined classes. Overloaded operators are syntactic sugar for equivalent function calls. They form a pleasant facade that doesn't add anything fundamental to the language (but they can improve understandability and reduce maintenance costs).

For example, suppose you have a class Number that supports the services add() and mul().

```
class Number {
public:
   friend Number add(Number a, Number b);
   friend Number mul(Number a, Number b);
};

Number f(Number a, Number b, Number c)
{
   return add(add(mul(a,b), mul(b,c)), mul(c,a));
}
```

Using named functions (that is, add() and mul()) makes f() unnecessarily difficult to read, write, and maintain. Instead, you can use operators + and * for class Number in the same way they are used for the built-in numeric types.

```
inline Number operator+ (Number a, Number b)
  { return add(a, b); }
inline Number operator* (Number a, Number a)
  { return mul(a, b); }

Number g(Number a, Number b, Number c)
{
  return a*b + b*c + c*a;
}
```

■

Cross references—

FAQ: 51, 343, 344
See Stroustrup: 7
See Ellis & Stroustrup: 5, 13.4
See Lippman: 6.3

F A Q
343

Is operator overloading good or bad?

Yes; it is good or bad.

Operator overloading is a powerful feature that can substantially improve the readability of user code. However, operator overloading should be used only in ways that are semantically familiar to users. For instance, it would be non-intuitive if a `class` used `operator+` for subtraction.

■

Cross references—

FAQ: 51, 342, 344
See Stroustrup: 7
See Ellis & Stroustrup: 5, 13.4
See Lippman: 6.3

What operators can be overloaded?

Almost all of them.

The only C operators that can't be overloaded are dot (.), arithmetic if (?:) and size (sizeof). C++ adds a few of its own operators, most of which can be overloaded except for :: and .*.

Here's an example of an array-like class without operator overloading.

```
class Array {
public:
  int& elem(unsigned i)    { return data_[i]; }
protected:
  int data_[100];
};

void
useArray()
{
  Array a;
  a.elem(10) = 42;
  a.elem(12) = 10;
  a.elem(12) += a.elem(10);
}
```

The member function elem(unsigned) returns a reference to the ith element of the Array. A better solution (that is, one whose user syntax is more intuitive) would replace elem with operator[].

```
class NewArray {
public:
  int& operator[] (unsigned i)    { return data_[i]; }

protected:            └──▶ formerly was "elem"
  int data_[100];
};

main()
{
  NewArray a;
  a[10] = 42;
  a[12] = 10;
  a[12] += a[10];
}
```

■

Cross references—

FAQ: 51, 342, 343
See Stroustrup: 7
See Ellis & Stroustrup: 5, 13.4
See Lippman: 6.3

F A Q
345

How can you create a `**` operator as an exponentiation operator?

You can't.

The names of, precedence of, associativity of, and arity (number of arguments) of operators is fixed by the language. There is no `**` operator in the base language C++, so you can't create one for a user-defined (`class`) type.

In fact, the expression `x ** y` is already syntactically legal C++. It means, "x multiplied by `*y`" (that is, `y` is treated like a pointer that is dereferenced). If C++ allowed users to provide new meaning to `**`, the compiler's lexical analyzer (the lowest level operation in the compiler) would need to be contextually dependent upon the semantic analyzer (the highest level operation in the compiler). This would probably introduce ambiguities and break existing code.

Operator overloading is merely syntactic sugar for function calls. Although syntactic sugar can be sweet, it is not fundamentally necessary. Raising a number to a power is best performed by overloading `pow(base, exponent)`, for which a double precision version comes standard in the `<math.h>` header file.

Another candidate for an exponentiation operator is `operator^`, but it has neither the proper precedence nor associativity.

Don't force-fit the semantics of an overloaded operator.

■

Cross references—

FAQ: 51, 342, 344
See Stroustrup: 7
See Ellis & Stroustrup: 5, 13.4
See Lippman: 6.3

How should you handle related operators such as +=, +, and =?

Don't shock your users.

In classes that define +=, + and =, the expressions a += b and a = a + b should generally have the same observable behavior. Similar comments can be made for the other identities of the built-in types (for example, a += 1 and ++a should have the same observable behavior; p[i] and *(p+i) are equivalent; and so on).

One way to enforce these rules is to implement constructive binary operators using the corresponding mutative operators. For example, the code below implements + using +=.

```
class X {
public:
  friend X operator+ (const X& a, const X& b);
  X& operator+= (const X& b);
};

X
operator+ (const X& a, const X& b)
{
  X result = a;
  result += b;
  return result;
}
```

Note that it is sometimes possible to implement constructive operators more efficiently by not using the corresponding mutative operators.

■

Cross references—

FAQ: 51, 342, 344
See Stroustrup: 7
See Ellis & Stroustrup: 5, 13.4
See Lippman: 6.3

FAQ
347

How are the prefix and postfix versions of `operator++()` differentiated?

A dummy parameter.

The postfix version (i++) is called `operator++`, and has a dummy parameter of type `int`. The prefix version (++i) is also called `operator++`, but without any dummy parameters.

Here's an example.

```
#include <iostream.h>

class X {
public:
  void operator++ ()        { cout << "prefix ++i\n"; }
  void operator++ (int)     { cout << "postfix i++\n"; }
};

main()
{
  X i;
  ++i;
  i++;
}
```

The output of this program follows.

```
prefix ++i
postfix i++
```

■

Cross references—

FAQ: 51, 342, 344, 348, 371
See Stroustrup: 7
See Ellis & Stroustrup: 5, 13.4
See Lippman: 6.3

What should be returned by the prefix and postfix versions of X::operator++()?

++i should return a reference to i; i++ should return either void or a copy of the original state of i.

X::operator++() (the prefix version, ++i) should normally return *this by reference (in this case, as an X&).

X::operator++(int) (the postfix version, i++) should return either nothing (void), or a copy of the original state of the object, *this. In any event, it should *not* return an X& because that would confuse users. For example, i = j++ would mean the same thing as i = ++j (assuming j++ returns *this by reference).

Normally X::operator++(int) is implemented in terms of X::operator++(), as shown below.

```
#include <iostream.h>

class X {
public:
  X& operator++ ()
    { cout << "do the increment here\n"; return *this; }
  X operator++ (int)
    { X old = *this;  ++(*this);  return old; }
};

main()
{
  X i;
  ++i;
  i++;
}
```

Note that users shouldn't use i++ unless they need the old state of i. In particular, assuming i is a user-defined (class) type, i++ may create an unnecessary copy of i when compared with ++i.

■

Cross references—

FAQ: 51, 321, 342, 344, 347, 371
See Stroustrup: 7
See Ellis & Stroustrup: 5, 13.4
See Lippman: 6.3

Are `inline` **functions relevant on modern hardware?**

Very.

Modern hardware is able to prefetch instructions along unconditional call paths such that the cost of the CALL instruction itself can be reduced to zero. However, the cost of the CALL instruction is a very small part of the overall cost of a function call, especially on RISC processors.

Assuming best-case cache line performance (zero cache line misses), a typical RISC machine might require 25 cycles for a function call. This figure includes all of the stack activity, setting up the activation record, the cost of the return linkage, the cost for the CALL instruction itself, and the lost optimization opportunity that would have occurred if the function had been expanded inline. If the function has several parameters, the cycle count rises accordingly.

The most significant cost of a function call on a RISC box is that the compiler is unable to optimize register usage *through* the call (procedural integration). Typically, the caller's temporaries are pushed onto some stack (possibly a register stack), then the called routine loads the parameters into some registers (possibly back into the same registers where they already reside), and computes temporary values (possibly regenerating the same temporaries that are already in some other registers). Register calling conventions and register stacks help, but the only way to fully exploit the power of a RISC box is for the optimizer to procedurally integrate the called code stream into the caller's code stream; in other words, to avoid the call entirely.

■

Cross references—

FAQ: 92
See Stroustrup: 1.5, 4.6, 5.3
See Ellis & Stroustrup: 7.1, 7.4, 16.1c
See Lippman: 3.2

**FAQ
350**

When should you use an `inline` function?

When performance is critical.

Define a function as `inline` when the function is called along a critical path, and when the overhead of the function call linkage is large compared with the cost of the work that the function will do.

Whatever you do, don't worry about it until you've actually measured your system to see where the bottlenecks are located.

■

Cross references—

FAQ: 351
See Lippman: 3.2

**FAQ
351**

What trade-offs are involved when using `inline` functions?

They aren't so obvious.

Trade-off #1: `inline` functions *can* improve performance, but they can also degrade performance.

Trade-off #2: `inline` functions *can* increase code size, but they can also decrease the code size.

Trade-off #3: `inline` functions *can* be easy to change, but they can also be impossible to change.

Please read the rest of this section, because these trade-offs are far too complicated to be reduced down to a simple sentence.

■

Cross references—
FAQ: 352, 353, 354

Do `inline` functions increase performance?

Not necessarily.

If an `inline` function expands to a lot of code, and if that function is called from many places in the code, there can be a significant increase in the size of the generated executable object code. This can eventually lead to thrashing on systems that use demand paged virtual memory.

Paging performance can also be improved by `inline` functions, since they provide locality of reference which improves both virtual memory performance and the hit ratio of the processor's cache lines. Thus, in practice, most systems can withstand modest code bloat before their performance begins to degrade. Naturally, memory-constrained systems have tighter requirements.

Fortunately, C++ makes it relatively easy to change functions from `inline` to non-`inline`, provided your `inline` function definition has been moved outside the class body. Thus, `inline` performance tuning can be done fairly late in the product cycle.

■

Cross reference—
FAQ: 356

Do `inline` functions increase code size?

Not necessarily.

First, some functions are so small that the compiler may generate more code to call the function than it would to expand the body of the function inline. Second, inlining a function allows the optimizer to procedurally integrate the code into the caller, improving its chances of detecting and removing dead (unreachable) code from the caller.

When compiling the following example, turning inline expansion on will probably produce smaller object and executable files, especially if optimization is also turned on (this experiment is highly system- and compiler-dependent).

```
class Stack {
public:
  Stack()                       : len_(0) { }
  void push(int elem)           { data_[len_++] = elem;     }
  int  pop()                    { return data_[--len_];     }
  int  top()     const          { return data_[len_-1];     }
  bool full()    const          { return len_ == dataMax_;  }
  bool empty()   const          { return len_ == 0;         }
protected:
  enum           { dataMax_ = 10 };
  unsigned   len_;
  int        data_[dataMax_];
};

main()
{
  Stack s;
  s.push(0);  s.push(1);  s.push(2);  s.push(3);  s.push(4);
  s.push(5);  s.push(6);  s.push(7);  s.push(8);  s.push(9);
  s.pop();    s.pop();    s.pop();    s.pop();    s.pop();
  s.pop();    s.pop();    s.pop();    s.pop();    s.pop();
}
```

One of the compilers we tested this with showed that inlining decreased the code size by better than 33%.

FAQ 354

What is the cost of changing an `inline` function?

It's a political issue, not a technical issue.

A fundamental property of inline expansion is that the compiler copies server code into the user's code stream. Therefore, if `inline` functions are visible to customers, releasing a subsequent version of your class(es) that has different `inline` code will force your customers to recompile their code. If your customers cannot or will not recompile their software, you may have to limit your use of `inline` functions, at least in those classes that are visible to customers.

Note that most compilers synthesize `inline` routines for default construction, copy construction, assignment, and destruction. Therefore, if your customers want to remain binary-compatible with subsequent releases of your software, you may need to explicitly define these infrastructure routines as non-`inline`, at least for those classes that customers use directly.

Should you turn on inlining when debugging code?

F A Q
355

Probably not.

Most compilers provide an option to turn `inline` expansion on or off. Turning it on actually inlines at least some functions declared as `inline`. Turning `inline` expansion off creates an out-lined copy of functions declared as `inline`, and generates a CALL when these functions are invoked.

Generally speaking, debugging through an `inline` expanded function is more difficult than debugging through a normal CALL, so normally you should turn inline expansion off during debugging.

An exception to this guideline occurs when a defect only surfaces later in the life cycle, after inlining has been turned on (indeed, some defects show their symptoms only when inlining is turned on). In this case, inlining must be turned on during debugging so the defect can be reproduced.

How can you make it easy to swap between `inline` and non-`inline` code?

F A Q
356

With a little macro magic.

Turning off inline expansion via a compiler option does not improve compile-time performance, because the compiler must still parse the bodies of `inline` functions. Furthermore, depending on the compiler, turning off inline expansion may increase code bulk, because the compiler may create duplicate `static` copies of each `inline` function seen by the compiler during every compilation unit.

Although the preprocessor is usually considered evil, this is one of the areas where it can be used to bypass the compile-time overhead previously mentioned. The strategy is straightforward. First, define all `inline` functions outside the class body in a separate file (call this the `.inl` file). Then, in the `.inl` file, change the keyword `inline` to the preprocessor symbol INLINE. Finally, conditionally #include the `.inl` file in either the `.h` file or the .C file, depending on whether or not the user wants INLINE to become inline, or wants INLINE to expand to nothing.

File inline.h, following, defines a macro INLINE to be either the keyword inline or nothing, depending on whether the USE_INLINE symbol is #defined. For example, if your compiler supports the -D option as a way to #define a symbol, compiling with -DUSE_INLINE causes INLINE to become inline.

```
//File "inline.h"
#ifdef USE_INLINE
  #define INLINE  inline
#else
  #define INLINE  /*nothing*/
#endif
```

File Fred.h, shown below, defines class Fred with two member functions, f() and g(). If USE_INLINE is #defined, file Fred.inl is #included from Fred.h.

```
//File "Fred.h"
#ifndef Fred_h
#define Fred_h

#include "inline.h"

class Fred {
public:
  void f();
  void g();
};

#ifdef USE_INLINE
  #include "Fred.inl"
#endif

#endif //Fred_h
```

File Fred.inl, shown below, defines Fred::f() as optionally inline. Note that Fred.inl does not #include "Fred.h".

```
//File "Fred.inl"
#include <iostream.h>
```

```
INLINE   // <--not 'inline'
void
Fred::f()
{
  cout << "Fred::f() is optionally inlined\n";
}
```

File `Fred.C`, shown below, defines `Fred::g()` as non-inline. If
`USE_INLINE` is not #defined, file `Fred.inl` is #included from `Fred.C`.

```
//File "Fred.C"
#include "Fred.h"
#include <iostream.h>

#ifndef USE_INLINE
  #include "Fred.inl"
#endif

void
Fred::g()
{
  cout << "Fred::g() is never inlined\n";
}
```

Finally, file `UserCode.C`, shown below, uses a `Fred` object.

```
//File "UserCode.C"
#include "Fred.h"

main()
{
  Fred fred;
  fred.f();
  fred.g();
}
```

This strategy can be easily modified to allow class-specific inlining. First,
replace `USE_INLINE` with `USE_INLINE_Fred`. Then, replace `INLINE` with
`INLINE_Fred`. Finally, move the #ifdef `USE_INLINE_Fred` logic from
`inline.h` into `Fred.h`.

FAQ 357

Where should an `inline` function be defined?

Normally, in the same header file where it is declared, or in a `.inl` file `#included` from that header file.

The most common violation of this rule is when an `inline` function is declared in a header file but defined in a `.c` file. When this happens, the usual symptom is a linker error. This is because `inline` implies `static`.

For example, if `f()` is declared in `A.h` and defined as `inline` in `A.c`, and if `B.c` calls `f()`, the compiler and linker won't know where to find the code for `f()`.

Note that a small percentage of `inline` functions are solely for use by a particular `.c` file. In these cases, the `inline` functions can be both declared and defined in the `.c` file.

■

Cross reference—
FAQ: 358

FAQ 358

Why is the linker complaining about undefined externals for my `inline` functions?

Probably because you've defined an `inline` function in a `.c` file.

Remember this simple rule of thumb: non-`inline` function should be defined in `.c` files; `inline` functions should be defined in `.h` or `.inl` files. As discussed in the previous FAQ, there are some minor exceptions to this guideline.

■

Cross references—
FAQ: 357, 359

FAQ
359

Why would the linker complain about multiply defined non-inline functions?

Probably because there's a non-inline function defined in a header file.

If a non-inline function is defined in a header file, and that header file is #included in several compilation units, the linker may see several definitions for the function. Either define the function with the inline keyword, or move the definition into a .c (or .cpp) file.

■

Cross references—
FAQ: 357, 358

FAQ
360

Why would the compiler complain about defining an inline function after it is used?

Inline functions must be defined before they are used.

The class developer typically must shuffle the definitions of inline functions until these errors go away. Some developers also declare their inline functions with the inline keyword (rather than just defining them with the inline keyword), however this makes it harder to move code between a .c file and a .h file.

■

Cross reference—
FAQ: 356

What's the cost of changing a default parameter?

The more existing users you have, the more expensive it is to change.

A function with N default parameters is like a function with N required parameters, plus N other `inline` functions that pass the default values to the function with N required parameters. So changing a default parameter has exactly the same problems as changing an `inline` function; users must usually recompile their code.

Thus, unless you are able to simulate the same observable behavior as the old default value yielded, you will break binary compatibility; users will have to recompile their code so that the compiler will use the new default value.

Worse, unless you are able to simulate the same observable behavior with the *new* default value, you will break source compatibility. Users will have to change their code explicitly to use the old default value.

Rule of thumb: Don't do it.

■

Cross reference—
FAQ: 354

What are reference and value semantics?

Reference semantics imply that assignment copies a pointer to the object; value semantics imply that assignment copies the state of the object.

With reference semantics, names for objects are implicitly pointers and assignment copies the pointer but doesn't change the object's state (assignment creates an alias). With value semantics (also known as copy semantics), assignment copies the state, not just the pointer.

Most OO programming languages other than C++ directly support reference semantics, and require an alternate user-defined syntax for copying state (for example, `clone()`, `shallowCopy()`, `deepCopy()`, and so on). C++ gives you a choice: use the assignment operator to copy the state (value or copy semantics), or use a pointer copy to copy the pointer (reference semantics). C++ allows you to override the assignment operator to do anything your heart desires, but the default (and most common) choice is to copy the state.

■

Cross references—
FAQ: 363, 364
See Stroustrup: 5.4
See Ellis & Stroustrup: 10.7c

What are some advantages of reference semantics?

Flexibility and dynamic binding.

Almost all flexibility in software comes with an extra layer of indirection (arrays, dynamic data structures, recursion, and so on). Not surprisingly, dynamic binding also depends on an extra layer of indirection.

```cpp
#include <iostream.h>

class Base {
public:
  virtual void f()     { cout << "Base::f()\n"; }
};

class Derived : public Base {
public:
  virtual void f()     { cout << "Derived::f()\n"; }
};

void
sampleUserCode(Base x, Base& y, Base* z)
{
  x.f();               //always calls Base::f()
  y.f();               //calls the "right" f()
  z->f();              //calls the "right" f()
}

main()
{
  Derived x, y, z;
  sampleUserCode(x, y, &z);
}
```

The output of this program follows.

```
Base::f()
Derived::f()
Derived::f()
```

■

Cross references—

FAQ: 16, 89, 362, 364
See Stroustrup: 5.4
See Ellis & Stroustrup: 10.7c

What are some advantages of value semantics?

Speed.

Even though value semantics produces slower assignment operations (the state must be copied, not just a pointer to the state), value semantics reduces the number of indirections, thereby enhancing the performance of other operations associated with an object. Thus using value semantics is often an overall performance winner, because an object is usually accessed more often than it is copied.

■

Cross references—

FAQ: 362, 363, 365, 366, 368
See Stroustrup: 5.4
See Ellis & Stroustrup: 10.7c

How can value semantics in C++ improve performance?

By eliminating function calls.

Virtual function calls can be inlined when the compiler can use static binding (that is, when it knows the object's exact class). If a function doesn't do very much (a candidate for inlining), then inline expansion of the function call can improve performance significantly.

As an extreme example, a simple fetch function might only do 3 cycles' worth of work, yet including the overhead of the virtual function call might cost a total of 30 cycles. In this case, it would take 27+3 cycles to do 3 cycles' worth of work. If this were on a critical path and the operation could be inlined, reducing the overhead of this operation by a factor of 10 could be significant.

■

Cross references—

FAQ: 93, 349, 362, 364, 366, 368
See Stroustrup: 5.4
See Ellis & Stroustrup: 10.7c

How can knowing an object's exact class improve performance?

This knowledge allows the compiler to de-virtualize calls to virtual member functions.

When an object's exact class is known, the compiler can use static binding even when calling virtual functions. In these cases, the overhead associated with dynamic binding can be bypassed.

For example, in the function pushStuff() following, the compiler cannot assume that the exact class of a is Stack, because pushStuff() may be called from places other than main() (that is, someone might pass an object of some class derived from Stack, and that class might override push() or pop()). In contrast, the compiler knows that the exact class of b is Stack, so b.push(42) can be statically bound to Stack::push(int). Since Stack::push(int) is defined as inline, all the overhead associated with the call to b.push(42) can be eliminated.

```
#include <iostream.h>

class Stack {
public:
  Stack()                    : numElems_(0) { }
  virtual void push(int x)   { data_[numElems_++] = x; }
  virtual int pop()          { return data_[--numElems_]; }
protected:
  int data_[10];
  int numElems_;
};

void
pushStuff(Stack& a)
{
  Stack b;
  a.push(42);    //must use dynamic binding
  b.push(42);    //can use static binding
}

main()
{
  Stack a;
  pushStuff(a);
}
```

■

Cross references—

FAQ: 93, 362, 364, 365, 367, 368
See Stroustrup: 5.4
See Ellis & Stroustrup: 10.7c

F A Q

367

When does the compiler know the exact class of an object?

When the object is a local variable, a global or static variable, or a fully contained member object of another class.

The most common (and therefore most important) of these is the last—the compiler knows the exact class of a member object. For example, the call x_.f() can be statically bound to X::f(), because the exact class of member object x_ is known to be X.

```
class X {
public:
  virtual void f() { }
};

class Y {
public:
  void g() { x_.f(); }
protected:
  X x_;
};

main()
{
  Y y;
  y.g();
}
```

■

Cross references—

FAQ: 362, 364, 365, 366, 368
See Stroustrup: 5.4
See Ellis & Stroustrup: 10.7c

How can fully contained member objects improve performance?

Eliminating freestore operations, layers of indirection, and function calls.

Compared to a pointer member that points to a freestore allocated object, fully contained member objects avoid the extra layer of indirection on each access, avoid the freestore operation on each construction and destruction, and the compiler can bypass the dynamic binding on each service invocation on the member object.

In the example following, `SampleClass::a_` is a `Stack*`, so the compiler knows that `*a_` is *at least* a `Stack`, but `*a_` isn't necessarily *exactly* a `Stack` (for example, member function `SampleClass::muddle()` might make `a_` point to something derived from `Stack`). In contrast, the compiler knows that the exact class of `b_` is `Stack`, therefore the invocation `b_.push(42)` can be statically bound to `Stack::push(int)`.

```
#include <iostream.h>

class Stack {
public:
  Stack()                      : numElems_(0) { }
  virtual void push(int x)     { data_[numElems_++] = x; }
  virtual int pop()            { return data_[--numElems_]; }
protected:
  int data_[10];
  int numElems_;
};

class SampleClass {
public:
  SampleClass() : a_(new Stack), b_() { }
 ~SampleClass() { delete a_; }
  SampleClass(const SampleClass& s);
  SampleClass& operator= (const SampleClass& s);
  void pushStuff();
  void muddle();
protected:
  Stack* a_;
  Stack  b_;
};
```

```
void
SampleClass::pushStuff()
{
  a_->push(42);    //must use dynamic binding
  b_.push(42);     //can use static binding
}

main()
{
  SampleClass x;
  x.pushStuff();
}
```

■

Cross references—

FAQ: 93, 362, 364, 365
See Stroustrup: 5.4
See Ellis & Stroustrup: 10.7c

Is bad performance a result of bad design or bad coding?

F A Q
369

All too often, bad performance is due to bad design.

When bad performance is due to bad coding practices, the correction is relatively inexpensive. However, when OO has been used improperly, the design is usually broken, and performance problems are not easily repaired.

Improper inheritance is typically the root problem. When inheritance is used improperly, the design often becomes brittle, and performance-related changes are prohibitively expensive. For example, some designs use inheritance as the means to put objects into a container. If you want to put objects in a List, for example, you inherit from a particular base class, often called ListElement, ListItem, or Linkable. The apparent motivation is to share the next pointer among all the derived classes, but the cost is enormous. In particular, the List class loses type safety (not all things that are linkable should be linked into the same list), and most importantly, user code becomes tacitly aware of the technique used to implement the list. This implementation dependency can inhibit performance tuning. These costs are manageable on a small ("toy") application, but as the application or system grows, the costs of improper inheritance become unbearable.

A better solution for the container problem is to use templates for type safety, and design a proper abstraction that hides the "list"ness from users. You can tell if your abstractions are designed well by asking: "Would it disturb user code if I changed this particular data structure from a linked list to an array?" If the answer is no, your abstraction will allow late life-cycle performance tuning, since you'll be free to change data structures or algorithms on an individual container-by-container basis. Code sharing among template classes can be accomplished by inheriting from a non-template base class.

■

Cross reference—
FAQ: 28

Can the language being used—rather than just the compiler—impact the performance of a software product?

Yes.

Statements such as, "C++ can ... produce faster executables" (FAQ-446) suggest that the efficiency of the executable is, at least in part, due to the language rather than simply the compiler. For example, compilers for dynamic typed languages cannot statically resolve member function invocations, because every member function is `virtual`, and every object is passed by pointer. Therefore, every member function dispatch needs to go through the dynamic-binding mechanism, which generally costs a function call. Thus, a member function with 10 statements will, in many OO languages, almost necessarily cost at least 10 function calls. The efficiency of the dynamic-binding mechanism can be improved, but it rarely can be improved enough to inline-expand these calls (a technique called customization can alleviate some of these issues in dynamically typed OO programming languages).

Languages such as C++ require the compiler to work harder, since not all member functions are necessarily `virtual`, and even if they are all `virtual`, not all objects are allocated from the heap. In addition, statically bound member functions can be expanded inline.

■

Cross references—
FAQ: 349, 368, 446

Should programmers use ++i or i++?

Use ++i unless you need the old value of i.

The expression i++ usually returns a copy of the old state of i. This requires that an unnecessary copy be created, as well as an unnecessary destruction of that copy. For built-in types (for example, int), the optimizer can eliminate the extra copies, but for user-defined (class) types, the compiler must retain the extra constructor and destructor unless it can guarantee they are free from side effects.

If you need the old value of i, i++ may be appropriate; but if you're going to discard the old value of i, ++i makes more sense.

Here's an example.

```
#include <iostream.h>

class Number {
public:
  Number()                       { }
  ~Number()                      { cout << "dtor "; }
  Number(const Number&)          { cout << "copy "; }
  Number& operator= (const Number&) { cout << "assign ";
                                   return *this; }
  Number& operator++ ()          { cout << "increment ";
                                   return *this; }
  Number  operator++ (int)       { Number old = *this;
                                   ++(*this);
                                   return old; }
};

main()
{
  Number n;
  { cout << "++n:  ";  ++n; } cout << '\n';
  { cout << "n++:  ";  n++; } cout << '\n';
}
```

The output of this program follows.

```
++n:  increment
n++:  copy increment copy dtor dtor
dtor
```

The postfix increment creates two copies of the Number—the local object inside Number::operator++(int), and the return value of the same. The third output line is the destruction of n itself.

Note that the postfix increment operator, Number::operator++(int), can be made to return void rather than the Number's former state. This puts the performance of n++ on a par with ++n, but forfeits the ability to use n++ in an expression.

■

Cross references—

FAQ: 51, 342, 344, 347, 348
See Stroustrup: 7
See Ellis & Stroustrup: 5, 13.4

FAQ 372

What is the performance difference between TypeName x(5); and TypeName y = 5; and TypeName z = TypeName(5);?

In practice, none. Therefore use the one that looks right.

Each of the above declarations initializes an object of type TypeName using the single-parameter constructor that takes an int (that is, TypeName::TypeName(int)). Even though the last two definitions use the equal sign, none of them use TypeName's assignment operator. In practice, none of them will create extra temporaries either.

```
#include <iostream.h>

class Fred {
public:
  Fred(int)                  { cout << "Fred ctor "; }
  Fred(const Fred&)          { cout << "Fred copy "; }
  void operator= (const Fred&) { cout << "Fred assign "; }
};

main()
{
  cout << "1: ";  Fred x(5);         cout << '\n';
  cout << "2: ";  Fred y = 5;        cout << '\n';
  cout << "3: ";  Fred z = Fred(5);  cout << '\n';
}
```

For most (if not all) commercial grade C++ compilers, the output of this program is the same.

```
1: Fred ctor
2: Fred ctor
3: Fred ctor
```

Because they cause the same code to be generated, use the one that looks right. If class Fred was actually Fraction, and 5 was the value of the numerator, the clearest would be the second or third. If Fred was actually Array, and 5 was the length of the Array, the clearest would be the first or the third.

Note that if the user cannot access the copy constructor (for example, if the developer of the class made the copy constructor private), only the first example is legal. Assuming the compiler makes the appropriate optimization (a fairly safe assumption), the copy constructor won't actually be called; the user needs access to it as if it was called.

■

Cross references—
FAQ: 168, 173
See Stroustrup: 7.6
See Ellis & Stroustrup: 8.4

What does I/O in C++ look like compared to I/O in C?

It looks funny. But you'll get used to it.

The functions `printf()` and `scanf()` are still supported, but `<<` and `>>` are preferred for the reasons discussed below.

The function `operator<<` (the left shift operator) is used for printing an object, while `operator>>` (the right shift operator) is used for reading an object. A comparison of the different I/O syntaxes follows.

```
/* C syntax */                 // C++ syntax
#include <stdio.h>             #include <iostream.h>

float                          float
readValue(int n)               readValue(int n)
{                              {
  float f;                       float f;
  printf("%d: ", n);             cout << n << ": ";
  scanf("%f", &f);               cin >> f;
  return f;                      return f;
}                              }
```

The overloaded shift operator syntax is strange at first, but it grows on you. However, syntax is just syntax; the real issues are deeper, as discussed in the following questions and answers.

■

Cross references—

FAQ: 374, 375, 376, 377, 378
See Stroustrup: 1.3, 10
See Lippman: Appendix A

FAQ 374

How can <iostream.h> **help reduce errors relative to** <stdio.h>**?**

Improved type safety and less duplication.

The functions scanf and printf are interpreters of a tiny language, made up mainly of "%" fields (format specifiers). The correct I/O primitive is selected dynamically by assuming the format specifier and the actual argument are compatible (if they aren't compatible, garbage is printed or your program crashes). The programmer is required to provide duplicate information in the format specifier and the actual argument.

With C++ I/O streams, users provide only the object to be read or written; the compiler selects the correct I/O primitive at compile-time via the rules of function overloading. Therefore, the selected primitive is always compatible with respect to the actual argument (that is, type safe).

■

Cross references—

FAQ: 373, 375, 376, 377, 378
See Stroustrup: 1.3, 10
See Lippman: Appendix A

FAQ 375

How can <iostream.h> **help improve extensibility relative to** <stdio.h>**?**

C++ allows I/O to occur on user-defined types as well as built-in types.

The C++ I/O mechanism allows new user-defined data types to be written and read using the same syntax as is used for built-in types (that is, << and >>). This extensibility would be analogous to adding new "%" fields to the switch statement that is used within the implementation of scanf() and printf().

C++ allows user-defined types (classes) to look and act like built-in types.

■

Cross references—

FAQ: 374, 376
See Stroustrup: 1.3, 10
See Lippman: Appendix A

How can `<iostream.h>` help improve flexibility relative to `<stdio.h>`?

C++ separates the code that formats an object from the code that performs I/O of the byte stream produced or consumed by such a formatting. This separation allows replacement of the underlying I/O mechanisms without the need to rewrite the formatting code.

In particular, classes `ostream` and `istream` (the C++ replacements for `FILE*`) are real classes; hence users can create derived classes. User-defined types can thus look and act like streams, but don't necessarily have to use the same underlying I/O mechanisms.

The formatting code written for both user-defined and built-in types will work correctly with these new classes derived from `ostream` or `istream`.

■

Cross references—
FAQ: 374, 375
See Stroustrup: 1.3, 10
See Lippman: Appendix A

How can you provide printing for objects of a class?

Provide a friend `operator<<`.

Here's an example.

```
#include <iostream.h>

class X {
public:
   friend ostream& operator<< (ostream& ostr, const X& x);
protected:
   int i_;
};

ostream&
operator<< (ostream& ostr, const X& x)
{
   return ostr << x.i_;
}
```

The function `operator<<` is a friend rather than a member because the x parameter appears on the right side of the <<.

∎

Cross references—

FAQ: 238, 241, 373, 374, 375, 376, 378
See Stroustrup: 1.3, 10
See Lippman: Appendix A

F A Q
378

How can you provide stream input for objects of a class?

Provide a friend `operator>>`.

Here's an example.

```
#include <iostream.h>

class X {
public:
   friend ostream& operator<< (ostream& ostr, const X& x);
   friend istream& operator>> (istream& istr, X& x);

protected:                                            ⌐→ not const
   int i_;
};

istream&
operator>> (istream& istr, X& x)
{
   return istr >> x.i_;
}
```

The x argument of `operator>>` is passed by reference (as opposed to by const reference) so `operator>>` can change the caller's x.

∎

Cross references—

FAQ: 238, 241, 373, 374, 375, 376, 378
See Stroustrup: 1.3, 10
See Lippman: Appendix A

STATIC CLASS MEMBERS | 33

What are static class members?

Data and functions that are associated with the class itself, rather than with any particular object of the class.

Static data members are often referred to as class data, and static member functions are often referred to as class services or class methods.

■

Cross reference—
See Lippman: 5.6

What is an analogy for static data members?

Static data members are like data located in the factory, rather than data located in the objects produced by the factory.

In Detroit, there's a big sign with a running total of the number of cars produced during the current year. But, you won't find that information under the hood of your car; all your car knows is a serial number indicating *its* ordinal number. The total number of cars produced is therefore factory data.

In the following example, class Car is the factory that is used to produce Car objects. Every car has a serial number (serial_). The factory keeps count of the number of existing cars via num_, which is a class datum; serial_ is an object (or instance) datum.

The constructors of class Car are responsible for incrementing the total number of cars; the destructor decrements the same.

```cpp
#include <iostream.h>

class Car {
public:

  Car()
    : serial_(num) { cout << "Car ctor\n"; ++num_; }
  Car(const Car& c)
    : serial_(c.serial_) { cout << "Car copy\n"; ++num_; }
  ~Car()
    { cout << "Car dtor\n";  --num_; }
  //explicit operator= isn't needed, it doesn't create Cars

  static int num_;    //class data

private:
  int serial_;        //object data
};

int Car::num_ = 0;    //class data is initialized before main
```

Just as a factory exists before it produces its first object, class data can be accessed before the first object is instantiated, as well as after the last object has been destroyed.

```cpp
main()
{
  cout << "Car::num_ = " << Car::num_ << '\n';
  {
    Car a;
    cout << "Car::num_ = " << Car::num_ << '\n';
    Car b;
    cout << "Car::num_ = " << Car::num_ << '\n';
    Car c = a;
    cout << "Car::num_ = " << Car::num_ << '\n';
  }
  cout << "Car::num_ = " << Car::num_ << '\n';
}
```

The output of this program follows.

```
Car::num_ = 0
Car ctor
Car::num_ = 1
Car ctor
Car::num_ = 2
Car copy
Car::num_ = 3
Car dtor
Car dtor
Car dtor
Car::num_ = 0
```

■

Cross reference—
See Lippman: 5.6

What is an analogy for static member functions?

Static member functions are like services attached to the factory, rather than services attached to the objects produced by the factory.

```
#include <stdlib.h>
#include <iostream.h>

class Car {
public:

  Car()
    : miles_(0) { cout << "Car ctor\n"; ++num_; }
  Car(const Car& c)
    : miles_(c.miles_) { cout << "Car copy\n"; ++num_; }
  ~Car()
    { cout << "Car dtor\n";  --num_; }
  //explicit operator= isn't needed, it doesn't create Cars
```

```
    static int num()   { return num_;   }   //class service
    int    odometer() { return miles_; }   //object service

    //object service (you drive a Car, not a factory):
    void   drive()     { ++miles_;      }

private:
  static int num_;     //class data
  int        miles_;   //object data
};

int Car::num_ = 0;     //class data initialized before main
```

Some services make sense only when applied to an object.

```
void
fiddleWithObject(Car& car)
{
  while (rand() % 10 != 0)
    car.drive();
  cout << "car.odometer() = " << car.odometer() << '\n';
}
```

Some services make sense only when applied to the factory.

```
void
fiddleWithClass()
{
  cout << "Car::num() returns " << Car::num() << '\n';

  #ifdef GENERATE_ERROR
    Car::drive();    //ERROR: can't drive a factory
    Car::odometer(); //ERROR: factories don't have odometers
  #endif
}
```

Since the factory exists before it produces its first object, you can request services from the factory before instantiating an object.

```
main()
{
  fiddleWithClass();

  {
    Car a;
    fiddleWithClass();
    fiddleWithObject(a);
  }

  fiddleWithClass();  ·
}
```

■

Cross reference—
See Lippman: 5.6

How is a static data member similar to a global variable?

A static data member is like a global variable with a funny name that needn't be public.

If your class has a static data member, there is only one copy of that datum even if there are many instances of the class. This is like a global variable. The difference is that a static data member has a funny (scoped) name (it doesn't pollute the global name space), and it needn't be public (static data members can be private, protected, or public).

These advantages allow you to use classes as your logical packaging device; modules are reduced to mere buckets of bits and code. You no longer use modules for hiding data (for instance, using file-scope static data to hide data in a module), since you can now hide data in a class. This distinction allows you to physically package your software in a way that may be different from the software's logical packaging. For example, you may wish to optimize your physical packaging based on page fault analysis, optimize for compile-time performance, optimize for maintainability, and so forth.

We rarely use global data any more. Normally we use objects and instance data, but when true global data is required, we almost always use static member data (that is, class-scope static data).

Cross reference—
See Lippman: 5.6

F A Q
383

How is a static member function similar to a friend function?

A static member function is like a friend function with a funny name that needn't be public.

Static member functions and file-scope friend functions are similar in that neither has an implicit `this` parameter, and both have direct access to the class's `private` and `protected` parts.

Except for overloaded operators, most of our friend functions end up actually being static member functions, because static member functions have a scoped name (they don't pollute the global name space), and static member functions don't have to be `public`—they can also be `private` or `protected`.

■

Cross reference—
See Lippman: 5.6

F A Q
384

What is the named constructor idiom?

An idiom that gives users a specific name for an operation that is similar to a constructor.

Occasionally, classes have a large suite of overloaded constructors. Because all constructors for a class have the same name, it can be confusing to select between the various overloaded constructors. When this happens, the named constructor idiom may be appropriate.

For example, consider a complex number class, Complex, that supports construction using either polar coordinates (magnitude, angle) or rectangular coordinates (real part, imaginary part). Unfortunately, these constructors are very similar; both constructors take two floats. Should Complex(2,1) be interpreted as specifying polar form ("2 at angle 1"), or as specifying rectangular form ("2 plus 1 times the imaginary constant")?

Many potential solutions exist to resolve this ambiguity; a boolean flag could indicate which is intended, or an extra dummy parameter on one of the constructors could be used to avoid run-time overhead by making the selection at compile-time rather than at run-time. However, the named constructor idiom is a bit more explicit.

```
class Complex {
public:
  Complex(float x=0.0)
    : a_(x), b_(0), rect_(true) { }
  static Complex rect(float real, float imag)
    { return Complex(real, imag, true); }
  static Complex polar(float mag,  float ang)
    { return Complex(mag, ang, false); }

private:
  Complex(float a, float b, bool rect)
    : a_(a), b_(b), rect_(rect)  { }
  float a_, b_;
  bool  rect_;
};
```

Both rect() and polar() are static member functions that operate like constructors. Users explicitly call whichever version they want.

```
main()
{
  Complex a;                         //0 + 0*sqrt(-1)
  Complex b = 3.14;                  //3.14 + 0*sqrt(-1)
  Complex c = Complex::rect(3,2);    //3 + 2*sqrt(-1)
  Complex d = Complex::polar(3,2);   //3 at 2 radians
}
```

■

Cross reference—

See Lippman: 5.6

FAQ 385

How should static member functions be called?

Explicitly name the class using ::.

For documentation purposes, calls to static member functions should be coded as `Classname::staticMember(...)` rather than coding it as `object.staticMember(...)` or `ptr->staticMember(...)`. The `::` reminds people that the member function is statically dispatched, and that the member function is attached to the class rather than to an individual object of the class.

Calling a static member function `Classname::f()` from another member function of class `Classname` is an exception to this rule. In this case, the call can be simply `f()`, since the meaning is usually clear in this context. When `Classname::f()` is a `protected` `static` member function of a base class, you must simply say `f()` rather than `Classname::f()`.

■

Cross reference—
See Lippman: 5.6

FAQ 386

Why is a class with static data members getting linker errors?

Static data members must be explicitly defined in exactly one module.

Here's an example.

```
class X {
public:
  static int i_;  //declare (vs define) static member X::i_
};
```

The linker will generate an error ("`X::i_` is not defined") unless (exactly) one of your source files defines `X::i_` as follows.

```
int X::i_ = 42;    //define (vs declare) static member X::i_
//int X::i_;        //without explicit initializer; also OK
```

You can (must) initialize X::i_ at file scope even when X::i_ is non-public. The usual place to define static member variables of class X is in the file X.C.

■

Cross references—

FAQ: 183, 185, 387
See Stroustrup: 5.4
See Ellis & Stroustrup: 3.1, 3.3, 9.4
See Lippman: 5.6

How is a constant static data member initialized?

F A Q
387

A constant static data member is declared in the class, and defined in some .C file. It must be initialized where it is defined.

Here's an example.

```
//File "Fred.h":
class Fred {
public:
  //public interface would go here...
private:
  static const int i_;
};

//File "Fred.C":
#include "Fred.h"
const int Fred::i_ = 100;
```

Constant static data members of type int are normally replaced by class scope enums. For example, the previous example can be replaced by the following enum.

```
class Fred {
public:
  //public interface would go here...
private:
  enum { i_ = 100 };
};
```

In either case, the constant is called Fred::i_.

■

Cross references—

FAQ: 183, 185, 386
See Stroustrup: 5.4
See Ellis & Stroustrup: 3.1, 3.3, 9.4
See Lippman: 5.6

How can C++ code call a C function?

You must tell the C++ compiler that the function has C linkage.

You do this with a declaration similar to the following.

```
extern "C" void f();
```

Specifically, the function prototype is preceded with extern "C". Be sure to include the full function prototype. A block of more than one C function can be grouped inside braces, as follows.

```
#include <stdlib.h>

extern "C" {
  void* malloc(size_t);
  char* strcpy(char* dest, const char* src);
  int   printf(const char* fmt, ...);
}
```

■

Cross references—

FAQ: 389, 390
See Stroustrup: r.2, r.18
See Ellis & Stroustrup: 16.2, 18.2
See Lippman: Appendix C

FAQ 389

How can you create a C++ function that is callable from C code?

You must tell the C++ compiler to provide the function with C linkage.

Use the same `extern "C"` construct as detailed in the previous FAQ, then define the function in your C++ code. The C++ compiler will ensure that the external information sent to the linker uses C calling conventions and name mangling. For example, the C++ compiler might precede the name with a single underscore, rather than the usual C++ name mangling scheme.

Obviously, you can't have several overloaded functions that are simultaneously callable by a C program, because name overloading isn't supported by C.

■

Cross references—

FAQ: 388, 390
See Stroustrup: r.2, r.18
See Ellis & Stroustrup: 16.2, 18.2
See Lippman: Appendix C

FAQ 390

Why is the linker giving errors for C functions being called from C++ functions and vice-versa?

Your `main()` should be compiled with your C++ compiler, and your C++ compiler should direct the linking process.

Your C++ compiler should be used to compile `main()` because it normally will embed C++ specific operations inside `main()` (for example, to deal with static initialization). Your C++ compiler should direct the linking process since it needs to deal with things such as C++ libraries, static initialization, and templates.

■

Cross references—

FAQ: 388, 389
See Stroustrup: r.2, r.18
See Ellis & Stroustrup: 16.2, 18.2
See Lippman: Appendix C

How can you pass an object of a C++ class to or from a C function?

With a layer of glue code.

The example that follows is a bilingual header file, readable by both a straight C compiler and a C++ compiler. Bilingual header files often use the preprocessor symbol __cplusplus, which is automatically #defined by C++ compilers, but is left undefined by C compilers.

```
/****** Bilingual C/C++ header file: Fred.h ******/
#ifdef __cplusplus
  class Fred {
  public:
    Fred()               : i_(0) { }
    void wilma(int i)    { i_ = i; }
  protected:
    int i_;
  };
#else
  struct Fred {
    int i_;
  };
#endif

#ifdef __cplusplus
  extern "C" {
#endif

extern void passClassToC   (struct Fred* p);
extern void passClassFromC(struct Fred* p, int param);

#ifdef __cplusplus
  }
#endif
```

The function passClassFromC() might be defined in a C++ file, such as cxx-code.C.

```
void
passClassFromC(struct Fred* p, int param)
{
  p->wilma(param);
}
```

The function `passClassToC()` might be defined in a C file, such as c-code.c.

```
void
passClassToC(struct Fred* p)
{
  passClassFromC(p, 123);
}
```

A `Fred` might be passed to the C code by `main()`. This is normally in a C++ module.

```
main()
{
  Fred fred;
  passClassToC(&fred);
}
```

Naturally, all of these .C and .c files would need to `#include "Fred.h"`.

Note that C code should not cast pointers that refer to C++ objects, because this can introduce errors, especially in cases where the pointer is returned to C++. For example, most compilers adjust the pointer during certain pointer casts involving multiple inheritance; the C compiler won't know how to do these adjustments.

The example code above assumes your C compiler supports ANSI-C function prototypes. Use `#ifdef __STDC__` to select code that only supports the old K&R C style.

■

Cross references—

FAQ: 392
See Stroustrup: r.2, r.18
See Ellis & Stroustrup: 16.2, 18.2
See Lippman: Appendix C

F A Q
392

Can a C function access data in an object of a C++ class?

Sometimes.

First read the previous FAQ on passing C++ objects to and from C functions. You can safely access a C++ object's data from a C function if the C++ class:

- has no virtual functions (including inherited virtual functions),

- has all its data in the same access level section (private, protected, or public), and

- has no fully-contained member objects that have virtual functions.

If the C++ class or its member object have any base classes, accessing the data will be technically non-portable, because the language does not mandate a specific class layout under inheritance. However, at least with non-virtual inheritance, all C++ compilers do it the same way—the base class object appears first (in left-to-right order in the event of multiple inheritance), and member objects follow.

If the class has any virtual base classes, it is more complicated and even less portable.

■

Cross references—

FAQ: 391
See Stroustrup: r.2, r.18
See Ellis & Stroustrup: 16.2, 18.2
See Lippman: Appendix C

Why does it seem that you are further from the machine when using C++ as opposed to C?

F A Q
393

Because you are.

Because C++ is an object-oriented programming language, it is designed to allow you to create and manipulate a model of the problem domain. Thus, C++ places a layer of abstraction between your software and the machine so that you can program in the language of the problem domain, rather than in the language of the computer.

■

Cross references—

FAQ: 29, 394
See Stroustrup: r.2, r.18
See Ellis & Stroustrup: 16.2, 18.2
See Lippman: Appendix C

Why does C++ do things behind your back?

Because it's not like C, where what you see is all you get.

One of C's great strengths is that it has no hidden mechanism. What you see is what you get. You can read a C program and see every clock cycle.

This is not the case in C++. As an OO programming language, C++ has different goals from C's. For instance, C++ calls constructors and destructors to initialize objects. Overloaded operators are another case in point— they provide a level of abstraction and economy of expression that lowers maintenance costs without destroying run-time performance. Long time C programmers are often ambivalent about these features, but they soon realize their benefits.

Naturally, you can write assembly code in any language; using C++ doesn't guarantee any particular level of quality, reusability, abstraction, or any other measure of goodness.

C++ enables reasonable developers to write superior software. It doesn't make it impossible for bad programmers to write bad programs.

■

Cross references—

FAQ: 29, 393
See Stroustrup: r.2, r.18
See Ellis & Stroustrup: 16.2, 18.2
See Lippman: Appendix C

How long does it take to learn C++?

One week for the basics, nine months for mastery.

In corporate settings, C programmers can learn the basics in a one week course; mastery takes experience, and there's no substitute for hands-on projects that allow concepts to gel.

■

Cross references—
FAQ: 396, 397
See Stroustrup: 12.1

How long does it take a good C programmer to become a good C++ programmer?

That's the wrong goal; instead become a good OO programmer who uses C++.

Using C++ as a better C will lead to only minor improvements in your software. Similarly, writing huge amounts of C++ code will not make you a good OO programmer. C programmers must learn to use the ++ part of C++, or the results will be lackluster. People who want the promise of OO must put the OO into OO programming.

For you and your organization to get the full benefits of OO technology, you must make the transition to OO design and OO programming. Using OO technology requires a new way of thinking—a paradigm shift—and this lets you make effective use of the facilities provided by C++.

■

Cross references—
FAQ: 395, 397
See Stroustrup: 12.1

How long does it take a good C programmer to become a good OO programmer?

Six months to three years, depending on your definition of good.

There are numerous plateaus of OO expertise. At each plateau you will become more proficient with OO technology. You will find new ways to use and combine OO features to develop more modular, robust, and extensible software. Becoming a good OO programmer is an iterative and incremental process.

It takes six to nine months to reach the first plateau. It takes three years of intense effort to reach the highest plateau.

■

Cross references—
FAQ: 395, 396
See Stroustrup: 12.1

What are the key factors in an organization's transition to using OO/C++ effectively?

There are five key factors.

1. **A commitment from corporate management.**

2. **High-quality trainers and training materials.**

3. A directed and focused training effort.

4. Intense application of OO technology on a realistic project.

5. Access to existing OO software that can serve as a model.

   Training an organization's individuals is not synonymous with transforming an organization. A cohesive technology transition plan must be developed and executed.

■

Cross references—
FAQ: 399, 400
See Stroustrup: 12.1

Why is corporate and management commitment important?

FAQ 399

Vision, resources, culture.

   While there are technical hurdles in moving to OO and C++, the most important factors are managerial and cultural. Management commitment is critical; without it, the transition will be slow and expensive. Thankfully, OO technology offers benefits that managers want, so management is generally willing to make the commitment. However, some organizations are unwilling to commit the resources that a long-term investment requires, such as appropriate training, tools, and schedules.

   The other issue affected by management's commitment is culture. This includes recognizing and rewarding development practices that promote reuse and reduce maintenance costs; adopting productivity metrics that encourage reuse; promoting reuse by ensuring that all components are properly specified and verified; investing in the establishment and maintenance of libraries and frameworks; and nurturing an environment that instills developers with team-oriented values such as altruism, selflessness, and cooperation.

■

Cross references—
FAQ: 398, 400
See Stroustrup: 12.1

400

What is the key goal of OO training?

Inspire developers to change the way they think and work.

OO instruction must describe more than the syntax of C++; the training must also include guidelines (so that developers know when to use a feature) and idioms (so that developers know how a feature can be combined with other features and with OO design methods). The instructor should be a practitioner in the field rather than merely a teacher who knows the syntax.

The instructor must do more than impart information. The instructor must change the way people think and work. This requires a significant emotional buy-in on the part of the students.

∎

Cross references—
FAQ: 399, 412, 413
See Stroustrup: 12.1

401

Why is intensity of use important?

Use it or lose it.

The sooner developers start using OO and C++, the more likely they are to retain the lessons and apply them effectively. It is also important to use the technology as intensely as possible. Dabbling with an OO design in your spare time is not nearly as effective as working with OO and C++ full time.

Developers can begin programming immediately after a good OO programming course, provided they have a decent design to work from. It takes a bit longer to develop the internal competence required to produce a good OO design, especially in the presence of conflicting priorities (for example, extensibility, high performance, and robustness).

∎

Cross references—
FAQ: 397, 398
See Stroustrup: 12.1

Why is access to good existing OO software important?

FAQ 402

Learn by emulation.

The time to master OO and C++ can be compressed if developers have regular access to both OO and C++ experts, and existing OO and C++ code that programmers can emulate and use. This process slows down if there isn't a good general purpose C++ class library available, or if the training doesn't provide a consistent philosophy for OO design and implementation.

■

Cross references—
FAQ: 398
See Stroustrup: 12.1

What are some strategies for training an organization to use OO and C++ ?

FAQ 403

In-house training, external professional classes, conference tutorials, self-training, videos, remote video links, and so forth.

■

Cross references—
FAQ: 398, 404
See Stroustrup: 12.1

Which strategy is the fastest and most effective?

FAQ 404

That depends on whether your organization is dabbling with the technology, or committed to applying the technology.

■

Cross references—
FAQ: 399, 403, 405, 406
See Stroustrup: 12.1

Does dabbling in OO produce representative results?

No.

OO is a strategic decision. If taught properly, it will impact the way your business operates from management through architecture, design, construction, testing, and maintenance.

If you want to dabble, you won't be able to build a business case for acquiring ideal training, therefore your people will not get a unified, cohesive philosophy that will bring stability to their organization and their software. In the long run, the lack of proper preparation will galvanize bad habits.

It's OK to run a pilot project, but if you want the results to mean something, you have to provide proper training, consulting, and tool support.

■

Cross references—
FAQ: 399, 403, 404, 406
See Stroustrup: 12.1

If you are committed to OO technology, which strategy is the fastest and most effective?

Active technology injection through interactive training provided by an experienced OO and C++ training organization.

This approach is the most appropriate when your organization sees the business value of OO and C++ and is fully committed to making the transition. In this case, active technology injection will get you to where you want to go as quickly as possible. Presumably the business value of making the transition to OO and C++ is significant (otherwise you wouldn't be going through all the hassle of it), so the relative cost of this approach is small.

■

Cross references—
FAQ: 398, 399, 400, 405
See Stroustrup: 12.1

What should programmers avoid when learning OO and C++?

Avoid reinventing the wheel.

- Do not invent your own training program.
- Do not invent your own consulting.
- Do not invent your own method.
- Do not invent your own language.
- Do not invent your own compilers and tools.
- Do not invent your own utility libraries.
- Do not invent your own coding standards.

Also, be aware that simply programming in C++ as a better C will give you only a fraction of the total benefits that OO technology offers. Issuing the developers a C++ compiler and letting them run with it is not the answer.

■

Cross references—
FAQ: 403, 406
See Stroustrup: 12.1

What are key qualities to look for in an OO and C++ training organization?

A symbiotic relationship between their organization and yours; and a trainer who is a practitioner who emphasizes a systematic approach, and who is teachable.

Symbiotic: Long-term consulting is grueling. The consultant shouldn't look at your training as just a job or money. The consultant's organization must have a long-term vision that provides an internal reason for *your* organization's success. Ask them if they have any motivation other than the immediate business opportunity. The *long*-term success of the consulting organization must be tied to your organization's *long*-term success.

Practitioner: Trainers and consultants must *earn* the trust of your organization's best developers. Find practitioners who can teach rather than teachers who know the material. If your project is large scale or complex, make sure you get practitioners with experience in large-scale or complex software systems. Experience is more valuable than theory.

Systematic: Find a training or consulting organization that emphasizes systematic solutions rather than random acts of heroism. Good systems make good people even better—good people with a good system outperform good people without a system.

Teachable: Beware of domain idiots. Domain idiots are the opposite of domain experts; they think their OO expertise makes them exempt from learning about your problem domain. High-quality results come from a marriage of domain expertise with OO expertise.

■

Cross references—

FAQ: 407
See Stroustrup: 12.1

F A Q
409

Who in the organization needs to learn OO?

Everyone.

It is important that everyone in the organization, including management, is acquainted with OO. OO has profound effects on all aspects of software development. Naturally, the needs of managers are different from those of developers, so the training will differ as well.

It is also critical that software architects learn about OO and C++, even if they do not normally write code. You cannot expect your organization to derive the benefits of OO technology unless that technology is effectively applied in all stages of product development. Some architects believe that they can't afford to write code; the truth is that they can't afford *not* to write code. If architects never write OO and C++ code, they'll never become effective OO architects. Software architects must write code, at least until they become unconsciously competent.

■

Cross references—

FAQ: 398, 399, 408, 411
See Stroustrup: 12.1

What else do you need to do to effectively use OO and C++?

Systemize.

A good software development process is critical to deriving the benefits of OO and C++ . This is because we demand so much more from OO than we do of procedural approaches—extensibility, maintainability, reusability, and so on. The only way to maximize all of these benefits is by using a disciplined software development process.

■

Cross references—
FAQ: 397, 398, 399, 406
See Stroustrup: 12.1

What are the stages of professional development?

Unconsciously incompetent, consciously incompetent, consciously competent, and unconsciously competent.

Someone at the unconsciously incompetent stage is typified by the haughty attitude that this is just another language or, "I've been using these techniques ever since I started programming." These are the people who don't listen long enough to discover how much they don't know.

A good trainer with good training materials will bring students up to the consciously incompetent stage before the first day is finished. Going to the next stage requires excellence on the part of the trainer and the materials, and drive on the part of the learner. Becoming unconsciously competent takes a long time and requires learning from your mistakes.

Certainly your OO trainers and consultants should be unconsciously competent.

■

Cross references—
FAQ: 397, 416

FAQ 412

Are all OO approaches the same?

No.

There are many different schools of thought in the OO world. If you randomly pick and choose OO courses and books, you will get conflicting and confused impressions of OO. The best way to avoid this is to choose one approach to OO and stick with it until you have enough experience to evaluate the other approaches. A directed training program provided by an experienced training organization will help guide you through this minefield.

■

Cross references—
FAQ: 400, 413
See Stroustrup: 12.1

FAQ 413

What does it mean that OO is evolving?

OO is a growing, changing field; new OO techniques are continually being discovered.

Your OO technology injection program can't ignore the innovations that are currently being added to the body of OO knowledge. A focused training program will bring you the latest ideas and techniques so that you don't have to stumble around for years learning all the lessons others have already learned.

One caveat—not everything that is new is also improved.

■

Cross references—
FAQ: 400, 412
See Stroustrup: 12.1

F A Q
414

Will OO succeed or will it eventually fail?

Both.

There is so much hype surrounding C++ and OO technology that people have unreasonable expectations that it is a silver bullet that will solve the software crisis. We believe this hype will create failures, and that there will be a crescendo of bad press about C++ and OO technology within 3 years. There are simply too many organizations that aren't properly preparing their troops to use OO, so failures are inevitable. Unfortunately, many people will blame the technology. In the mean time, other organizations will successful deploy the technology because they have reasonable expectations and are properly preparing their people.

In some cases, C++ and OO will succeed because it is properly applied in an environment where there are realistic expectations. These will be unqualified successes.

In some cases, C++ and OO will succeed because the project sponsors cannot afford for it to fail and, therefore, they will interpret any outcome as some sort of success. These will be questionable successes.

In some cases, the use of C++ and OO will be considered a failure because even though it is applied properly, it will not meet the (unrealistic) expectations of the project sponsors.

Finally, there will be cases where C++ and OO will fail simply because it is applied or executed improperly.

■

Cross references—
FAQ: 406, 407

F A Q
415

How risky is C++ and OO technology?

It all depends on how your organization deploys OO technology.

There is always a risk when adopting new technology. However, the risk associated with using C++ and OO technology is manageable and the potential payoff is significant. Using C++ and OO technology is generally not a gamble.

Defining a suitable plan for the transition to C++ and OO technology is the best way to manage this risk.

■

Cross reference—
FAQ: 416

How can you maximize your chances of success with OO technology?

Prepare. Prepare. Prepare.

First, define a transition plan. This plan should define specific business goals, should set realistic expectations, and should include a training program.

Defining specific business goals ensures that you know where you are going, why you are trying to get there, and what you will look like when you arrive.

Having realistic expectations ensures that you recognize what the capabilities of C++ and OO technology are, and that you do not oversell the technology. Having unrealistic expectations is the surest way to fail with C++ and OO technology.

Professional consulting and training services ensure that your team doesn't waste resources in reinvention.

■

Cross references—
FAQ: 407, 415

What is the potential payoff from using OO technology?

Faster, cheaper, better.

Faster because OO technology can reduce development time and speed time to market, especially for enhanced products (but beware of eating your seed corn; if you're never willing to invest, you'll never get the benefits of extensibility or reuse).

Cheaper because OO technology can reduce development, maintenance, and enhancement costs (but only if you've made some investment in developing software that is maintainable and extensible).

Better because OO technology can improve quality and increase customer satisfaction (but only if you're willing to shuffle your resource allocation to avoid big-bang testing and inspection).

When properly applied, OO technology is a key element in improving the software developed by your organization.

■

Cross references—
FAQ: 33, 38, 227

Are coding standards necessary?

Yes.

Coding standards discourage petty fragmentation when organizations coordinate the activities of diverse groups of programmers. They also promote portability of developers between different parts of the organization. Finally, the structure provided by coding standards gives neophytes one less degree of freedom to worry about.

Unfortunately, in some organizations coding standards have been created by those unfamiliar with the language or paradigm. In these cases, the standards end up based on what the state of the art *was* when those who set the standards were involved in implementation activities. Such impositions generate an attitude of mistrust for coding standards in general, and for those who set the standards in particular.

■

Cross references—
FAQ: 419, 420
See Stroustrup: 11, 12, 13

Are coding standards sufficient?

Never.

Coding standards—even OO coding standards—do not make non-OO programmers into OO programmers. Only training and experience make non-OO programmers into OO programmers.

■

Cross references—
FAQ: 418, 420
See Stroustrup: 11, 12, 13

FAQ
420

What else do you need besides coding standards?

A consistent design and implementation philosophy.

Such a philosophy deals with issues such as:

- static typing versus dynamic typing,

- references versus pointers in interfaces,

- stream I/O versus standard I/O,

- inter-language calling conventions, and

- guidelines for using ABCs, dynamic binding, inheritance, classes, encapsulation, exception handling, const correctness, and so on.

■

Cross references—
FAQ: 418, 419
See Stroustrup: 11, 12, 13

FAQ
421

How can an organization establish and promote its design philosophy?

Training, consulting, and libraries.

This three-pronged approach can be effective at establishing and promoting an organization's design and implementation philosophy. Training provides intense instruction, consulting galvanizes and focuses that training, and high quality C++ class libraries provide long-term instruction. There is a thriving commercial market for all three kinds of training.

Advice from members of organizations who have already made the transition to the object-oriented paradigm is consistent with the view, "Buy, don't build." Buy training, buy consulting, buy tools. Companies who have attempted to become self-taught tool shops as well as application or system shops have found success difficult.

Naturally, the three-pronged strategy is most effective when there is a consistent and practical philosophy behind the training, consulting, and using of libraries.

■

Cross references—
FAQ: 407, 408, 419, 420
See Stroustrup: 11, 12, 13

Should you develop your design philosophies based on your C experience?

F A Q
422

No!

No matter how vast your C expertise, being a good C programmer does not make you a good OO and C++ programmer.

OO and C++ coding standards and design philosophies should be developed by OO and C++ experts. Seek out experts who can help guide you away from pitfalls.

■

Cross references—
FAQ: 407, 408, 419, 420, 421
See Stroustrup: 11, 12, 13

Should you ever break your coding standards?

F A Q
423

Yes, carefully.

The real goal is a design philosophy, not just "pretty printing" standards. Design philosophies should have sufficient depth that they are, by their nature, guidelines rather than inflexible rules.

For example, redefining an inherited non-virtual member function is generally immoral, but is is sometimes necessary (for example, to get around the hiding rule).

It takes judgment to know which guidelines are flexible, what degrees of freedom are available, and if a given situation is one of the exceptions to the guideline.

■

Cross references—
FAQ: 139, 140, 418, 419, 420
See Stroustrup: 11, 12, 13

F A Q
424

Should local variables be declared at the top of a function or near first use?

Near first use.

C++ allows objects to be created at any statement within the block. Because an object is initialized (constructed) the moment it is declared, empty initialization followed by assignment (`x x; x = y`) often has inferior performance when compared with proper initialization (`x x = y`). Therefore, declaring all locals at the opening brace of a function results in unnecessary performance degradation.

The idea that this guideline can affect performance is unfamiliar to C experts, but new doesn't necessarily mean bad.

■

Cross references—
See Stroustrup: 2.1, 4.6

F A Q
425

What is the C++ naming convention?

What follows is a naming convention (there is no definitive naming convention).

Class names begin with a capital letter (`Shape`, `Stack`). Subsequent words in multi-word class names are introduced with a capital letter (`SymbolTable`, `ForeignCar`). Class names don't contain underscores. Class names are singular (`Stack` rather than `Stacks`).

Member function names begin with a lower-case letter, and are generally verb phrases (`push()`, `unlockGate()`). Subsequent words in multi-word class names are introduced with a capital letter (`openFile()`) or an underscore (`open_file()`).

Data member names begin with a lower case letter, and have an underscore ("_") suffix. Subsequent words in multi-word class names are introduced with a capital letter (`firstNode_`) or an underscore (`first_node_`).

The names for global data begin with // (in other words, avoid global data). You should also avoid file-scope static data. Use class-scope static data instead. Similar comments apply to file-scope static functions, as well.

F A Q

426

What is the difference between 123 and 0123?

Forty.

The leading zero in `0123` makes it an octal number. Its decimal value is `83`.

In general, avoid leading zeros in integer literals (unless you really want an octal constant). Note that `0xFF3C` is fine because the `0x` makes it explicit that the number is hexadecimal.

■

Cross references—

See Stroustrup: 2.4
See Ellis & Stroustrup: 2.5
See Lippman: 1.1

F A Q

427

What is the proper way to test a boolean value encoded in an int?

Use `false` or `0`; don't use `1`.

In C and early C++, we encoded boolean values in an `int`. We used `0` or `FALSE` to mean false, and an arbitrary non-zero value (often `1` or `-1`) to mean true. Since any non-zero value is considered true, you cannot assume that a true `int` value is necessarily `1`. When booleans are encoded in `int`s, falsehood is well defined as false or `0` but there are many true values.

Note that the C++ intrinsic data type `bool` remedies this situation. The two values for type `bool` are `true` and `false`. When a `bool` is converted to an `int`, `true` becomes `1` and `false` becomes `0`. When an `int` is converted to a `bool`, `0` becomes `false` and anything else becomes `true`.

In new C++ code, boolean values should be encoded in a `bool` rather than an `int`.

■

Cross references—
See Stroustrup: 4.7, 6.4
See Lippman: 2.14

FAQ 428

What is the best way to compare a `char*` and a string literal?

Use a `String` object, or `strcmp()`.

In general, don't compare a `char*` and a string literal using `==`, `!=`, and so on. It is unlikely that the two could be equal, because the string literal may have a unique address. The only way to get the address of the string literal is by accident. The right way to do the comparison is either to convert the `char*` to a `String` object, or to use `strcmp()`.

FAQ 429

How should you express `char` literals?

Avoid explicit numeric values for `char` literals, and for characters inside a string literal.

For example, use \r rather than \015. The rationale is that the symbolic names (for example, \r) are portable across different character sets.

■

Cross references—
See Stroustrup: 2.4
See Ellis & Stroustrup: 2.5
See Lippman: 1.1

Is `sizeof(NULL)` **the same as** `sizeof(void*)`**?**

Not necessarily.

In ANSI-C, the macro `NULL` is often defined as `((void*)0)`. However, this is unacceptable in C++, because the C++ compiler does not allow automatic conversion from `void*` to any other pointer type (fortunately). For example, the following is illegal in C++.

```
main()
{
  #ifdef GENERATE_ERROR
    int* p = (void*)0;  //ERROR: can't convert void* to int*
  #endif
}
```

The compiler uses the context of the token `0` to indicate whether it is the `0` integer, the `0` floating point number, or the `0` pointer. Therefore, `sizeof(NULL)` is probably the same as `sizeof(int)`, which is not necessarily the same as `sizeof(void*)`.

Using the token sequence `sizeof(NULL)` in C++ is a bad programming practice.

Note that the `NULL` pointer may contain some non-zero bits.

∎

Cross references—
FAQ: 319
See Stroustrup: 2.4, 2.5, r.4, r.5
See Ellis & Stroustrup: 4.6
See Lippman: 2.6

What source file name extension means the file contains C++ code?

The most common is `.C`**, but** `.cpp` **and others are also used.**

Most compilers on case-sensitive file systems (for example, UNIX) accept `.c` for C++ source files; some prefer `.cc`; and some also accept `.c`. Most compilers on case-insensitive file systems (DOS, OS/2, VMS, and so on) differentiate C++ from C by using `.cpp` for C++ and `.c` for C.

Most compilers on case-insensitive file systems have an option to always compile with C++ rules. You can use .c on both case-sensitive and case-insensitive file systems, and tell your Makefile to pass the "C++ always" option to the compiler. When your system has a mixture of C++ and C modules, and when those C modules don't yet compile under your C++ compiler, you'll need a slightly more complicated Makefile to keep track of which .c files should get the "C++ always" option.

Many organizations simply never use straight C compilers; they use C++ compilers for all of their C and C++ development.

■

Cross references—

FAQ: 432
See Stroustrup: 4.3

F A Q
432

What header file name extension means the file contains C++ code?

The most common is .h, but .H and others are also used.

Almost all vendors ship their C++ header files using a .h extension, so you can reliably write code such as the following.

```
#include <iostream.h>
```

Some tools utilize a file's extension to determine the language of the file (for example, an editor might highlight C++ keywords if the header file ends with .H, and might highlight only C keywords if the header file ends with .h).

Here again, if you use a C++ compiler for all of your code, even if it is C style code, then your environmental tools can be told to always use the C++ rules.

■

Cross references—

FAQ: 431
See Stroustrup: 4.3

What is a leaf class?

The tip at the end of the inheritance tree.

A leaf class is a class that permanently forbids derived classes. Any such class should be marked as a leaf class. An example follows.

```
class Shape {
  //...
};

/*leaf*/ class Circle : public Shape {
  //...
};
```

A leaf class shouldn't have a `protected` section, nor should it declare any new virtual functions (though it will often override inherited virtual functions).

C++ provides no formal support for leaf classes and does not enforce the guidelines listed above. A class should be declared as a leaf with some caution, but it is sometimes useful, as demonstrated in the following FAQs.

■

Cross references—
FAQ: 77, 434, 435
See Stroustrup: 5.4
See Ellis & Stroustrup: 9.3, 10.2

FAQ 434

What is a leaf member function?

One that derived classes are permanently forbidden from overriding.

Any such member function should be marked as a leaf member function.

```cpp
class Shape {
public:
  virtual void draw() const = 0;
  virtual ~Shape() { }
};

class Circle : public Shape {
public:
  /*leaf*/ void draw() const;
};
```

A member function should be declared as a leaf with some caution, but is sometimes useful, as shown in the following FAQs. Note that all member functions of a leaf class are implicitly leaf member functions, because a leaf class isn't allowed to have derived classes.

■

Cross references—
FAQ: 433, 435, 436
See Stroustrup: 5.4
See Ellis & Stroustrup: 9.3, 10.2

FAQ 435

How often should you use leaf member functions and leaf classes?

Rarely, and with caution.

Using the preceding example, class Circle inherits from an abstract base class, Shape. Suppose the system is designed so that users pass a Shape& rather than a concrete class (for example, Circle doesn't add any new services beyond those declared in Shape). In these cases, making Circle a leaf class won't sacrifice much flexibility, because someone wishing to create a kind-of Shape that reuses the code from Circle can inherit from Shape and have-a Circle.

■

Cross references—

FAQ: 433, 434, 436
See Stroustrup: 5.4
See Ellis & Stroustrup: 9.3, 10.2

What good are leaf member functions?

They can increase performance.

Leaf functions can be called using full qualification ("::"). This allows the compiler to employ static binding, thereby reducing or even eliminating the cost of dynamic binding. An example follows.

```
class Shape {
public:
  virtual void draw() const = 0;
  virtual ~Shape() { }
};

class Circle : public Shape {
public:
  /*leaf*/ void draw() const;
};

void f(Circle& c)
{
  c.Circle::draw();

}          └───► OK: Circle::draw() is a leaf member function
```

This is safe because leaf functions are never overridden in derived classes.

■

Cross references—

FAQ: 92, 93, 94, 433, 434, 435
See Stroustrup: 5.4
See Ellis & Stroustrup: 9.3, 10.2

When should you use full qualification on a non-leaf virtual function?

You shouldn't.

An invocation of a virtual member function p->f() should avoid full qualification (that is, avoid p->X::f(), where X is the class of *p). This is because full qualification subverts dynamic binding. If the actual class of the referent is something derived from X, the wrong member function may be invoked. An example follows.

```
class Shape {
public:
  virtual void draw() = 0;
  virtual void hide() = 0;
  virtual ~Shape() { }
};

class Circle : public Shape {
public:
  /*leaf*/ void draw();
           void hide();
};

void f(Circle& c)
{
  c.Circle::draw();    //OK: Circle::draw() is a leaf
  c.Circle::hide();    //BAD: subverts dynamic binding
  c.hide();            //OK
}

class FancyCircle : public Circle {
public:
  void hide();
};
```

In f(Circle& c), if c actually refers to a FancyCircle rather than a plain Circle, the call to c.Circle::hide() invokes the wrong member function.

■

Cross references—

FAQ: 93, 94, 433, 434, 435, 436
See Stroustrup: 5.4
See Ellis & Stroustrup: 9.3, 10.2

Should full qualification be used when calling another member function of the same class?

Only if the other member is a leaf member function.

If `X::f()` calls `this->g()`, full qualification (for example, `this->X::g()`) should only be used if `X::g()` is a leaf member function, or if `X` is a leaf class.

```
class X {
public:
  void f();
  /*leaf*/ virtual void g();
           virtual void h();
};

void
X::f()
{
  g();       //OK
  X::g();    //OK: X::g() is a leaf
  h();       //OK
  X::h();    //BAD: X::h() is not a leaf
}
```

Note that this is simply a specialization of the previous guideline.

■

Cross references—

FAQ: 92, 93, 94, 434, 436, 437
See Stroustrup: 5.4
See Ellis & Stroustrup: 9.3, 10.2

What is Smalltalk?

The other object-oriented programming language.

C++ and Smalltalk are, respectively, the first and second most widely used OO programming languages.

Smalltalk is called a pure OO programming language because everything is an object of some class. C++ is called a hybrid OO programming language because not everything is an object of some class (for example, you can't inherit from built-in types like int or char).

■

Cross references—

FAQ: 440–442
See Stroustrup: 6.2, 12.1
See Ellis & Stroustrup: 6.2

What are the major differences between C++ and Smalltalk?

They are based on different philosophies.

1. C++ performs type checking at compile-time; Smalltalk performs type checking at run-time.

2. C++ fully supports both reference and value semantics; Smalltalk fully supports reference semantics only.

3. In C++, inheritance is tied to the kind-of relationship; in Smalltalk, inheritance is not tied to the kind-of relationship.

4. C++ memory management is explicitly controlled by the programmer; Smalltalk provides a built-in garbage collector for memory management.

5. C++ has a number of features that are only indirectly related to the OO paradigm, including templates, exceptions, constructors, destructors, operator overloading, and so on; Smalltalk does not have these features.

6. C++ supports multiple inheritance; Smalltalk programmers use idioms to simulate multiple inheritance when needed.

■

Cross references—

FAQ: 15, 76, 152, 153, 362, 363, 364, 439, 441, 444, 446
See Stroustrup: 6.2, 12.1
See Ellis & Stroustrup: 6.2

FAQ 441

Which is better, C++ or Smalltalk?

Whichever is better for the job at hand.

Each language has its own strengths. The right language for you depends on your application.

■

Cross references—

FAQ: 439, 440
See Stroustrup: 6.2, 12.1
See Ellis & Stroustrup: 6.2

FAQ 442

Is one OO language better for writing OO programs?

No.

Both languages provide comprehensive support for OO programming.

■

Cross references—

FAQ: 439, 440, 441
See Stroustrup: 6.2, 12.1
See Ellis & Stroustrup: 6.2

F A Q
443

Does one OO language prevent you from writing bad software?

No.

You can write bad OO programs (or even non-OO programs) in either C++ or Smalltalk. For example, both languages allow you to create spaghetti inheritance hierarchies, abuse dynamic typing, or have a procedural mindset. You can write software that is hard to maintain, non-reusable, and buggy in any language.

Programming languages are tools, and the tool is only as good as the person using it. If you don't know what you are doing, neither language will save you.

You can write bad software in any language.

■

Cross references—
FAQ: 440, 441, 442
See Stroustrup: 6.2, 12.1
See Ellis & Stroustrup: 6.2

F A Q
444

What are some C++ features that make OO programming convenient?

Static typing, exception handling, automagically called destructors, value semantics, and operator overloading.

With static typing, the compiler checks the type correctness of every operation at compile-time (that is, statically), rather than generating code that checks the types at run-time (that is, dynamically). For example, the signature matching of function arguments is checked by the compiler and an improper match is flagged as an error at compile-time.

Other C++ features such as templates, exception handling, constructors, destructors, value semantics, operator overloading, and so on, give flexibility when constructing OO software, often making it possible to meet both short-term and long-term goals.

Some say that C++'s features and flexibility make it overly complex and cumbersome. Naturally, this depends on your perspective. In particular, C++ was designed for solving complex problems in a wide range of application domains. To meet this goal, it supplies a full range of features and facilities.

■

Cross references—

FAQ: 11, 51, 52, 53, 152, 153, 170, 244, 275, 342, 362
See Stroustrup: 5.4, 5.5, 6.2, 7, 8, 9, 12.1
See Ellis & Stroustrup: 6.2, 12.1, 12.3, 13.4, 14, 15

F A Q 445

How can you make C++ look and act like Smalltalk?

Don't try.

There have been many attempts to make C++ look and act like Smalltalk, even though the languages are very different. This has lead to a lot of needless frustration and expense. Bjarne Stroustrup said it best, "Smalltalk is the best Smalltalk around."

Note that C++ is flexible enough so that you can make it look like Smalltalk (by using pointer casts, unions, and `#defines`), but there's no real reason to do so.

■

Cross references—

FAQ: 439, 440
See Stroustrup: 6.2, 12.1
See Ellis & Stroustrup: 6.2

F A Q 446

What are the practical consequences of the differences between C++ and Smalltalk inheritance?

C++ is more restrictive, but can produce faster executables.

Because Smalltalk doesn't require users to use inheritance in order to create a kind-of, users can be carefree about putting data (bits, representation, data structures) into a class. After all, if you don't like the implementation, you can make a new kind-of with a completely different implementation.

For example, let's say you have an implementation of a `Stack` class that has-a linked list. Later, if you want another `Stack` based on an array, you don't have to inherit from `Stack` if you are using Smalltalk; you can go off and make a new stand-alone class. Smalltalk even allows you to inherit from class `Array`, even though the new class is not a kind-of `Array`!

In C++, you can't be nearly that carefree. Once you place a data structure in a class, that data structure is inherited by all derived classes. Therefore, derived classes are stuck with the base class's data structures, even if they don't like those data structures. That's why you use abstract base classes—to delay the decision about what data structure to put into a class until you are near the leaves of the inheritance hierarchy.

You can think of the difference between Smalltalk and C++ as being similar to the difference between an all terrain vehicle (ATV) and a Maseratti. An ATV (like Smalltalk) is more flexible and fun, because you can drive through fields, streams, forests, and the like. A Maseratti (like C++) gets you there faster, but it forces you to stay on the road.

The best advice to C++ programmers is simple: *Stay on the road.* Even if you like the expressive freedom of driving through the bushes, don't do it in C++; it's not a good fit.

■

Cross references—
FAQ: 15, 76, 370, 439, 440
See Stroustrup: 6.2, 12.1
See Ellis & Stroustrup: 6.2

Do you need to learn a pure OO programming language like Smalltalk before learning C++?

F A Q
447

No.

Having trained thousands of software professionals in OO technology, we can state with some authority that the purity of the OO programming language doesn't make the transition to OO and C++ significantly easier. Those of our C++ students who came from a Smalltalk background did not have a significant advantage over those who came with a background in a traditional programming language.

In the long run, learning Smalltalk as a way of learning C++ is a waste of corporate assets. If your developers are going to use C++ for their OO development, learning OO and C++ directly is a more efficient use of human resources.

We would caution, however, that many OO and C++ training organizations emphasize only the C part of C++. The previous advice applies only if your training organization places an appropriate emphasis on the ++ part of C++. If what you learn is C++ syntax and semantics rather than a new way of thinking, you may be better off staying with C; the relative value-add of C++ as a better C is not that great, and the cost of training is high.

■

Cross references—

FAQ: 29, 153, 154, 395, 412
See Stroustrup: 6.2, 12.1
See Ellis & Stroustrup: 6.2

F A Q
448

What does a Smalltalk programmer have to learn to master C++?

A Smalltalk programmer needs to learn nine things.

1. Substitutability—beware of bad inheritance.

2. How to use static typing—break your reliance on dynamic typing.

3. How to use destructors for reclaiming resources.

4. How to use value semantics.

5. How to use constructors.

6. Where `friend`s can help you—break your reliance on `get` and `set` methods.

7. How to exploit `private`.

8. How to use templates for containers—break your reliance on inheritance-based containers.

9. How to use exception handling—break your reliance on error codes.

■

Cross references—

FAQ: 11, 15, 29, 76, 152, 153, 168, 170, 395, 439, 440, 444
See Stroustrup: 6.2, 12.1
See Ellis & Stroustrup: 6.2

What are private inheritance and protected inheritance?

Syntactic variants of composition.

From the user's perspective, private and protected inheritance are semantically similar. They both hide the relationship between the base class and the derived class (neither private nor protected inheritance provides the kind-of relationship that public inheritance supports). This means that a user cannot pass an object of the derived class to a function whose parameter type is a private or protected base class. Also, public members of the base class will generally not be available as public members of the private or protected derived class.

In private inheritance, the relationship with the base class is a private decision; only members and friends of the privately derived class can exploit the relationship with the private base class. In protected inheritance, the relationship with the base class is a protected decision, so members and friends of the protected derived class, and members and friends of classes derived from the protected derived class can exploit the protected inheritance relationship, but normal users cannot.

Protected inheritance is less restrictive than private inheritance, and therefore introduces more coupling between the derived class and the base class. With protected inheritance, if you change the relationship between the protected base class and the derived class (or if the protected operations of the protected base class change), the effects may reach beyond the protected derived class and its friends. This potentially affects classes derived from the protected derived class, classes derived from those derived classes, and so on.

This is a for-better-and-for-worse situation; derived classes have more coupling, but they also have the ability to exploit the relationship between the derived class and the base class.

■

Cross references—

FAQ: 14, 87, 450, 451
See Stroustrup: 6.6, 12.2, r.4
See Ellis & Stroustrup: 4.6
See Lippman: 8.5

F A Q

450

How is private or protected inheritance similar to composition?

You can think of private or protected inheritance as a syntactic variant of part-of.

For example, the part-of relationship between Engine and Car can be expressed in two ways. The first is with private inheritance.

```
class Engine { };

class Car : private Engine {
  //private inheritance; a Car is NOT a-kind-of Engine
  //protected inheritance is conceptually similar to this
};
```

The second is with part-of.

```
class Car2 {
  //normal composition; a Car2 is NOT a-kind-of Engine
  Engine e;
};
```

There are several similarities between these. In both cases there is exactly one Engine member object contained in a Car and in both cases users (outsiders) are prevented from converting a Car* to an Engine*.

There are also several differences. Private or protected inheritance allows members and friends of the derived class (Car) to access the protected members of the base class (Engine). Private or protected inheritance allows members and friends of Car to convert a Car* to an Engine*. Private or protected inheritance is usually used for the first of these—to gain access to the protected: members of the base class. Note that the extra authority of private or protected inheritance carries with it extra responsibility.

There are also several caveats when using private or protected inheritance. Simple composition (has-a) is needed if you want to contain several member objects of the same class; and private or protected inheritance can introduce unnecessary multiple inheritance.

■

Cross references—

FAQ: 14, 87, 451
See Stroustrup: 6.6, 12.2, r.4
See Ellis & Stroustrup: 4.6
See Lippman: 8.5

F A Q
451

Should you use normal has-a, or private or protected inheritance?

Use normal has-a when you can, use private or protected inheritance when you have to.

Simple composition (has-a) is preferred because it leads to fewer dependencies between classes. Private and protected inheritance are more expensive to maintain because they increase the number of classes that have access to the protected parts of other classes—they increase coupling.

Private or protected inheritance is often used when you want to use simple composition, but the interface of the class to be used is insufficient. In this case, an alternative to private or protected inheritance is improving the public interface of the base class so that simple composition can be used. If you cannot change the interface of the base class (for example, because the source code is not available), you can create *one* derived class (often using public inheritance) that has an improved interface. This derived class with its fixed interface is then used via simple composition (has-a).

■

Cross references—

FAQ: 14, 87, 450
See Stroustrup: 6.6, 12.2, r.4
See Ellis & Stroustrup: 4.6
See Lippman: 8.5

FAQ
452

What are the access rules for public, protected, and private inheritance?

Consider the following classes as examples.

```
class B                     { protected: int prot; };
class PrivD : private    B {                       };
class ProtD : protected B {                       };
class PublD : public     B {                       };
class User                  { B b;                 };
```

With private inheritance, the public and protected parts of B become private in PrivD. This means that PrivD can access these services, but user code and classes derived from PrivD cannot access them.

With protected inheritance, the public and protected parts of B become protected in ProtD. This means that members and friends of ProtD can access these services, as can classes derived from ProtD, but user code cannot access them.

With public inheritance, the public parts of B become public on PublD, and the protected parts of B remain protected in PublD.

In all three cases, the private parts of B are inaccessible to the derived classes (PrivD, ProtD, and PublD) as well as to user code.

■

Cross references—
FAQ: 82, 449
See Stroustrup: 6.6, 12.2, r.4
See Ellis & Stroustrup: 4.6
See Lippman: 8.5

FAQ
453

In a private or protected derived class, how do you make a service public that was public in the base class?

Special syntax.

You declare the name (not the entire signature) of the member function in the public interface of the derived class. For example, to make the member function B::f(int,char,float) public in ProtD, you would say this.

```
class B {
public:
  int f(int, char, float);
};

class ProtD : protected B {
public:
  B::f;    //note: omit the parameter declarations
};
```

The syntax to do this with private inheritance is identical.

There are two limitations to this technique: you can't distinguish over-loaded names, and you can't make a feature public if it was protected in the base class. When necessary, you can get around these limitations by defining a call-through service in the derived class.

```
class ProtD2 : protected B {
public:
  int f(int x, char y, float z) { return B::f(x, y, z); }
};
```

■

Cross references—
FAQ: 452, 454
See Stroustrup: 6.6, 12.2, r.4
See Ellis & Stroustrup: 4.6
See Lippman: 8.5

Should you cast a pointer from a private or protected derived class to its base class?

No.

Within a service of a private or protected derived class (that is, in the body of members or friends of a private or protected derived class), the relationship to the base class is known, and the upward pointer or reference conversion takes place automatically without a cast.

In normal user code, the relationship to a private or protected base class is inaccessible, therefore the conversion requires a cast. Users should not perform this cast, because private or protected inheritance is a non-public decision of the derived class. The cast will fail if the private or protected derived class chooses to change or remove the inheritance relationship.

The conclusion is that only a class and its friends have the right to convert a pointer to a non-public derived class into a pointer to its base class. The services of a class don't need a cast, because the relationship with the base class is accessible to them.

Here's an even simpler conclusion—don't user pointer casts!

■

Cross references—

FAQ: 85
See Stroustrup: 6.6, 12.2, r.4
See Ellis & Stroustrup: 4.6
See Lippman: 8.5

F A Q
455

What is the type of a pointer to a nonstatic member function?

A pointer to the nonstatic member function with signature void Fred::f(int) **has type** void(Fred::*)(int).

Here's an example.

```
#include <iostream.h>

class Fred {
public:
  void f(int i) { cout << "Fred::f(int); i=" << i << '\n'; }
  void g(int i) { cout << "Fred::g(int); i=" << i << '\n'; }
  void h(int i) { cout << "Fred::h(int); i=" << i << '\n'; }
};

typedef void(Fred::*FredMemberPointer)(int);

main()
{
  FredMemberPointer p = Fred::g;
  Fred fred;
  (fred.*p) (42);     //same as "fred.g(42)"
}
```

The output of this program is as follows.

```
Fred::g(int); i=42
```

A pointer to a nonstatic member function of class `Fred` is a totally different type from a pointer to a function. For example, the pointer type `void(Fred::*)(int)` is totally different from the pointer type `void(*)(int)`.

A pointer to a static member function of class `Fred` has the same type as a pointer to a file-scope function. In other words, you can convert a file scope function or static member function to the same pointer to function type, but you cannot convert a pointer to nonstatic member function to a normal pointer to function type.

■

Cross references—
FAQ: 456, 457, 458
See Stroustrup: 5.4, r.5
See Ellis & Stroustrup: 5.4, 5.5, 8.1c
See Lippman: 4.3

F A Q
456

How do you pass a pointer to a nonstatic member function to a signal handler, X event call-back, and so on?

You can't do this directly, because a nonstatic member function is meaningless without an object to which the nonstatic member function can be applied.

Use a file scope function as a wrapper that takes an object obtained through some other technique (held in a global, perhaps) and calls the desired nonstatic member function.

For example, suppose you want to call `x.f(int)` on interrupt, where `f(int)` is a nonstatic member function of the class of object x. The following would accomplish this.

```
#include <iostream.h>
#include <sys/signal.h>

class X {
public:
  void f(int n) { cout << "X::f()\n"; }
  static void staticMethod(int n);
  static X* signalHandlerObject;     //the handler object
};
```

```
void
XMethodWrapper(int n)
{
  X::signalHandlerObject->f(n);
}

void
X::staticMethod(int n)
{
  X::signalHandlerObject->f(n);
}

main()
{
  //signal(SIGINT, X::f);           //Can NOT do this
  signal(SIGINT, XMethodWrapper);   //OK
  signal(SIGINT, X::staticMethod);  //Also OK
}
```

■

Cross references—
FAQ: 455, 457, 458
See Stroustrup: 5.4, r.5
See Ellis & Stroustrup: 5.4, 5.5, 8.1c
See Lippman: 4.3

F A Q
457

Why would someone have trouble taking the address of a nonstatic member function?

This is a corollary to the previous question; please read it first.

Nonstatic member functions have an implicit parameter that points to the object—the pointer that is called this inside the member function. You can think of normal C functions as having a different calling convention from that of nonstatic member functions, so the types of their pointers are different and incompatible—pointer to nonstatic member function versus pointer to function.

C++ introduces a new type of pointer, called a pointer to nonstatic member, which can be invoked only by providing an object. Do *not* attempt to cast a pointer to nonstatic member function into a pointer to function or vice versa; the result is undefined and probably disastrous. For example, a pointer to nonstatic member function probably doesn't contain the machine address of the appropriate function. As noted in the last example, if you want a regular C function pointer, use either a file-scope (non-member) function, or a static (class) member function.

■

Cross references—
FAQ: 455, 456, 458
See Stroustrup: 5.4, r.5
See Ellis & Stroustrup: 5.4, 5.5, 8.1c
See Lippman: 4.3

FAQ 458

How do you declare an array of pointers to nonstatic member functions?

Consider the following class declaration.

```
#include <iostream.h>

class Fred {
public:
  void f(int i) { cout << "Fred::f(int); i=" << i << '\n'; }
  void g(int i) { cout << "Fred::g(int); i=" << i << '\n'; }
  void h(int i) { cout << "Fred::h(int); i=" << i << '\n'; }
};

typedef void (Fred::*FredMemberPointer) (int);
```

An array of pointers to nonstatic member functions is declared as follows.

```
FredMemberPointer p[3] = { &Fred::f, &Fred::g, &Fred::h };
```

To call one of the nonstatic member functions, supply a Fred object, and use the .* operator.

```
main()
{
  Fred fred;
  for (int i = 0; i < 3; ++i)
    (fred.*p[i]) (42 + i);
}
```

The output of this program is as follows.

```
Fred::f(int); i=42
Fred::g(int); i=43
Fred::h(int); i=44
```

■

Cross references—

FAQ: 455, 457
See Stroustrup: 5.4, r.5
See Ellis & Stroustrup: 5.4, 5.5, 8.1c

What is a baby String**?**

A String **class that's good enough for small examples.**

To avoid unnecessary code duplication, the FAQ examples that use String objects #include the following header file.

```
//String.h
#ifndef String_h
#define String_h

#include <string.h>
#include <iostream.h>

class BadIndex { };

class String {
public:

  String()
    : len_(0), data_(new char[1])
    { data_[0] = '\0'; }

  String(const char* s)
    : len_(strlen(s)), data_(new char[len_ + 1])
    { memcpy(data_, s, len_ + 1); }

 ~String()
    { delete [] data_; }

  String(const String& s)
    : len_(s.len_), data_(new char[s.len_ + 1])
    { memcpy(data_, s.data_, len_ + 1); }
```

```
    String& operator= (const String& s)
      {
        if (len_ != s.len_) { //makes self-assignment harmless
          char* newData = new char[s.len_ + 1];
          delete [] data_;
          data_ = newData;
          len_ = s.len_;
        }
        memcpy(data_, s.data_, len_ + 1);
        return *this;
      }

    unsigned len() const
      { return len_; }

    char& operator[] (unsigned i)
      { indexTest(i); return data_[i]; }
    char  operator[] (unsigned i) const
      { indexTest(i); return data_[i]; }

    friend ostream& operator<< (ostream& o, const String& s)
      { return o.write(s.data_, s.len_); }

    friend int operator== (const String& a, const String& b)
      { return a.len_ == b.len_ &&
              memcmp(a.data_, b.data_, a.len_) == 0; }
    friend int operator!= (const String& a, const String& b)
      { return ! (a == b); }

  private:
    void indexTest(unsigned i) const
      { if (i >= len_) throw BadIndex(); }
    unsigned len_;   //ORDER DEPENDENCY; see FAQ 190
    char* data_;     //ORDER DEPENDENCY; see FAQ 190
  };

  #endif //String_h
```

■

Cross references—

FAQ: 85, 208, 228, 259, 276, 278, 328, 329, 332, 336
See Stroustrup: 6.6, 12.2, r.4
See Ellis & Stroustrup: 4.6

What is a baby HeapPtr?

A HeapPtr **class template that's good enough for small examples.**

To avoid unnecessary code duplication, the FAQ examples that use HeapPtr objects #include the following header file.

```
//HeapPtr.h
#ifndef HeapPtr_h
#define HeapPtr_h

#include <stdlib.h>
#include <assert.h>

template<class T>
class HeapPtr {
public:

  HeapPtr(T* ptr=NULL)   : ptr_(ptr) { }
 ~HeapPtr()              { deallocate(); }
  void deallocate()      { delete ptr_; ptr_ = NULL; }
  HeapPtr<T>& operator= (T* ptr)
    { deallocate(); ptr_ = ptr; return *this; }

  T* operator-> ()    { assert(ptr_ != NULL); return ptr_; }
  T& operator* ()     { assert(ptr_ != NULL); return *ptr_; }

  T* relinquishOwnership()
    { T* old = ptr_; ptr_ = NULL; return old; }

private:
  T* ptr_;
  HeapPtr<T>& operator= (const HeapPtr<T>&); //unimplemented
  HeapPtr            (const HeapPtr<T>&); //unimplemented
};

#endif //HeapPtr_h
```

∎

Cross references—

FAQ: 204, 205, 316, 317, 320
See Stroustrup: 6.6, 12.2, r.4
See Ellis & Stroustrup: 4.6

Is there a difference between `Stack a;` **and** `Stack a();`**?**

YES!

`Stack a;` defines a as an object of class `Stack`. The default constructor for `Stack` (the one that can be called with no arguments) will initialize a.

`Stack a();` declares a to be a function that returns a `Stack` by value, and that takes no parameters (hence the empty parenthesis in `a()`). However, a is not an object of class `Stack`.

■

Cross references—
FAQ: 182
See Stroustrup: 4.6, 5.2, 5.5
See Ellis & Stroustrup: 8.2, 9.1

Why can't you overload a function that differs only in its return type?

It can't always be determined which one you want the compiler to call.

Return types are not considered when determining unique signatures for overloaded functions; only the number and type of parameters are considered. Otherwise, it wouldn't be clear which function should be called if the caller chose to ignore the return value.

Consider the following example.

```
char  f(int i);
float f(int i);
```

```
main()
{
  f(3);  //which version of f() should be invoked?
}
```

The compiler generates an error message for the preceding example.

■

Cross references—

See Stroustrup: r.13
See Ellis & Stroustrup: 13.1, 13.3

FAQ
463

What is a persistent object?

An object that can live longer than the program that created it.

Loosely speaking, a persistent object is one that lives after the program that created it has terminated. A persistent object can even outlive various versions of the creating program, the disk system, the operating system, or even the hardware on which the operating system was running when it was created.

The challenge with persistent objects is to effectively store their member function code on secondary storage along with their data bits (and the data bits and member function code of all member objects, and of all their member objects, and so on). This is non-trivial when you have to do it yourself. In C++, you have to do it yourself. OO/C++ databases can help hide the mechanism for all of this.

FAQ
464

Is there a TeX or LaTeX macro that displays "C++" correctly?

Yes, here are two.

```
\def\CC{C\raise.22ex\hbox{{\footnotesize
+}}\raise.22ex\hbox{\footnotesize +}}

\def\CC{{C\hspace{-.05em}\raisebox{.4ex}{\tiny\bf ++}}}
```

What's a good interface that allows elements to be accessed (retrieved, changed, removed, inserted) at any of several positions in a container (linked list, hash table, binary tree, and so forth)?

Here is a prototypical example, inserting into a linked list.

The obvious approach is to provide services for inserting at the head and tail of the list and tell users to iterate over the list by directly accessing the elements of the list. However, this would produce a class that is too weak. A weak class is one that does not provide the services that users want. When this is the case, it may be that the class's public interface needs enhancing. If the list allows users to add elements only at the front and tail, it definitely needs more strength.

Since this is a subtle topic that may be difficult for those new to C++, here are several options. The first is the easiest, though the second option is better. There is also a third option, which has certain advantages and disadvantages over the second option.

1. Let the list have the concept of a "current element." Provide the list with services such as `advance()`, `backup()`, `atEnd()`, `atBegin()`, `rewind()`, `fastforward()`, and `getCurrent()`. The `getCurrent()` service returns the element of the list that is currently under the cursor. Finally, you'll need to add a few more member functions to mutate the list, such as `changeTo(x)`, `insert(x)`, `remove()`, and so on.

2. Separate the concept of "current element" from the concept of "list." In this case, a separate class is provided, such as `ListIndex`. `ListIndex` would have services similar to those listed previously. The `List` itself would not have any services that access the "current element," since the current element is determined by the `ListIndex` rather than by the `List`. Class `ListIndex` would probably be a `friend` of `List`, since `ListIndex` would need to have access to the implementation of `List`. Thus `ListIndex` allows outside users to access the abilities of `List` without allowing normal users to see the underlying implementation of `List`.

3. The third possibility treats the entire iteration as an atomic event, where an object is created that embodies this event; this object is normally created using a template. This technique allows the iteration to avoid public access member functions (which may be virtual functions) during the inner loop, thus enhancing performance. Unfortunately it can increase the size of the application's object code,

because templates gain speed by duplicating code. This third technique was developed by Andrew Koenig (Templates as interfaces, JOOP, 4, 5: Sept 91). You can also get a taste of it in Bjarne Stroustrup's book, *The C++ Programming Language*, Second Edition (look for Comparator in the index).

The reason option 2 is better than option 1 becomes apparent when you use classes that support only option 1. With option 1, if you pass a list to a subcall, you'd better hope that the subcall doesn't change the list's "current position," since this can make your code fail. For this reason, it is very difficult to do things such as operate on all *pairs* of elements. The concept of using a distinct class as an iterator, option 2, removes these restrictions.

■

Cross reference—

See Stroustrup: 13

What books are available on C++?

Here are a handful of references. A complete list is updated on the electronic FAQ, posted monthly on the electronic news group comp.lang.c++.

Barton, John J. and Nackman, Lee R. (1994), *Scientific and Engineering C++: An Introduction with Advanced Techniques and Examples*, Addison-Wesley Publishing Company, Inc.

Budd, Timothy A. (1994), *Classic Data Structures in C++*, Addison-Wesley Publishing Company, Inc.

Cargill, Tom (1992), *Elements of C++ Programming Style*, Addison-Wesley Publishing Company, Inc.

Ellis, Margaret A. and Stroustrup, Bjarne (1990), *The Annotated C++ Reference Manual*, Addison-Wesley Publishing Company, Inc.

Lippman, Stanley C. (1991), *C++ Primer, Second Edition*, Addison-Wesley Publishing Company, Inc.

Martin, Robert, C. (1994), *Designing C++ Applications Using the Booch Notation*, Prentice Hall.

Meyers, Scott (1992), *Effective C++: 50 Specific Ways to Improve Your Programs and Designs*, Addison-Wesley Publishing Company, Inc.

Murray, Robert B. (1992), *C++ Strategies and Tactics*, Addison-Wesley Publishing Company, Inc.

Plauger, P.J. (1993), *The C++ Library*, Prentice Hall

Pohl, Ira (1994), *C++ for C Programmers, Second Edition*, Benjamin-Cummings Publishing Company

Stroustrup, Bjarne (1994), *The Design and Evolution of C++*, Addison-Wesley Publishing Company, Inc.

Stroustrup, Bjarne (1991), *The C++ Programming Language, Second Edition*, Addison-Wesley Publishing Company, Inc.

Teale, Steve (1993), *C++ IOStreams Handbook*, Addison-Wesley Publishing Company, Inc.

Vilat, Michael (1993), *C++ Programming Powerpack*, Sams.

Waldo, James (1993), *The Evolution of C++: Language Design in the Marketplace of Ideas*, MIT Press.

■

Cross references—
FAQ: 460, 461, 462

FAQ 467

What periodicals are related to C++?

- *The C++ Report,*
- *Journal of Object-Oriented Programming,*
- *Journal of C++,* and
- The working papers of the ANSI/ISO C++ committee.

■

Cross references—
FAQ: 459, 461, 462

FAQ 468

What conferences and conference proceedings are related to C++?

- Proceedings of the OOPSLA conferences,
- Proceedings of the ECOOP conferences,

- Proceedings of the C++ At Work conferences , and

- Proceedings of the USENIX C++ conferences.

■

Cross references—
FAQ: 459, 460, 462

What Internet news groups and mailing lists are related to C++?

- comp.lang.c++,

- comp.std.c++,

- comp.object, and

- BIX.

■

Cross references—
FAQ: 459, 460, 461

Where can I get a copy of the latest ANSI/ISO C++ draft standard?

You can get a hard copy by sending a request to:

> x3 Secretariat
> CBEMA
> 1250 I St., NW, Suite 200
> Washington, DC 20005

Ask for the latest version of "Working paper for draft proposed American national standard for information systems—programming language C++."

ANSI standards and drafts are *not* available in machine-readable form from any source, since CBEMA finances standards activities through the sales of standards documents.

■

Cross references—
FAQ: 49
See Stroustrup:
See Ellis & Stroustrup: 1.1

INDEX

Note: All references in the index are to FAQ (Frequently Asked Questions) numbers.